Successful
Beverage
Management

Proven Strategies for the On-Premise Operator
by Robert Plotkin with Steve Goumas

BEVINCO

PRECISION POUR
3 BALL LIQUOR POUR

BERG COMPANY

Libbey

We're proud to have the support and endorsement
of these fine companies.

x

BarMedia
Tucson, AZ
©2001

Dedication

This book is dedicated to my youngest daughter,
Hannah Marie Plotkin,
who even at the age of ten
exhibits every indication of being an outstanding human being.

RP

Other books by Robert Plotkin

¡Toma! Margaritas!: The Original Guide to Margaritas and Tequila (1999)
Preventing Internal Theft: A Bar Owner's Guide - 2nd Edition (1998)
Bar Sales: Creative Twists to Bigger Profits (1997)
The Bartender's Companion: A Complete Drink Recipe Guide - 3rd Edition (1997)
The Commercial Bartender's Training Manual - 2nd Edition (1994)
Reducing Bar Costs: A Survival Guide for the '90s (1993)
501 Questions Every Bartender Should Know How to Answer:
    A Unique Look At The Bar Business (1993)
The Professional Guide to Bartending: An Encyclopedia of American Mixology (1991)
The Intervention Handbook: The Legal Aspects of Serving Alcohol - 2nd Edition (1990)

Publisher: Robert Plotkin, Carol Plotkin
Editors: Karen Schmidt, Sheila Berry
Managing Editor: Robert Plotkin
Production Manager: Carol Plotkin
Cover Design: Miguel Castillo, Carol Plotkin
Book Design: Miguel Castillo
Photography: Seagram Americas — Bulleit Bourbon Frontier Whiskey photograph, and project partners Berg, Bevinco, Libbey and Precision Pours — respective photography.

Published by: **BarMedia**

P.O. Box 14486
Tucson, AZ 85732
520.747.8131
www.barmedia.com
www.barprofits.com

Library of Congress Card Catalog Number: 00-091416

ISBN 0-945562-27-6

Printed in the United States

Second Printing

Successful Beverage Management
Proven Strategies for the On-Premise Operator

Table of Contents

II. Section Two: Developing a Profitable Beverage Operation

III. Section Three: Professional Beverage Management

Acknowledgements

In many respects this book was years in the making. Countless people have contributed to its content in one way or another. No one is born with the inherent abilities and knowledge to manage a beverage operation profitably. I am no exception. So to all of the bartenders, managers, owners, and clients that I have worked with over the years, my sincere thanks.

On behalf of everyone at BarMedia, I want to take this opportunity to thank our partners on this project. We sought out the support of four companies in whom we have unwavering confidence in their products or service. These companies will continue to positively affect our industry for the foreseeable future and I felt compelled to mention their products or service where appropriate. We are proud to be associated with them.

Libbey Glass afforded us the opportunity of working with corporate communications manager David Pett and a tremendous glassware selection to showcase. His considerable efforts on behalf of this project are greatly appreciated.

We also appreciate the working relationship that has developed with Rick Sandvik and Bill Slattery of Precision Pours. They have been enthusiastic supporters of the project since its inception.

Another staunch supporter of our efforts has been Terry Singer, vice president of the Berg Company. He is a dedicated professional, a pleasure to work with, and has helped to bring beverage management controls into the 21st century.

President of Bevinco, Barry Driedger's vision and dedication to this project has proved enormously beneficial to our efforts. I would also like to thank Bevinco franchisees John Hennessey and Ian Foster for their contributions.

Last but not least, I would like to express my gratitude to Steve Goumas for writing the chapter on point of sale systems for this book. Founder of the Madison Group, a food and beverage consulting company located in Scottsdale, Arizona, Steve is a genius in a number of areas, point of sale systems being one of them.

Producing a book like this one is a monumental task, not one recommended for anyone who values free time or weekends. This book would not have become a reality without the extraordinary efforts of the president and publisher of BarMedia, Carol Plotkin. I also received invaluable editorial support from Karen Schmidt and Sheila Berry. Without their assistance and encouragement I would not have completed this project.

All of us at BarMedia want to acknowledge the invaluable contributions of Miguel Castillo. He is a highly creative and talented individual, and is responsible for this book's graphic design and layout.

Introduction

Long-term success in this industry requires stability. Place a poorly conceived operation without a stable infrastructure in a magnificent facility at a prime location and eventually the inefficiencies and unprofitable ways of the business will bring about its demise.

You must not only put the right operation with the right concept into the right facility at the right location, but as important is the business infrastructure — the systems, policies, procedures, training programs, menus, cost controls, point-of-sale marketing and merchandising. Add to that the need to have it all properly implemented by trained and fully capable personnel in order to achieve long-term success, and you may wonder where to start.

It all looks so easy. Pour drink, sell drink, and ring-in the profits. In fact, extracting profits out of a beverage operation can be quite challenging. Between waste, spillage, free drinks, over-pouring, theft and other operational maladies, profit is typically the first casualty.

The lack of educational requirements and the availability of excellent resources adds to the challenges. People very often have to learn about beverage management on the job. It also means that when an individual applies for a management position that there are no assurances about what the person knows and the validity of the person's knowledge.

We've taken care of that and more. This is a real guide for working professionals, written by working professionals. Everything contained in this book has been field-tested, stripped down to its basic elements and proven by the test of time.

This book deals with every topic that affects a beverage operation's level of profitability, including cost-control issues, human resource issues and issues pertaining to the physical layout. Following is what you can expect to get out of this book.

Profit. There are cost-saving, profit-generating idea concepts on nearly every page. *Managerial Discipline.* Success equals a few simple disciplines practiced every day. Whereas failure is a few mistakes repeated every day. *Confidence.* If some of what you're currently doing is working well, stay with those aspects of your present program. But work to incorporate the information and recommendations contained in this book. Staying open to possibilities creates new opportunities for success. In the end, you will have the confidence of knowing that you've created the best possible management program for your beverage operation.

The authors of this book know this business. They have incorporated their excellent organizational skills, years of data collected through hands-on experience, and the tenacity (gruesome!) to put it all together in an easy to use, sensible format that allows you to make it all work for you, guaranteed. So role up your sleeves, get involved and increase your operation's profits.

Conducting Your Own
Market Research

Typically people have a limited amount of discretionary funds to spend on entertainment. If you're going to successfully compete for those dollars, you need to assess the marketplace from the consumers' point of view. They have to pass a lot of your competitors before they reach your front door. The bottom line is, there is no way that you can be an effective beverage manager without knowing what is happening in the marketplace.

What sort of information are you looking for? You need to learn what your direct competitors are doing to entice those same people into their front door. Are they trying to out compete you by reducing prices, increasing portion sizes or offering better entertainment?

Making sound decisions requires you to have an accurate, realistic perspective of your market position. This information will have a significant impact on decisions such as pricing, well liquor selection, portion control, glassware selection and formulating house drink recipes. Knowing what your competition is doing will also affect your marketing and promotion, inventory selections, and the services that you may want to offer your clientele.

Market research is nothing more than a logically organized survey of the marketplace. Rarely is there money in the budget to hire a company to analyze your marketplace for you, which means that to be effective, you're going to have to leave your place of business and personally pay your competitors a visit. Do not send other people to gather these insights for you. While second-hand information may be useful, first-hand knowledge is invaluable.

There are two basic aspects to knowing the market. The first is understanding what your direct competitors are doing, or not doing. Direct competition is a driving force behind this industry. Not only are your direct competitors vying for the same dollars that you are, how you position your business in relation to your direct competitors will greatly affect how people perceive your business.

**Making
sound
decisions
requires
you to have
an accurate,
realistic
perspective
of your
market
position.**

The second aspect is acquiring a clear understanding of what your clientele wants and desires are. It's not until you really understand who you're catering to, and what they want, that you can successfully deliver the goods and services.

SHOPPING YOUR COMPETITION

Sit at an active bar and listen to the regulars. They'll provide you with a complete run-down on the market—including information on pricing, drink specials, and on-premise promotions. They know which bars are doing good business, and those that don't. It's called "bar-hopping." They leave one place and patronize another.

To succeed in this business, you have to routinely hit the road and shop the competition. These excursions should be aimed at learning more about the market than your customers know.

Shrewd, "street smart" operators do it all the time. They frequent their competitors, spend some money, make friends, and in a relatively short amount of time, gather a virtual bonanza of information about the competition. They probably drum up business for themselves in the process.

There are some basic rules and guidelines that should be followed. After all, you are a representative of your business and must subscribe to certain rules of conduct. Don't be covert. When natural to do so, introduce yourself to the server, bartender, or the manager and let them know that you own the establishment down the road. Be warm, open, and genuinely complimentary. They must be doing something right if they're still in business, so make a point of being positive. Regardless of the field of endeavor, it's an impressive quality when someone can bestow praise on a competitor.

Remember, you're there to have a drink or two, eat some appetizers, and enjoy the ambiance. Equally important, don't over-imbibe or forget to tip well. The employees you see at that bar or restaurant today, may soon be applying for employment at your business tomorrow.

When shopping your competition, here are some important things to look for:

Products — What products do your competitors carry that you don't? What quality grade of liquor do they stock in the well, e.g., pouring brands, call or premium brands, etc.? Do they stock an

> To succeed in this business, you have to routinely hit the road and shop the competition.

extensive line of super-premium spirits, such as cognacs, single malt Scotches, single barrel bourbons, or 100% agave tequilas? Do they have a wide array of house specialty drinks? Are your competitors known for any particular house signature drinks? What brands of draft beer do they carry? How many handles of draft do they have? Do they offer micro-brew drafts? How many labels of beer do they carry? Do they have a good selection of micro-brews in the bottle? What is their house wine? Do they offer varietal wines by-the-glass?

2 Pricing — How do your competitors prices compare to yours? What do they charge for a well highball, such as a gin and tonic, or Scotch and soda? What are their call and premium prices? What is the price range of the house specialty drinks, such as margaritas, daiquiris? What does the competition charge and what products are put on special during happy hour? How much is a draft of American premium beer, such as Budweiser or Miller Lite? What do they charge for American premium beers by the bottle? What are their import bottle and draft prices? How much is a glass of house wine?

3 Marketing — Is there a demand for the products that your competitors stock that you don't? What type of happy hour promotions do they run? Do they use bar menus to promote their house specialty drinks and bar appetizers? Do they have a wines by-the-glass program? Do they promote a "drink of the day" or "shooter of the day"? Does their service staff attempt to up-sell or use suggestive selling techniques? Do they offer complimentary bar food (bar munchies)? Do they serve food at the bar?

4 Portioning and Glassware — What size drinks do they serve, and what size liquor portion do they pour? How do they dispense alcohol; shot glasses, free pour, or electronic liquor dispensers? What size draft beer does the competition serve? Do they offer more than one serving size? Do they serve draft beer by the pitcher? If so, what size pitchers do they have? What size is their wine serving?

5 Staff — How does the competition's staff compare with your own? Do they appear better trained than your employees? Are they more motivated? Do they conduct themselves more professionally?

6 Ambiance — What type of background music does your competition play? What kind of atmosphere does it help to create? What type of lighting are they using, and what mood does the lighting create?

7 Entertainment — What types of promotions do your competitors run? How do they advertise those promotions? Does your competition have coin-op machines, e.g., video games, pinball, etc.? Do they have pool tables? Does your competition feature dancing? Do they use a disc jockey? Do they offer kareoke? Are there other types of entertainment being offered?

From this information you will be in excellent position to identify what market advantages you enjoy over your competition, what advantages they have over you and how to best counter those advantages.

SHOPPING YOUR CLIENTELE

Clearly, success greatly depends on knowing who your clientele is, understanding their wants and desires, and then somehow finding a way of providing it for them.

Success greatly depends on knowing who your clientele is and understanding their wants and desires.

While you already probably know who is coming into your establishment, demographic shifts do occur. Sometimes the changes happen slowly, almost imperceptibly. Other times the changes to the make-up of your clientele can occur rapidly. A new business complex opens nearby. A manufacturing plant shuts down and goes out of business. A new road is completed making your establishment more accessible.

If there is a significant shift in your demographics underway, one way to confirm the trend is to analyze your sales mix. A change in your sales mix often signals a change in your client base. For example, if a major corporation's headquarters opened its doors down the street, the likely result would be a more professional clientele during lunch, and more people dressed in suits during happy hour. Your credit card sales, especially American Express, would likely increase. Predictably, sales of premium and super-premium spirits would increase as well. You may also notice a change in the sales of certain menu items, as well as an increase in bottled wine sales.

Make note of subtle changes in your sales mix. Ask your bartenders and servers if they have seen any changes in the clientele base. Are different people coming in than before? Is the cast of regulars changing? Often your employees can prove to be an invaluable source of information about your clientele.

There are, however, more deliberate ways to quantify changes in your sales mix. Track the ratio in sales between your major product categories. Begin by tracking the ratio in gross sales between food and beverage. The ratio between food and beverage sales for most operations remains relatively static, so a shift one way or another may prove significant.

For the beverage operation, track the ratio in sales between liquor, beer, wine, and non-alcoholic beverages. They're important percentages to know, and a shift in the sales mix is often the earliest indicator of a changing client base. It is also revealing to analyze the bar's liquor sales. If your clientele is changing, it will likely reveal itself in the sales mix between well liquors, and premium and super-premium liquors. A shift toward a more blue-collar, working crowd is often indicated by an increase in well liquor sales in relation to the top-shelf spirits. A shift toward a more professional, white-collar crowd will likely be revealed by an increase in the premium and super-premium spirits.

How can you find out what your clientele's wants and desires are? One approach is to ask them directly. Walk the floor and talk to your guests. Find out if they are enjoying themselves, and if everything was to their liking. Who doesn't like the owner to come over to pay a brief visit? It's good public relations, and it creates a good opportunity to ask them questions about what they'd like that you don't have, or what they'd like to change. One caution, most people are hesitant to say anything negative to the owner, so gauge the responses accordingly. Nevertheless, it's a good way to stay in contact with your clientele.

How can you find out what your clientele's wants and desires are?

One of the most direct, and effective means of learning what your clientele want and don't want is to routinely ask the bartenders and servers. They're at the point of every sale, practically making them the resident experts. Your staff possesses first-hand knowledge about how customers respond to new products, specials, and menu items. They also see how customers react to your prices.

Another approach is to incorporate your clients in the decision-making process. For instance, instead of you determining which of several new micro-brews to put on tap, why not conduct a beer tasting for your clients, with the consensus choice earning the handle. The same approach can be taken when selecting which new house specialty drinks to feature, or what labels of varietal wines to promote, or which new desserts to add to the menu.

Also consider using comment cards. It's a non-obtrusive method of asking your customers for their comments, opinions, and criticisms.

QUESTIONS LEAD TO ANSWERS
WHICH LEAD TO SUCCESS

- Who are your clientele? What is their estimated range in age and income?
- What affect does your location have on the demographics of your clientele?
- How do your business hours affect the demographics of your clientele?
- Who are your establishment's direct competitors?
- How does the competition's price and products compare to yours?
- What services do you offer your clientele that your direct competitors don't?
- What services do your competition offer the public that your operation doesn't?
- What type of well liquors do your competitors pour and how much do they charge for well drinks?
- What marketing advantages do you enjoy over your competition?
- What marketing disadvantages do your competitors enjoy over you?

Chapter 2

Facility Design,
Beverage Equipment and Smallwares

If you've ever worked behind a bar on a busy shift, then you already know that there isn't such a thing as a perfectly designed bar. Ill-devised layouts and poorly placed equipment can prove to be insurmountable obstacles and leave bartenders incapable of performing their duties behind the bar in a timely and efficient manner.

The likely explanation is that designers and owners are frequently forced to make compromises between concept and function. Often it's unavoidable. Unfortunately, while the compromises may result in an inviting, attractive looking bar, one very much in keeping with the concept of the operation, it may also cause operational chaos. The design changes might work on paper, but the ramifications they have on bartender productivity may end up costing lost sales for the life of the business.

If when designing a bar, too much emphasis is placed on facilitating concept, the smooth operation of the bar will likely suffer. Poor bar design frequently results in delayed service, which will negatively affects sales and customer satisfaction. A poorly designed facility may also result in increased labor costs if one bartender is not able to work the bar alone. Conversely, erring too heavily on the side of function to the detriment of concept is equally harmful and may undermine the viability of the business.

Designing a bar involves determining the specific size and shape of the physical bar structure and the precise layout of the equipment. The optimum design allows bartenders to work at peak efficiency, servers to receive their drink orders quickly, and most importantly, for patrons to enjoy the bar's products and ambiance. All of these must all work in synergy if the operation is to perform at its highest level of profitability and remain within concept.

Many operators do not have extensive practical experience behind the bar, and therefore, do not have a hands-on perspective to draw from when working with a designer or architect. The following will explore the numerous considerations to bar design, and the selection and placement of the equipment.

The optimum design allows bartenders to work at peak efficiency, servers to receive their drink orders quickly, and most importantly, for patrons to enjoy the bar's products and ambiance.

DESIGN AND LAYOUT OF THE FACILITY

There are a number of specific factors that affect the physical shape of the bar, not the least of which is the area in which the bar is to be situated. Popular shapes include linear (straight) bar, L-shaped, horseshoe, and oval (or island) bar. Each type of bar has its advantages and disadvantages.

The linear bar is the easiest shape for bartenders to work efficiently. It allows for unobstructed vision of the patrons seated at the bar and often can be worked by only one bartender in non-peak hours of business. The linear bar design is also the easiest of the various shapes in which to position equipment, outfit with workstations and properly merchandise inventory. The linear bar typically requires less square footage to accomplish the same volume of business and to accommodate the same number of bar stools as other shaped bars. It is, however, the least interesting and appealing shape from a design standpoint.

There are specific factors that affect the physical shape of the bar.

The L-shaped bar is an often used shape because it is relatively easy to incorporate in most floor plans and to outfit with equipment and work stations. It can usually be worked by only one bartender. The L-shape does, however, obstruct the bartender's line of vision. A bartender standing at one end of the bar often cannot see patrons seated at the other end, which may lead to delayed service.

Horseshoe and oval bars are the most challenging shapes for bartenders to work. They require constant movement on the bartender's part to ensure that all the patrons seated at the bar receive proper service. These bars are also the most labor-intensive. Horseshoe and oval bars require more bartenders to work during hours of peak business to provide the same level of service. They are the most difficult in which to adequately position equipment and merchandise inventory.

Regardless of the actual shape of the bar facility, the bartender workstations should be positioned so that there is an equal distance between them, reducing the amount of distance and time necessary for a bartender to reach a workstation to make a drink order. If there are two work stations at a linear bar, for example, the stations should be positioned five or six feet from each end. If there are three stations, the third station should be located in the middle of the bar, providing easy access to all bartenders.

If there are two workstations at an L-bar, they are typically positioned five or six feet from each end. If three workstations are required, two should be positioned on the longest side of the bar with the third located on the short side of the facility.

If there are two workstations at a horseshoe bar, they are most strategically positioned on each of the straight sides. If a third station were required, it would likely be located in the center of the curved portion of the bar. Again the oval or island bar is the most challenging in this regard. If two stations are required, they would be positioned at each of the curved ends of the oval. Should a third station be necessary, it would be advisable to position the three stations an equal distance from each other.

BAR SPECIFICATIONS

There are certain specifications that must be incorporated into the bar facility and design. Deviating from these standard specifications will unnecessarily burden your bartenders and needlessly hamper your operation. For example, the standard distance between the back bar face and any piece of under bar equipment (including the speed racks) is 30-36 inches. If there is less space than this, the bartenders will be cramped and often have difficulty moving behind the bar. If the distance is greater than 36 inches, the bartenders will be constantly wasting time and motion traveling between the work-

There are certain specifications that must be incorporated into the bar facility and design.

The following are standard bar specifications:

a.	Width of back bar	24 inches
b.	Width of liquor display shelves	12-16 inches
c.	Height of back bar	42 inches
d.	Distance between back bar and front bar equipment	30-36 inches
e.	Distance between edge of speed rack and bar rail	14 inches
f.	Height of underbar	30 inches
g.	Width of underbar	18 inches
h.	Width of underbar including speed rack	23-24 inches
i.	Distance from underbar to bar top	12 inches
j.	Width of bar top	24 inches
k.	Width of speed rack	5-6 inches
l.	Distance between bar rail and front edge of underbar	7-8 inches
m.	Height of bar top	42 inches
n.	Distance between outside edge of bar top and speed rack	37 inches
o.	Height of bar die	40 inches
p.	Distance between bar die and back of underbar equipment	3 inches
q.	Distance from back wall to outer edge of bar top	91 inches

Illustration 2.1

station and the back bar. The cumulative effect of such a miscalculation is surprisingly costly, and will continue to be so for the useful life of the facility.

BARTENDERS' WORK STATIONS
AND ENSURING PEAK PRODUCTIVITY

Bartending at a high-volume bar is a highly choreographed art, and properly designed workstations will directly affect bartender productivity. Armed with well-devised and fully functional stations, bartenders can work quickly and efficiently.

When standing in front of the workstation, nearly everything a bartender needs to fill any drink order should be positioned within a six-foot radius. In this case, a six-foot radius realistically translates to a step and a reach. The ice bin is the focal point of the bartender's workstation. It should be constructed of 20-22 gauge stainless steel, with rigid frame construction, and contain a completely sealed, full-sized cold plate. The balance of the equipment and supplies should be positioned around the station to create an effective use of space so that drink orders can be made with a minimum of wasted motion. Wasted motion equates to lost sales.

Create an effective use of space so that drink orders can be made with a minimum of wasted motion.

Basic items should be duplicated at each station: ice bins, liquor speed racks, glass storage, beverage dispensers (a.k.a. soda gun), condiment trays, jockey boxes with drink mixes and juices, waste containers, P. O. S. terminal(s) or cash registers, and cash drawer(s). The equipment and supplies used most frequently should be placed closest to the ice bin, minimizing the amount of time and motion it takes for the bartender to reach them.

Since most bartenders are right-handed, equipment and supplies should be positioned so that there is a minimum of cross-handed operations required to make drinks. For example, right-handed bartenders naturally pick-up bottles with their right hands and glasses with their left. To maximize efficiency, glasses should be stored to the left of a workstation, allowing the bartender to pick-up the glasses with their left-hand and add the ice using the scoop in the right hand. Mixing equipment and blenders should be positioned to the right. A hand sink is ideally positioned to the right of the work station allowing the bartender to dump the excess ice and fluid from his mixing equipment, blender or returned glasses with a minimum of movement.

If a hand-held jigger is used, it should be placed on the pour mat to the left of the bartender. This will allow the bartender to hold it in the left hand while pouring a bottle with his or her right. The soda gun(s) should be positioned to the right side of the ice bin so that the bartender is capable of using it without reaching across the body.

If bartenders are allowed to free-pour, or if you use the Precision Pour control spouts, the soda gun(s) should be positioned on the left side of the station, allowing the bartender to hold a bottle in the right hand while operating the soda gun with the left.

Well liquors are positioned in a speed rack mounted to the front of the workstation for immediate access. A speed rack is a stainless steel, enclosed shelf designed specifically to hold liquor bottles. Two-tiered (double) speed racks are also available. Call brand liquors and liqueurs can be placed in speed racks to the left and right of the bartenders' workstation. These speed racks are frequently mounted on the sides of top-loading beer boxes or four-compartment sinks.

Premium, super-premium and top-shelf liquors and liqueurs should be merchandised in display cases optimally located directly behind the workstation on the back bar above 42 inches. This will allow bar patrons to see the products and prevent bartenders from having to stoop down to retrieve them. To save on storage space behind the bar, design the shelves of the display case wide enough (approximately 12-16 inches) to accommodate positioning bottles two deep. This will allow you to shelve a back-up of each brand (with some exceptions) and eliminate some of the need for undercounter liquor storage.

Equipment and supplies should be positioned so that there is a minimum of cross-handed operations required to make drinks.

When designing the liquor display cases, an estimate needs to be made as to how much shelving is required to display the liquor inventory. This projection is critical to the operation. Estimate too low and you'll wind up without enough display shelving to adequately merchandise your inventory. Over-estimate the amount of shelf space and you'll have a back bar dominated by shelving to the detriment of the design.

As mentioned, glassware should be stored to the left of the workstation. The most frequently used bar service glasses should be stored in sufficient quantity closest to the station. Beer glasses should be positioned within easy reach of the draft beer dispenser.

Other necessary equipment that should be located near the bartenders' work station include the draft beer dispensing system and the refrigeration equipment, such as the reach-in cooler and top-loading beer box. Reach-in doors should be hinged so they open toward the bartenders' workstation for easy access. Shared equipment or areas, such as the glassware drain boards, automatic glass washer or a three- (four-) compartment sink unit should be positioned between the workstations, reducing the amount of crossing between bartenders working adjacent stations.

This compact positioning of equipment, supplies and inventory should allow the bartenders to fill the majority of drink orders without having to take more than a few steps away from the workstation.

It is important that bartenders have adequate lighting behind the bar for drink making. Florescent lighting mounted underneath the bar top and abutting the bar die is usually all that is necessary. Track lighting behind the bar may also be highly effective.

The bar top area directly in front of the bartenders' workstation serves several functions. Frequently used single service items, such as straws, sip sticks, sword picks, and cocktail napkins or drink coasters are placed on the bar top in front of the station for easy access to both the bartenders and servers. The condiment tray is also typically found here.

This area is also where servers pick-up their drink orders and return dirty glassware. The surface area for beverage pick-up must be large enough for drink orders to be placed on cocktail trays for several servers. Efficient service is slowed down and a backlog occurs if there isn't adequate space in the pick-up area for drinks that have been prepared. Brass rails are normally used to delineate this section of the bar top as a service area.

It is also advisable to use the surface area adjacent to the workstation for the sundry smallwares and tools the bartenders need. This shelf area is ideal for storing a mixing tin, mixing glass, bar spoon, spring strainer, bottle opener, wine opener, cutting board, and paring knives. The surface of this shelf should be covered with glassware netting to allow the wet mixing equipment to air dry.

Food service at the bar is essential to the success of many beverage concepts. Accommodation should be made for the storage of such items as menus, silverware, napkins, plates, water glasses and assorted condiments (e.g. salt, pepper, Lea & Perrins, etc.) behind the bar. This will allow the bartenders to professionally serve the guests eating food at the bar. It is also advisable to reserve an area behind the bar for a bus tub to hold dirty flatware and silverware. It is a modification that will likely bolster food sales at the bar.

This compact positioning of equipment should allow the bartenders to fill the majority of drink orders without having to take more than a few steps away from the workstation.

Make sure that your facility has the storage space necessary to store adequate quantities of back-up liquor, dry goods, canned juices, clean towels, cleaning solutions, disposable supplies, back-up matches and pens, internal forms (e.g. requisitions, bar par, spillage & wastes, drink/food checks), back-up syrups and mixes, and glass washing solutions. Insufficient storage behind the bar may cause shortages of some items.

Trash disposal is an often over-looked design consideration behind the bar. A busy bar generates a surprising amount of trash. Insufficient trash disposal behind the bar creates an unsightly and often disruptive problem. Imagine the impression patrons seated at the bar form when they see overflowing trash containers. Trash containers should be located conveniently by each workstation, out of sight to the public whenever possible. There should also be trash containers on the public side of the bar for servers' use. They should be emptied frequently during the course of a busy night.

The final design element crucial to the smooth operation of the bar is a functional, well-positioned employee entry to the bar, also known as a pass-through. It may be hard to conceive, but many designers give little to no thought where the pass-through is located or what type of pass-through is incorporated into the bar design.

The pass-through should provide easy passage from behind the bar. Often bartenders are required to provide tableside service during non-peak hours of business. The entry should be located at the end of the bar where the least amount of bar traffic is anticipated. An entry that is narrow and difficult to negotiate will needlessly hamper the operation. Some entries are designed such that you have to stoop underneath the bar top to get behind the bar. It is a slow means of passage, and when your back aches after a long shift, you'll curse the designers. Do not underestimate the importance of a well-designed entry.

Food service at the bar is essential to the success of many beverage concepts.

SERVICE BARS

In high-volume operations, incorporating a service bar into the design may be advisable. A service bar is intended solely for indirect service, meaning the bartender working that station makes drinks for servers only. Service bars are most frequently located either in the kitchen or in a centrally located area of the facility. The service bar must be conveniently located for server access. As the distance of the bar from guest area increases, service time also increases. If possible, the service bar should be positioned in the operation such that servers do not have to walk through crowded, heavy traffic areas to reach the service bar or to deliver drink orders.

The service bar is designed solely for function and to improve drink service. No real consideration to concept is necessary. The service bar is a compact area designed for optimum bartender productivity. The bar is designed around the bartenders' workstation. Everything the bartender requires to fill drink orders should be positioned within a six-foot radius.

BEVERAGE EQUIPMENT PURCHASING AND PLACEMENT CRITERIA

The pass-through should provide easy passage from behind the bar.

As with any business decision, budget constraints are a consideration in determining what equipment to purchase for the bar. While there are usually sufficient reasons for eliminating the purchase of a given piece of equipment based on budget, serious consideration should be given to the savings that a particular item will provide long term. In selecting a specific piece of equipment for your operation, do not only consider its initial cost. Unless you are contemplating a quick turnaround, you and your employees will have to work with the equipment for years. The lowest price today may prove to be the least economical in the long run. Here the adage, "Always buy quality," is most appropriate and applicable.

The small cost differences in quality equipment today will pay dividends in lower maintenance and operating costs over the useful life of the equipment. A refrigerator unit with poor insulation and improperly designed gaskets will cost more to operate long term than the initially more expensive, but properly constructed equipment. An inexpensive refrigeration system will be more costly to maintain than a well designed unit.

Quality equipment works more efficiently and reliably for a longer period of time. Equipment breakdowns are costly in both time and money. They also cause customer service delays and result in poor quality drinks, both of which often create negative customer impressions. Quality cannot be determined by price alone. Quality is judged by performance, ease-of-use, aesthetics, warranties, and the availability of convenient, timely service when needed.

The following are some important criteria to use when evaluating whether to purchase a piece of equipment for the bar.

1 **Need** — Every piece of equipment must be justified from the standpoint of need. Thought must be given to whether purchasing a certain piece of equipment will generate additional revenue due to its impact on merchandising and customer satisfaction, making it a worthy investment. Equipment must have the proper capacity and be suited for the tasks it is to perform in the operation. Often the basic model of equipment is sufficient. High capital cost items, such as refrigeration units and glass washing machines (or sinks), are shared between the bartenders' workstations.

2 **Cost** — The initial cost of equipment is frequently misleading. A piece of equipment that is initially more expensive is often more economical in the long term. Factors to consider are the cost of regular maintenance, cleaning, repair, supplies, training, financing, insurance, and anticipated operating costs.

3 **Performance** — Performance must be measured by how well the equipment being considered carries out its specific tasks. For example, does a certain blender prepare drinks quickly and efficiently, or is it inadequate for demands of commercial use? Is a reach-in cooler or top-loading beer box large enough to stock inventory for an entire shift? Will a glass washing machine clean the volume of glasses necessary during a busy shift? Will the glasses get clean and come out of the rinse cycle cool enough to use immediately?

Quality equipment works more efficiently and reliably for a longer period of time.

4 **Safety and Sanitation** — Are there any equipment safety concerns, such as sharp or protruding edges, or poorly insulated electrical cords? These hazards can prove to be a constant headache to your business and staff. Beverage equipment must also be sanitary. Of major concern are defects in the design and construction to the equipment that prevent them from ever being cleaned to the point of being sanitary. Equipment with the National Sanitation Foundation (NSF) or the Underwriter's Laboratory (UL) approval are easily cleaned and therefore suitable for purchase.

There are other factors that should be considered before investing in beverage equipment. Those factors are specified in the following:

5 **Ice Machines** — Ice machines are generally located near the rear of the operation as they are accessed only several times during the course of a day's business. They are, however, indispensable to the smooth operation of the business. The capacity of the machine must be adequate to keep pace with the demands of the operation.

If an ice machine is unable to produce enough ice for the business, you will be forced to purchase retail ice from an outside vendor. On a long-term basis this is an expensive and unacceptable business practice.

The ice machine should be outfitted with a remote condenser that is located on the exterior roof. The remote condenser will exhaust its heat outside, instead of building up the heat in the back of the house. Heat build-up will negatively affect the ice machine's production levels.

The size and the shape of the ice cube are also important. The smaller the ice cube, the more cubes will fit into your bar service glassware, reducing a glass's capacity. This will allow you to use a standard measurement of liquor (1 to 1.25 ounces) and less mixer, resulting in a smooth, good tasting drink. There are numerous different shaped cubes (e.g. rectangular, round, etc). Cubes with rounded surfaces help prevent the "splash-out" effect, where the liquor splashes off the surface of the ice cube and out of the glass. This is a wasteful practice and should be avoided.

Heat build-up will negatively affect the ice machine's production levels.

Recent innovations and advances in ice making technology have made a considerable impact on the purchase and economical operation of ice machines. Today, ice machines are operated by microchip technology. The inboard computer is capable of monitoring every phase of ice production, making the entire process more energy and water efficient. The computer will also monitor every function of the machine, and will shut itself down in the event of a malfunction. The control panel will indicate if there is a problem and exactly what the problem area is.

Coolers and Refrigerators — There are essentially two types of refrigeration units necessary behind your bar. An undercounter reach-in cooler resembling a small refrigerator should be positioned directly behind or adjacent to the bartenders' workstation. The reach-in is ideally suited for storing back-up mixes, cream, juices, garnishes, and bottles of wine. The door(s) should be hinged to open toward to the bartenders' workstation. The unit must have a thermometer.

The shelves in the reach-in cooler should be adjustable. Both the interior and exterior of the reach-in should be easy to clean and the unit should meet NSF standards for sanitation. Units not on enclosed bases must be on legs high enough to permit sweeping and mopping underneath.

The top-loading cooler (a.k.a. beer box) is an essential piece of equipment. They are available in a variety of styles and usually range in length from four to six feet. The equipment is best suited for bottled beer storage with capacities ranging from 14 to 28 cases of beer. This type of storage capacity will prevent bartenders from having to restock bottled beer during a busy shift. The unit must have a thermometer.

The beer box(es) should be located close to the bartenders' workstations, and if possible an equal distance between stations for easy access.

7 **Post-Mix Beverage Dispensers** — Post-mix beverage dispensers are considered an indispensable piece of bar equipment. The device, also known as a soda gun, is capable of cost-effectively dispensing carbonated beverages and juices more quickly and conveniently than pouring from individual containers. The system operates by mixing concentrated syrups and carbonated water in the exact proportion in the dispenser head. The syrups are stored in five-gallon containers or boxes either behind the bar or at a remote site, typically in the kitchen or pantry.

Bartending is an art form that requires its own tools of the trade.

The post-mix beverage dispenser equipment is installed and maintained (normally free of charge) in exchange for the operator purchasing the purveyor's syrups and juices. A soda gun sits in a specially designed receptacle or holster at each bartenders' workstation.

BAR SUPPLIES AND SMALLWARES

Bartending is an art form that requires its own tools of the trade. Optimum drink production depends on providing your bartending staff with the necessary labor and time saving devices. The following is a complete alphabetical list of all the supplies and smallwares necessary to operate an efficient, high-volume beverage operation.

1 **Anti-Fatigue Floor Mats** — During a busy shift, the floor behind a bar gets wet and slippery, posing a safety hazard for the bartenders. The solution is hard rubber floor mats. Not only do they provide badly needed traction behind the bar, they also greatly reduce breakage. Perhaps their greatest benefit is the affect they have on reducing bartender back strain and leg fatigue. Standing and working on a hard surface can be brutal on the back and legs.

2 **Blenders** — The electric blender is considered a necessary piece of beverage equipment. While some beverage operations may receive fewer requests for blended (frozen) cocktails than others, there will undoubtedly still be guests that request an occasional frozen margarita or strawberry daiquiri.

Consider getting more than one canister for your blender. This will allow you to quickly make more than one blended drink per order. It also allows you to make swirl drinks, which require making two frozen drinks nearly simultaneously, and then combining them in one glass for a fantastic effect.

3 **Bottle Opener** — Most top-loading coolers are outfitted with a mounted bottle opener that is partially enclosed and designed to prevent the bottle caps from flying off and landing on the floor. These types of openers are preferable over the hand-held style.

4 **Cutting Board and Paring Knives** — Several washable, wooden cutting boards should be procured for the preparation of fruit garnishes. The health department dictates the use of wooden boards over the hard plastic or Lucite kind. Sharp paring knives are essential. A dull knife poses a much greater hazard to bartenders than one that is extremely sharp.

5 **Glassware Shelving Netting** — The health department requires glassware to be placed on shelving lined with plastic netting to allow the free flow of air to circulate inside the glassware. This netting can be purchased at most restaurant supply outlets.

6 **Ice Scoops** — The health department considers ice a food substance, which means that it cannot be touched or come in contact with skin. Hard plastic or Lexan ice scoops are preferable to metal scoops. Metal scoops may scrape against the cold plate in the ice bin, possibly resulting in metal shavings in the ice. Bartenders are never permitted to use a glass to scoop ice.

7 **Jiggers** — Hand-held measuring is the most cost-effective means of pouring liquor at the bar. There are several types of hand-held measuring devices that can be used. The most common is the double-sided, stainless steel jigger. It is available in a variety of measurement combinations. Their principle drawback is that they are opaque and don't allow patrons or supervisors to visually confirm how much liquor is being poured. Clear plastic or glass measures are preferable.

8 **Mixing Equipment** — The traditional bartender mixing set consists of a stainless steel mixing tin (16 oz.), mixing glass (16 oz.), spring strainer and long-handled bar spoon.

The health department considers ice a food substance.

9 Optics — Long popular in Europe, optics are a gravity feed measuring system in which liquor bottles are inverted in specially designed racks on the back bar. The optic devices are inserted into the necks of the bottles. The optic device has a reservoir that fills with liquor, and when the activator arm is depressed, the device dispenses the liquor in the reservoir. These devices come in different portion sizes, ranging from ⅞ ounce to 1½ ounces.

10 • Pour Mats — Pour mats are ribbed rubber mats that are placed on the bar top directly in front of the bartenders' workstation where the drinks are made. The mats are designed to hold any spilled fluids from dripping into the ice bin below or pooling on the bar top.

11 • Pour Spouts — Reusable spouts used in liquor or liqueur bottles. Some styles of spouts pour faster than others and are therefore harder for bartenders to control and deliver accurate measurements. The opening on the spout determines the speed of the pour. Medium pour spouts are more cost-effective than speed (fast) pours.

12 • Wine Openers — The most widely used commercial wine opener is the French waiters' corkscrew. When selecting which wine opener to purchase, choose one equipped with a blade for cutting away the foil on the neck of a wine bottle. A straight blade is preferable to one that is curved; the curved blade has a tendency to tear the foil. Choose an opener that has a worm (the screw portion of the opener) with five curls instead of four, and preferably one that has a center groove etched down the middle of the curls. The groove will reduce friction and is easier to use.

The traditional bartender mixing set consists of a stainless steel mixing tin, mixing glass, spring strainer and long-handled bar spoon.

Wall mounted wine openers are also an option. These devices are capable of removing the cork from a bottle in one smooth, effort-less motion. They are a fast and efficient method of opening a bottle of wine at a bar.

QUESTIONS LEAD TO ANSWERS WHICH LEAD TO SUCCESS

- Does the design and layout of your bar slow bartender productivity?
- Is the equipment behind the bar in the best possible location?
- Are there design elements behind the bar that require modification?
- Are there pieces of equipment behind the bar that need to be replaced? Are all of the operation's equipment needs behind the bar currently being met?
- Are your bar's workstations set-up to best meet the bartenders' needs. Do you have all of the smallwares necessary for efficient drink making?
- Do you have sufficient refrigeration behind the bar to meet operational demands?
- Is there everything a bartender will require to professionally serve food located behind the bar?
- Do you have adequate waste/trash disposal behind the bar?
- Is there a need for a service bar in your operation?
- If you have a service bar, is it laid-out and equipped to best meet the operation's demands?
- Is the production capabilities of your ice machine sufficient to meet operational demands?
- Do you have anti-fatigue mats behind all of your bars?

Chapter 3

Well Liquor:
The Most Important Bottles in the House

Well liquors (a.k.a. house liquor) are used in drinks when the guest specifies no brand name preference, or in drink recipes in which a liquor is used only as a base, e.g. Singapore Sling. Approximately half of your operation's liquor depletion will likely come from the well. As a result, the quality and cost of the featured house liquors are of primary importance. Considerations to weigh when selecting well liquor include their perceived quality versus their cost per ounce, the importance of name-brand recognition, the demographics of your clientele, and the concept of your operation.

Since the well products will sell at the same price, it is advisable to evaluate the cost-effectiveness of well liquors collectively. For a standard well (gin/bourbon/vodka/Scotch/rum/tequila), add the wholesale costs of the six products together and then divide by six to arrive at the average liter cost. Divide the average liter cost by 33.8 ounces to determine the well liquor's average cost per ounce.

How you sequence the well liquor in your speed rack will have an impact on waste and spillage. The traditional well series—bourbon/Scotch/gin/vodka/rum/tequila—increases costs as a result of positioning the dark liquors together and light liquors together. Contrast that with the more contemporary "light/dark series"—gin/bourbon/vodka/Scotch/rum/tequila—where each light liquor is separated by one that is dark. When busy, bartenders are less apt to mistakenly pour one liquor thinking it's another.

There are basically three grades of liquors to choose from. Each grade has its advantages and disadvantages, the merits of which should be carefully considered.

How you sequence the well liquor in your speed rack will have an impact on waste and spillage.

POURING BRANDS IN THE WELL

These inexpensive spirits are produced at varying degrees of quality and taste. They are typically spirits that, unless you're in the industry, have unfamiliar brand names. While prices vary, pouring brands usually cost between $.20 to $.35 per ounce and yield drink prices between $2.00 to $3.00.

The advantages of featuring pouring brand liquors in your well include their low cost per ounce and reduced carrying cost. Carrying cost is the total dollar value of the inventory. If you stock pouring brands in the well, your carrying cost will be less than if you stocked more expensive premium brands.

Among the disadvantages, pouring brands have little or no name-brand recognition or consumer loyalty. They are frequently chosen for operations that cater to a clientele that is predominantly price-conscious—meaning the patrons are more concerned with what a drink costs than what brand of liquor is used in its preparation. If in their minds the drink prices are even a quarter or two too high, they will often go to another establishment.

Pouring brands are frequently chosen for a clientele that is price-conscious.

The following is an example of a well comprised of pouring brands. The average liter cost for the six products is $7.19, or an average cost of $.2 per ounce. Five retail price points are listed, ranging from $2.00 to $3.00, with the corresponding cost percentages and gross profit figures.

Brand Name	Liter Cost	Cost Per Ounce	Retail Price	Cost Percentage	Gross Profit
Bartons Vodka	$4.72	$ .14			
Bartons Gin	$5.40	$ .16	$2.00	10.5%	$1.79
Castillo Rum	$7.44	$ .22	$2.25	9.4%	$2.04
Tempo Tequila	$7.54	$ .22	$2.50	8.4%	$2.29
Beam Eight Star Bourbon	$8.02	$ .24	$2.75	7.6%	$2.54
Clan MacGregor Scotch	$10.02	$ .30	$3.00	7.0%	$2.79
Average Liter Cost	$7.19	$ .21			

Pouring Brands

Illustration 3.1

SEMI-PREMIUM BRANDS IN THE WELL

Semi-premium brands are a grade of spirits from the low-cost end of the call brands. These are name brand spirits that most consumers have heard of, yet they come with a reasonable price tag. Semi-premium brands usually cost between $.25 to $.50 per ounce and yield drink prices in the $2.50 to $4.50 range.

The advantages of featuring semi-premium liquors in the well include their moderate cost per ounce and enhanced name-brand recognition. This grade of liquor is often marketed through P. O. S. displays ("We proudly pour...").

The downside to featuring semi-premium liquors in your well include their slightly elevated cost per ounce and a minimal increase in carrying cost. Although with this type of well you eliminate stocking any pouring brands, the operation's carrying costs will increase somewhat because of the larger inventory of call brands. It should be noted, however, that these are brands that the bar would likely be carrying regardless.

Semi-premium brands are typically featured in operations where the clientele can be characterized as being value-conscious—meaning they are individuals who are willing to spend a little more to receive a better quality drink. Semi-premium wells are popular in mid-scale restaurants, bars and hotels, establishments that cater to people who are looking for a good drink at a reasonable price.

The following is an example of a well comprised of semi-premium brands. The average liter cost for the six products is $11.28, or an average cost of $.33 per ounce. Five retail price points are listed, ranging from $2.50 to $4.50, with the corresponding cost percentages and gross profit figures.

Semi-premium brands are typically featured in operations where the clientele is value-conscious.

Brand Name	Liter Cost	Cost Per Ounce	Retail Price	Cost Percentage	Gross Profit
Seagram's Gin	$8.80	$ .26			
Bacardi Light Rum	$9.48	$ .28	$2.50	13.2%	$2.17
Smirnoff 80 Vodka	$10.25	$ .30	$3.00	11.0%	$2.67
Jim Beam Bourbon	$10.76	$ .32	$3.50	9.5%	$3.17
Cuervo Especial Tequila	$13.98	$ .41	$4.00	8.2%	$3.67
White Horse Blended Scotch	$14.40	$ .43	$4.50	7.3%	$4.17
Average Liter Cost	$11.28	$ .33			

Semi-Premium Brands

Illustration 3.2

PREMIUM BRANDS IN THE WELL

These spirits are likely to be selected from the top-end of the premium brands, or the least expensive super-premium brands. These brands usually cost between $.30 to $.55 per ounce and yield drink prices in the $3.50 to $5.50 (or more) range.

The advantages of featuring these call brands in your well include their unsurpassed quality, high name-brand recognition and staunch consumer loyalty. Premium brands are successfully marketed through P. O. S. displays ("We proudly pour..."). If you're going to feature quality at the bar, make sure you announce the fact to your clientele.

Included among the disadvantages of featuring premium brands in the well are their extremely high cost per ounce and the elevated carrying cost. Also, when premium liquors are used in the well, the sales of call brands and other premium products are greatly reduced. As a result, many bars featuring a premium well simply do not carry many standard call and premium selections.

Premium brands are typically featured in operations where the clientele are brand-conscious

Premium brands are typically featured in operations where the clientele are brand-conscious—meaning the patrons are more conscious of what they are drinking than how much it costs. Premium wells are most often found in upscale restaurants, hotels and nightclubs.

The following is an example of a well comprised of premium brands. The average liter cost for the six products is $17.53, or an average cost of $.52 per ounce. Five retail price points are listed, ranging from $3.50 to $5.50, with the corresponding cost percentages and gross profit figures.

Brand Name	Liter Cost	Cost Per Ounce	Retail Price	Cost Percentage	Gross Profit
Tanqueray Gin	$16.58	$ .49			
Appleton Estate Rum	$16.60	$ .49	$3.50	14.9%	$2.98
Absolut 80 Vodka	$16.69	$ .49	$4.00	13.0%	$3.48
Maker's Mark Bourbon	$16.88	$ .50	$4.50	11.5%	$3.98
Sauza Hornitos	$18.90	$ .56	$5.00	10.4%	$4.48
Dewars White Label	$19.54	$ .58	$5.50	9.5%	$4.98
Average Liter Cost	$17.53	$ .52			
Premium Brands					

Illustration 3.3

PARTING SHOT

Marketing the wrong type of well liquor to your clientele can be damaging. Consider what the ramifications would be of promoting pouring brand liquors to an affluent clientele at an upscale establishment. The guests would likely be negatively impressed by the apparent lack of quality in the house drinks. They might take it to mean that if quality is not a benchmark in the front of the house, then it probably isn't the standard in the back of the house either. The net effect would be a loss of credibility and consumer perception.

Conversely, what if premium products are featured at a bar with a price-conscious clientele? The elevated cost of these name-brand liquors may raise the price of the drinks out of most of the guests' reach. These are people who are more interested in how much a drink costs than what brand of liquor is used in its preparation.

Finally, do not think that the above examples limit the realm of possibilities when it comes to putting together a successful well. For example, the operator of an Irish pub may very well decide to feature only Irish brands in the well, spirits such as Boru Vodka, Cork Dry Irish Gin and Jameson Irish Whiskey.

QUESTIONS LEAD TO ANSWERS
WHICH LEAD TO SUCCESS

- What types or brands of well liquors do your direct competitors pour and how do they compare to the brands featured in your well?
- What criteria did you use when selecting your well liquor?
- What is your clientele most interested in regarding mixed drinks—the cost of the drink, its perceived value, or the brand of liquor used in its preparation?
- What do your bartenders think about the brands featured in the well? How does your clientele react to your choices of house liquors?
- What is your speed rack order and is it the most cost-effective arrangement?
- What is your well's average liter cost per ounce?
- What is your well's cost percentage?
  (portion cost ÷ sales price x 100)
- Do you purchase your well liquor by the case?
- Do you buy your well liquor from more than one distributor? Purchasing comparable brands, would you receive better discounts purchasing from just one distributor?

Chapter 4

Selecting Your
Top-Shelf Products

The average bar in the United States carries roughly 130 liquors and liqueurs in their inventory. And while consumption of distilled spirits has dropped steadily since the mid-1980s, the number of liquors and liqueurs stocked at the average American bar has remained relatively constant.

There are certainly many bars and restaurants in this country that carry a large number of liquors and liqueurs. An expansive back bar with scores of mirror-backed shelves lined with bottles is for many operations an integral aspect of their marketing concept. If a spirit is available and potentially may hold some intrigue for a guest, the establishment may stock it. The marketing concept here is, "If one of our guests might request it, we should have it."

Each strategy has its merits.

Some operations opt for a more conservative approach to marketing. They will offer a limited selection of spirits and liqueurs, each product carefully chosen to be a reasonable choice of a specific category. So, for instance, instead of carrying a broad selection of imported vodkas, the establishment may only stock Absolut and Stolichnaya, or Tanqueray and Beefeater as their gin. The marketing concept being, "We may not carry everything, but what we carry we can serve with pride."

Other bars may choose to carry a sufficiently broad selection of products dominated by conventional brands without venturing into the unusual. For example, the bar might carry a wide selection of Scotch whiskies, comprised of five blended, 8-year old Scotches, several 12-year old blends, and a half dozen single malts. All of the selections are conventional, mainstream brands, offerings designed to meet most customers' requests. Here the marketing concept is, "Unless you throw us a curve, we likely carry it."

Each strategy has its merits. Conversely, each has its shortcomings. What is critically important is to use a marketing strategy best suited for your establishment and the clientele to whom you will be catering. Once again market research is crucial to your decision-making process.

Your understanding of the market will help you answer two fundamentally important operational questions. One, how much inventory is right for your establishment? And two, which products should you carry in your inventory?

Before setting about answering those questions, two business-related concepts need to be examined.

1 **Carrying Cost** — As it pertains to the beverage end of the food & beverage equation, your carrying cost is the combined dollar value of the liquor, beer, wine, and non-alcoholic inventories. The cost of your inventory will remain relatively constant, fluctuating somewhat with seasonal demands. It is important to maintain your inventory levels as low as possible without experiencing shortages of products, and while still remaining in your marketing concept.

From a business perspective, it is crucial to keep your working capital flowing through your checking account and not needlessly tied-up in inventory. Determine the exact number of each product you carry, and maintain your inventory at those levels. You should occasionally take advantage of special deals offered by your wholesalers on select products that you know turnover rapidly. Do not purchase large quantities of products, regardless of their discounted cost, that will take you many months to turnover. As will be mentioned again later, only purchase products by the case that you estimate will sell in 4-5 weeks or less.

2 **Capital Risk** — There is another reason to keep your inventory levels as low as you can feasibly maintain them. Once you take inventory out of the relative security of the liquor storeroom, the money you have invested in those products essentially becomes "capital at risk." Once requisitioned to the bar, those products can be wasted, spilled, given away, drunk by employees, or otherwise stolen.

Maintaining tight inventory levels, carrying as little inventory as is reasonable, and implementing an effective inventory control program will greatly reduce your exposure to losses.

Your carrying cost is the combined dollar value of the liquor, beer, wine, and non-alcoholic inventories.

SETTING INVENTORY LEVELS

So how do you determine how much inventory is right for your establishment? If you're just starting out in business, the best piece of advice is to be conservative, and start small. For most operations, opening with an adequate selection of the most popular call and premium brands is sufficient. For example, instead of initially carrying three or four premium gins, stock the two best-selling brands. Do the same for the imported vodkas, super-premium tequilas, and so forth. As your business grows, your customers will begin requesting certain products, and your inventory will slowly grow.

Be especially conservative when purchasing super-premium products. They naturally take a longer amount of time to turnover, and their relatively high cost means that if you make a mistake by ordering an unpopular brand, or too much of a certain brand, more of your capital will be tied-up and "at risk" for a longer period of time.

While there is no such thing as a typical beverage line-up, illustration 4.1 is an example of the categories and products that might comprise a liquor, beer and wine inventory.

Over time, most beverage operations let their inventory grow to the point of being unmanageable. New products are added to the inventory, while older, slower moving products are allowed to remain on the back bar. Unless offering an extensive array of liquors and liqueurs is part of your marketing concept, there is a physical limit to how many products you can adequately market on your back bar. There is only so much space available behind the bar.

Track each product's depletion rate.

One way to cull through the inventory is to track each product's depletion rate. This is best accomplished with a liquor requisition tracking form. If a product takes more than six months to turnover, it's likely that one or two customers order it occasionally, and you may therefore deem it worth hanging on to. However, it should be considered "on the bubble," and if the product remains on the shelf much longer, you would be well advised dropping it from your inventory.

If a product doesn't turnover in nine months to a year, than it should definitely be considered "dead stock." Dead stock is a problem for nearly all bars. Products fall out of fashion, while others were never in fashion to begin with. As a result you will have products with old, tattered labels taking valuable display space on your back bar. This space could be put to much better use either marketing products that people actually want, or by simply increasing the amount of space between the bottles, making the remaining stock seem more exclusive.

What should you do with dead stock? There are essentially only two strategies that can implemented to rid your bar of slow moving/non-moving inventory. The first method to sell-off the product is to devise a specialty drink or shooter that uses the unwanted item as its base. For some products, however, incorporating them in even the most bizarre concoctions will do little to attract consumer interest. When all else fails, it's best to remove the dead stock from the back bar, and place it in the liquor room until an effective strategy to "blow-out" the products can be formulated.

One way or another, dead stock needs to be removed from your display shelves, the area that your clientele look at when they're sitting at the bar. Dead stock is unsightly, and gives the back bar a neglected, disheveled appearance.

SELECTING A LIQUEUR INVENTORY

Liqueurs are typically more expensive than distilled spirits, so some care is needed when selecting which products to stock. Begin by reviewing what type of drinks you'll be preparing. If you anticipate marketing a wide range of shooters, ice cream drinks, and tropical drinks, you'll need products such as creme de cacao, banana liqueur, sloe gin, blue Curaçao, and creme de noyaux. If you're not planning on marketing many exotic concoctions, but you would like a fully stocked back bar, consider purchasing these cordials in 750ml or 500ml bottles. You'll still have them on your back bar, but you'll have made a smaller investment.

Before you invest in a liqueur, have an idea why you're stocking it and how you'll be using it.

The same is true for the flavored brandies. These products have largely gone out of fashion, primarily because they are too sweet and syrupy for contemporary tastes. If you're catering to an older crowd and feel that you need to carry apricot-, cherry-, and blackberry-brandy, consider purchasing smaller bottles until you've established exactly how quickly you're depleting them.

Before you invest in a liqueur, have an idea why you're stocking it and how you'll be using it. If you're not planning on serving many Rusty Nails, for instance, you probably don't need to invest in a liter-sized bottle of Drambuie. The same holds true for liqueurs such as Benedictine D.O.M., Chartreuse, ouzo, sambuca, anisette, and Galliano. Before you begin investing your working capital, make sure there is a legitimate demand for products.

There is a vast array of flavored schnapps, ranging in flavors from chocolate, spearmint and blueberry, to cinnamon, root beer and watermelon. With so many flavors, and new flavors seemingly introduced every month, it may take an exceedingly long time to turnover these products. They do make excellent flavoring agents in drinks though. So before you become overwhelmed with flavored schnapps, have a clear idea of how you're going to market them.

Example Liquor, Beer and Wine Inventory

AMERICAN WHISKEY
Jack Daniel's (well)
Jack Daniel's Single Barrel
Jim Beam
Jim Beam Bookers
Jim Beam Knob Creek
Makers Mark
Seagrams 7

BRANDY
Christian Brothers (well)
Hennessy VSOP
Kelt XO
Remy XO

CANADIAN WHISKY
Canadian Club
Crown Royal
Seagrams VO

GIN
Bombay (well)
Beefeater
Plymouth
Tanqueray

IRISH WHISKEY
Black Bush
Bushmills Irish
Bushmills 16 yr
Jameson Gold
Jameson Irish
Jameson 1780
Midleton Irish

RUM
Appleton XO
Bacardi Añejo
Bacardi Limón
Bacardi Rum (well)
Captain Morgan's
Cruzan Single Barrel
Malibu Rum
Mount Gay Eclipse
Myers's Jamaican Rum

SCOTCH WHISKY
Aberlour 18
Chivas Regal
Dalmore 21
Dewars Scotch (well)
Glenlivet
Glenlivet 18
Glenlivet French Oak
Glenmorangie Port
J & B Scotch
J Walker Black Label
J Walker Gold Label

TEQUILA
Cuervo Especial (well)
El Tesoro Silver
Chinaco Añejo
Patron Añejo
Sauza Hornitos
Sauza Triada

VODKA
Absolut 80°
Absolut Citron
Belvedere
Ketel One
Original Crystal
Smirnoff Black Vodka
Stolichnaya
Stolichnaya Gold

LIQUEURS
Bailey's Irish Cream
B & B
Campari
Chambord
Cointreau
Di Saronno Amaretto
Drambuie
Frangelico
Godiva
Goldschläger
Grand Marnier
Harvey's Bristol Cr. Sherry
Irish Mist
Jägermeister

LIQUEURS (Cont.)
Kahlúa
Midori
Rumple Minze
Sambuca Romana
Southern Comfort

BOTTLED BEERS
Amstel Light
Bass Ale
Beck's Light
Bud Light
Budweiser
Coors Light
Corona
Foster's Lager
Guinness Stout
Harp's
Heineken
Miller Lite
O'Douls
Rolling Rock
Samuel Adams

DRAFT BEER
Bass Ale
Guinness Stout
Harp's
Anchor Steam
Pilsner Urquell
Woodpecker Cider

WINES
Chardonnay, Woodbridge (house)
Chardonnay, K. Jackson
Chardonnay, Sonoma Cutrer
Merlot, Vichon
Merlot, Frogs Leap
White Zinfandel, Sutter Home (house)
White Zinfandel, Bel Arbres
Cabernet, Columbia Crest (house)
Cabernet, Stags Leap
Champagne, Domaine Chandon
Champagne, White Star

Illustration 4.1

There are companies that produce "knock-off" or substitute liqueurs, products that are devised to taste similar to name-brand liqueurs. Naturally, these substitute liqueurs are less expensive, and in many cases, their taste profile is extremely close to their well-known counterparts.

The problem with substitute products, however, is that when a customer orders a drink made with Kahlúa, for example, and another brand is substituted instead, the customer is likely to object. He or she will feel somehow cheated. Over a matter of a few cents per ounce, customer good will is jeopardized. While there may be opportunities to use these substitute liqueurs, exercising care is nevertheless advised.

There are also numerous, truly exceptional liqueurs that are produced in small quantities and not heavily marketed. It may prove highly beneficial to stock several of these lesser-known liqueurs, and use them to add intriguing new dimensions to your signature cocktails that your competition can't duplicate. Consider them your secret ingredients.

For example, the producers of Patrón tequila make a tequila-based coffee liqueur named St. Maarten X.O. Café. It has a delicious, singular flavor, one different than Kahlúa, which is made from a base of cane spirits, or Tia Maria, which is made from a base of Jamaican rum. Another example is Whidbey's Liqueur. It is made from Washington State loganberries. It has a fabulous flavor, similar to Chambord, yet different.

Search out these types of liqueurs. Give them to your bartenders to experiment with. You may find that you've stumbled on a gem, a product that adds a distinctive flavor to your specialty drinks, and yet unknown to your competitors.

QUESTIONS LEAD TO ANSWERS WHICH LEAD TO SUCCESS

- Have you determined a marketing orientation for your back bar? Does this marketing strategy dictate the selection of products on your back bar?
- Are there shortcomings to the particular marketing orientation you've chosen?
- Have you determined the ideal amount of inventory to stock behind the bar?
- Have you devised a strategy for eliminating dead stock from your back bar?

Chapter 5

The Profit Potential
of Glassware

Over the years, scores of companies have introduced plastic glass-ware in hopes of it catching on in bars and restaurants. Admittedly, their claims have some validity. Made from high-tech polymer plastic, plastic glasses are durable to the point of being nearly indestructible and are also now available in numerous shapes and contemporary styles.

Plastic glassware has made some in-roads in the industry, most notably in establishments catering to a younger clientele and those featuring outdoor patios or volleyball pits. The question remains, however, why hasn't plastic glassware caught on industry wide? Perhaps the follow-up question should be why haven't paper cups or pewter mugs caught on either?

The secret to glassware's success lies in its elegance, transparency and relative fragility. There is no other known medium that is capable of showcasing a cocktail with the same style and sophistication as glass. Its transparency makes it an ideal vehicle for presenting drinks of all types. In addition, glass is an excellent insulator that helps keep cold drinks cold and hot drinks hot.

Premium cocktails command significantly higher prices, and must therefore be presented in glassware that properly showcases the creation. The best way to make a cocktail look as good as it tastes is to present it in a fabulous looking glass. The glass used to present a drink is one of the most important elements in defining its style, much in the same way a great plate presentation increases an entrée's perceived value. A little elegance goes a long way toward creating a dramatic presentation and conveying a quality message.

Glassware is a singularly important means of marketing and merchandising drinks. Long gone are the days of relying on a few styles of stock glasses. Briefly peruse the Libbey glassware catalog and you'll quickly appreciate the wide and diverse selection of glassware styles available.

There are several crucial aspects to effectively managing a glass-ware inventory, each of which will be covered in this chapter.

> **The best way to make a cocktail look good is to present it in a fabulous looking glass.**

Fundamentally important is the selection process, determining that you have invested in the most beneficial lines of glassware for your operation's needs. That investment then must be protected by training employees how to properly wash and handle the glassware.

GLASSWARE SELECTION PROCESS

The first step when selecting bar service glassware is determining the types and ounce capacities of the glasses that will be necessary to stock. The decision as to what types and sizes of glasses you will need should be based on the types of drinks you will be serving. For example, if you intend on serving champagne-based cocktails you will not only need to stock champagne glasses, they must have the capacity to accommodate a larger serving portion.

Determine the serving portion for cocktails. Similarly, if you anticipate serving classic cocktails, you will first have to determine the serving portion for cocktails such as the martini and Manhattan. The size of the drink portion will dictate to a large degree the capacity of the cocktail glass you stock. If, for instance, you decide to offer your clientele a generously portioned martini of 2½ ounces of liquors you need a glass with a minimum of five-ounces capacity. Drink portioning is discussed in detail in Chapter 7.

To ease the glassware selection process, the following is a list of the primary types of beverage, wine and beer service glassware you will want to consider. The references to Libbey glassware contained in the information below are intended as excellent representations of the quality, style, size and shape of glasses being referenced.

A. Libbey Rocks Glasses — 6-8 oz.

Service of liquors and liqueurs on-the-rocks; and chilled shooters served neat.

Gibraltar	Dakota	Super Sham	Lexington	Quantum	Everest
No.15241	No.15601	No.1654SR	No.2328	No.15690	No.15433

B. Libbey Highball Glasses — 9-10 oz.

Service of highballs (e.g. gin and tonic, Scotch and soda).

Chivalry	Winchester	Inverness	Lexington	Gibraltar	Nob Hill
No.2485	No.15456	No.15485	No.3537	No.15242	No.23256

C. Libbey Double Rocks / Bucket Glasses — 11-14 oz.

Service of tall highballs and all-purpose beverage glass (i.e. soft drinks, fruit juice, and lemonade).

Presidential	Heavy Base	Gibraltar	Paneled Tumbler	Squire	Lexington
No.9171CD	No.139	No.15233	No.15644	No.5630	No.2339

D. Libbey Snifters — 6-14 oz.

Service of brandies, whiskies, and liqueurs, neat.

Citation	Domaine	Embassy	Citation	Michelangelo
No.8402	No.8905	No.3705	No.8405	No.C49ZX

E. Libbey Tall, Specialty Drink Glasses — 10-16 oz.

Service of tall iced specialty drinks (e.g. Long Island Iced Tea, Blue Hawaiian).

Chivalry	Paneled Tumbler	Metropolis (Iced Tea)	Super Sham	Napoli Grande
No.2486	No.15642	No.3648	No.1661SR	No.1619

Embassy Royale	International	Stratus	Nob Hill	Cooler
No.3750	No.197	No.2257	No.23106	No.32802

F. Libbey Specialty Drink Glasses — 10-16 oz.

Service of frozen/blended specialty drinks (e.g. Margarita, Piña Colada).

Domaine	Embassy Royale	Squall	Metropolis Margarita	Hurricane
No.8905	No.3715	No.3616	No.3646	No.850

Fountainware	Impressions	Squire	Heavy Base (Finedge)	Scandinavia
No.5110	No.1767790	No.5631	No.817CD	No.5298

G. Libbey Classic Cocktail Glasses — 6-9¾ oz.

Service of Classic cocktails served straight-up (e.g. Margaritas, Daiquiris).

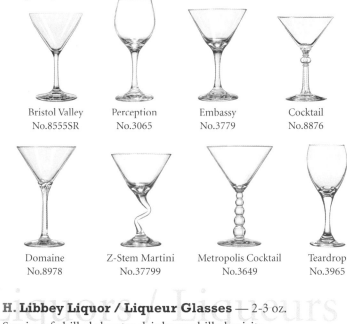

Bristol Valley No.8555SR	Perception No.3065	Embassy No.3779	Cocktail No.8876

Domaine No.8978	Z-Stem Martini No.37799	Metropolis Cocktail No.3649	Teardrop No.3965

H. Libbey Liquor / Liqueur Glasses — 2-3 oz.

Service of chilled shooter drinks or chilled spirits.

Cordial No.1650SR	Prism No.5277	Cordial No.3826	Whiskey No.2303	Whiskey (Fluted) No.5126	Georgian No.8089

I. Libbey Shot Glasses — 1¾ - 2¼ oz.

Service of shots of liquors and liqueurs, neat.

Whiskey (Fluted) No.5126	Whiskey No.5120	Spirit Glass No.155	Shooter No.5109	Tequila Shooter No.9562269

J. Libbey Hot Drink Glasses — 8-10 oz.

Service of hot coffee, tea, and hot specialty drinks (e.g. Irish Coffee, Keoki Coffee).

| Mug
No.5213 | Tall Mug (w/Starburst)
No.5091 | Irish Coffee
No.5295 | Irish Coffee
No.5293 | Irish Coffee
No.5304 |

Caution:

Before pouring "steaming" hot drinks, always pre-heat the glass or be sure to insert a metal spoon to help absorb the heat.

K. Libbey Cocktail Glasses, Martini Type — 4-6 oz.

Service of cocktails requested straight-up.

| Bristol Valley
No.8555SR | Citation
No.8455 | Embassy
No.3771 | Cocktail
No.8882 | Z-Stem Martini
No.37719 |

L. Libbey Mixing Glasses — 14-16 oz.

Use with the mixing tin; alternative use beverage.

| Gibraltar
No.15230 | Mixing Glass
No.1639HT (5139) | Cooler
No.15141 | Mixing Glass
No.1637HT (5137) |

M. Libbey Soda Glasses — 14-16 oz.

Service of sodas, juices and non-alcoholic drinks.

Bell Soda	Cascade	Comet	Governor Clinton	Footed
No.535HT	No.29811HT	18191HT	No.1713HT	No.1452HT

Everest	Heavy Base (Finedge)	Dakota	Gibraltar	Gibraltar
No.15437	No.817CD	No.15604	No.15230	No.15642

WINE SERVICE GLASSWARE:

A. Libbey Red Wine Glasses — 8-15 oz.

Service of red wines.

Bristol Valley	Citation	Napa	Perception	Charisma	Domaine
No.8541SR	No.8471	No.8771	No.3056	No.4114SR	No.8911

B. Libbey White Wine Glasses — 8-15 oz.

Service of white and blush wines.

    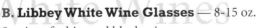

Perception	Citation	Chivalry	Bristol Valley	Charisma	Domaine
No.3065	No.8472	No.3264	No.8573SR	No.4113SR	No.8957

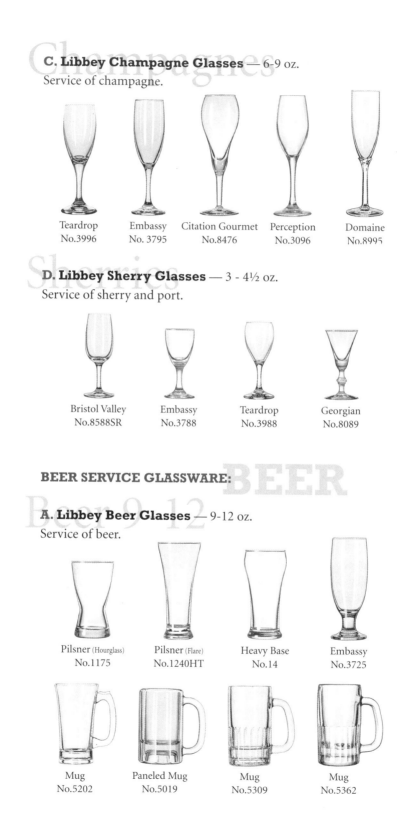

C. Libbey Champagne Glasses — 6-9 oz.
Service of champagne.

Teardrop	Embassy	Citation Gourmet	Perception	Domaine
No.3996	No. 3795	No.8476	No.3096	No.8995

D. Libbey Sherry Glasses — 3 - 4½ oz.
Service of sherry and port.

Bristol Valley	Embassy	Teardrop	Georgian
No.8588SR	No.3788	No.3988	No.8089

BEER SERVICE GLASSWARE:

A. Libbey Beer Glasses — 9-12 oz.
Service of beer.

Pilsner (Hourglass)	Pilsner (Flare)	Heavy Base	Embassy
No.1175	No.1240HT	No.14	No.3725

Mug	Paneled Mug	Mug	Mug
No.5202	No.5019	No.5309	No.5362

B. Libbey Beer Glasses — 14-18 oz.
Service of draft beers.

| English Pub Glass | Cooler | Mixing Glass | Teardrop |
| No.14806HT | No.15141 | No.15230 | No.3915 |

| Chivalry | Maritime Mug | Paneled Mug | Schooner |
| No.2487 | No.5027 | No.5020 | No.1785473 |

C. Libbey Beer Glasses — 20 oz. + (optional)
Service of 20 oz. + draft beers.

| Giant Beer | Giant Beer | Sport Mug | Mug |
| No.1610 | No.1611 | No.5272 | No.5360 |

GLASSWARE SELECTION CRITERIA

After deciding which types and sizes of glasses that will be needed for the bar, you'll be faced with the challenge of selecting the particular style of each type of glass to purchase. This will require that you study the manufacturers' glassware catalogs to assess what's available.

Purchasing your operation's glassware inventory will be a sizeable investment. You will, therefore, want to be as prepared as possible and to have considered all of the factors prior to making your purchase. There are a number of selection criteria that should be factored into your decision. These considerations include:

1. **Budgetary Constraints** — There are scores of different styles of glassware from which to choose. Libbey alone offers over 80 different lines of glassware. These various lines of glasses vary considerably in cost. It is necessary to know in advance how much capital you have to invest in glassware. In addition to the initial purchase price, consider also the ongoing expense of replacement costs.

2. **Versatility of Function** — Rarely is there an abundance of storage space for glassware behind a bar, making versatility an important selection factor. The more types of drinks that may be appropriately presented in a particular glass, the more valuable it will be to your operation. The fewer types of glasses carried allow more of each to be stocked.

3. **Durability** — Glassware must be durable enough to withstand the rigors of commercial use. It is advisable to obtain a sample of each glass you're considering investing in and washing them vigorously in the bar's sinks, putting them through the same paces they would be subjected to during a busy shift. This will give you an appreciation for how durable a glass is.

   The less frequently a glass is used, the less important durability becomes as a selection factor. There are several factors that affect the durability of glass. The most significant variable is heat-tempering, a process in which molten glass is cooled rapidly making it more durable and shock resistant. While more expensive than other types of glass, heat-tempered glassware has a considerably longer useful life and is therefore exceptionally cost-effective. Some stemware is produced as one piece, others are made in two pieces with the stem epoxied to the base of the glass. In most cases, the compound glass is more durable than its counterpart since the epoxy is stronger than the glass itself.

4. **Aesthetic Considerations** — The glassware you purchase will have a dramatic impact on defining your operation's image and concept. There are bars that serve drinks in Mason jars and do so well, while other operations merchandise their specialty drinks in elegant stemware and snifters. Take into consideration the image you want your establishment to project, and purchase glassware that works within that concept.

5. **Availability** — It is important to set reasonable assurances from the local glassware distributor that the line of glasses you're investing

in will be available for the foreseeable future. The discontinuation of your primary line of glassware is definitely something you'll want to avoid. Practically speaking, the relative worth of the remaining glassware stock would then be relegated to salvage value and the entire process would have to start anew. This is more an issue if you select a small glassware producer than a well known, widely distributed line, such as Libbey.

SELECTING SPECIALTY GLASSWARE

Conventional wisdom suggests that the better a drink looks, the better the drink will be received and the more you can charge for it. While difficult to prove, it does stand to reason. Thus the need for specialty glassware to merchandise your signature drinks. It is advisable to have a minimum of two styles and sizes of specialty glasses in which to present your bar's signature creations.

The better a drink looks, the more you can charge for it.

The first style and size of specialty glass to choose will be used for frozen or blended drinks. These glasses typically range in capacity from about 12 to 16 ounces and are available in a wide variety of intriguing styles and shapes.

The second recommended style and size of specialty glass to carry will be used to merchandise tall, iced specialty drinks. These glasses typically range in capacity from 7 to 13 ounces and are also available in a wide variety of styles and shapes.

There are scores of creative options available to you when it comes to selecting specialty glassware. Depending on the concept, a 12-ounce brandy snifter is a superb glass to serve frozen signature drinks, in a red wine bowl or handled beer mug are creative ways to present iced signature drinks. You may opt to market your bar's martinis and Manhattans in a sophisticated over-sized cocktail glass-6 to 9½ ounces in capacity. Likewise, you may choose to serve 100% agave tequilas in a 3-ounce sherry glass. It's an elegant, stylish way to present these expensive tequilas.

Leaf through the pages of the Libbey catalog for inspiration. You'll quickly realize that there are scores of options on how to present nearly every type of drink. Don't get locked into convention. Kick out all the stops and look to wow your clientele.

ESTABLISHING GLASSWARE PAR LEVELS

Once you have selected the types and styles of glassware you will be purchasing, you'll be faced with the final challenge of determining the number of glasses to order. The following is a step-by-step plan on how to arrive at the appropriate quantities of each glass to order.

1 **Step One** — There is a limited amount of space for storing glassware behind a bar. The first step in the process of establishing your opening glassware order is to determine how much space you will be devoting to shelving glasses behind the bar. The glassware catalog will give you the exact specifications for each glass. You can use these specifications to determine how many of each type of glass you will be able to shelve behind the bar.

2 **Step Two** — You will need to make some sweeping assumptions as to glass usage. For example, in nearly all bars, usage of highball glasses will far exceed the number of rocks glasses used during the course of a shift. The usage of cocktail and wine glasses varies considerably with the type of establishment. For some operations, a dozen cocktail and wine glasses behind the bar would be sufficient; in others, stocking such low par levels of these glasses would cause an operational nightmare.

3 **Step Three** — Armed with the estimate of how many of each type of glass you'll be able to stock behind your bar(s), you are now in a position to establish the minimum order for each glass.

Glassware is typically ordered by the case. Determine the number of glasses contained in a case for each type of glass being ordered. Divide the estimated number of each type of glass needed by the quantity contained in a case. This will derive the minimum number of cases you will need to initially purchase.

4 **Step Four** — If you've ever worked behind a busy bar you can appreciate the need for an adequate supply of back-up glassware. There are a number of reasons to have a reserve of each type of glassware. A drink promotion may increase the demand for a particular glass and require you to dip into the reserves. You will suffer breakage over time. You may have underestimated the usage of a certain type of glass.

Regardless of the reason, running out of a particular type of glass during a shift is disruptive to the operation and can lead to lost sales or drinks being presented to guests in the inappropriate glasses. It is, therefore, advisable to purchase a minimum of an extra case of each type of glass to be kept in reserve. To best protect your investment store the back-up glasses in their original packing case.

Step Five — Regularly inspect the glassware inventory and confirm that you still have an adequate stock of each glass to meet anticipated demand. The use of a glassware inventory form helps this process.

Illustration 5.1 is a representation of a Glassware Par Form. Every glass carried in the inventory is identified by type, style, size, product code and supplier. The par levels and reserve quantities for the glass are then listed. The total of those figures will reveal each item's build-to quantity, the minimum number of cases to have on-hand at any point in time.

Glassware Par Form

Libbey Glass Type	Size	Product Code	Case Size	Par Bar 1	Par Bar 2	Par in Reserve	Build-To Quantity
Gibraltar Rocks	7 oz.	#15241	36	24	18	36	78
Gibraltar Rocks	9 oz.	#15242	36	36	24	36	76
Gibraltar Dbl Rocks	13 oz.	#15233	36	24	18	36	78
Embassy Snifter	9 oz.	#3704	24	18	12	24	54
Cyclone Specialty	15 oz.	#3617	12	18	12	24	54
Viva Grande	13 oz.	#8413	12	18	12	24	54
Coupette	7 oz.	#8428	12	18	12	24	54
Lexington	3 oz.	#2303	36	18	12	36	66
Fluted Lined Whiskey	2 oz.	#5126	36	18	12	36	66
Irish Coffee	8¼ oz.	#5293	36	18	12	36	66
Z-Stem Martini	5 oz.	#37719	12	18	12	24	54
Mixing Glass Faceted	16 oz.	#15230	24	36	24	48	108
Bell Soda	16 oz.	#535HT	36	18	12	36	66
Bristol Valley Red Wine	8½ oz.	#8541SR	12	18	12	24	54
Bristol Valley White Wine	8½ oz.	#8564SR	12	24	18	36	78
Bristol Valley Champagne	6 oz.	#8595SR	24	18	12	24	54
Bristol Valley Sherry	3¾ oz.	#8588SR	24	12	8	36	56
Mixing Glass	16 oz.	#1639HT	24	36	24	48	108
Footed Pilsner	12 oz.	#8425	24	48	36	48	132
English Pub Glass	20 oz.	#14801HT	36	36	24	48	108

Illustration 5.1

CONTROLLING GLASSWARE BREAKAGE

While losses through breakage are inevitable, there are measures you can take that will greatly increase your glassware's chances of survival. Glasses stocked behind the bar may need to be returned to the bar for cleaning. Without direct supervision and training, breakage in the dish room can be astronomical. Other leading causes of breakage include:

1. **Mechanical Impact** — The leading cause of glassware and china breakage is due to mechanical impact. This is the result of glass or china coming in direct contact with a solid object, be it another glass or some other hard object. The contact causes a minute abrasion invisible to the naked eye. These abrasions weaken the surface of the glass making it more susceptible to breakage from impact or thermal shock. Glassware or china with noticeable abrasions should be remove from service.

   The staff should be instructed to never carry an excessive number of glasses at once, either stacked in their hand, pyramided or in a "bouquet." Limits should also be set on how many glasses can be carried on a service tray. Glasses should never be placed in bus tubs with dinnerware or flatware. Consider providing your bartenders with plastic or Lexan ice scoops instead of ones made of die-cast metal. The number of chipped rims should drop accordingly.

2. **Thermal Shock** — Thermal shock is caused by subjecting glass or china to a sudden change in temperature. Glass retains heat and a sudden change in temperature can cause sufficient stress to shatter the glass. Cracks that result from thermal shock usually form around existing abrasions. The thicker the item the more time is required for it to return to room temperature.

   Bartenders should pre-heat glasses with warm water before pouring in hot coffee of tea whenever possible. Glasses right out of the glass washer should be allowed to cool prior to use. The same is true about emptying ice out of a glass and immediately plunging it into extremely hot water.

3. **Improper Handling** — Despite the obvious temptations, don't stack glasses on top of one another. Rotating the stock on a regular basis will lessen the chances of glasses sticking to the shelf matting. The resulting tug on the matting often is enough to topple other glasses off the shelf. Hanging glass racks are notorious for causing breakage through frequent glass-to-glass contact or vibration shock caused by shimmy.

4 **Theft** — Some of your glasses leave the premise in pockets, purses and backpacks. Prime targets are shot glasses, snifters, cordials, sherry glasses and small, house specialties. Employees walk out with glasses too. In some cases it's inadvertent, so a tactfully worded reminder posted by the back door is appropriate and advisable.

PROPER GLASS HANDLING PROCEDURES

Training your staff on how to properly handle glassware and china is a money-making idea. Improved handling results in less breakage, increased employee productivity and reduced risk of accidental injury. The following are items that should be conveyed to your staff regarding the proper handling of glassware.

- Always handle glassware by the outside bottom half, avoiding areas of the glass that come in contact with the customer's mouth. It is unsanitary and unprofessional to ever handle the rim or inside of a glass.

- Bartenders should practice holding two or more glasses at a time in one hand. This can make a big difference in their productivity, since the less time it takes to select and ice down glassware, the less time it takes to prepare each order. Also, they need to become proficient at holding different combinations of glasses. It will inevitably save valuable time behind the bar and reduce breakage.

- Never use a glass to scoop ice from the bin, or allow anyone else behind the bar to. The glass could chip or break in the ice, resulting in a customer being served a drink with a glass shard hidden in the ice.

- In the event of glass breakage anywhere near or in the ice bin, all of the ice must be immediately removed and replaced. This is an absolute rule of safety behind the bar. It is impossible to see and remove pieces of broken glass from amidst ice cubes.

- The expense of replacing glasses is significant and the staff should be trained to handle the operation's glassware carefully. Special care should be taken when handling delicate, stemmed glassware as shimmy and contact frequently cause breakage.

- Bartenders need to inspect glasses before adding ice or products. They must be observant for abrasions, spots, lipstick smudges, grease or oily deposits, chips, cracks, off-odors, or anything that is in any way unappealing or potentially harmful.

- Clean glasses must be stored properly so they stay clean until needed again. Glassware should be inverted and stored on level

Improved handling results in less breakage.

shelves covered with open matting that allows air to circulate under the glass.

• Glasses should never be stored in a refrigerator or glass-chiller that is not clean and odor-free. Odors in the glass will affect the flavor of many beverages, particularly wine and beer.

• Glasses should be stored in areas away from smoke, grease, or dust. This is often not the case, however, with overhead racks used for hanging wine and cocktail glasses.

QUESTIONS LEAD TO ANSWERS WHICH LEAD TO SUCCESS

• Does your glassware inventory provide your bartenders sufficient drink vehicle options?

• Are there glasses behind the bar that are rarely used and whose function is easily replaced?

• Do you stock the bar with sufficient numbers of each type of glass?

• Are your glasses durable enough to withstand the rigors of your business?

• Do your glasses enhance the presentation of your drinks?

• Is there a need to stock plastic, unbreakable glasses?

• Are glassware handling procedures taught in your bartender training program?

• Do bartenders use plastic (Lexan) or metal ice scoops?

• Do your bartenders periodically rotate the glassware inventory and wash the shelf netting?

• Do you use imprinted or silk screened artwork on your glassware?

• Do you pre-heat glasses and coffee mugs prior to serving a hot beverage?

Chapter 6

The Mathematics
of Profit

As an income producing entity, a beverage operation cranks out a constant stream of information. To be an effective beverage manager you're going to have to regularly crunch some numbers. It will be necessary to decipher those facts and figures, understand their meaning and to rely on those to better manage the business.

One of the business principles that serves as a foundation of this book is "if you can't measure it, you can't manage it." It means that if you can't detail exactly what is happening within your business, you won't be in a position to effectively manage it. Without hard data, you're flying blind. How will you know if you're operating profitably without determining each department's gross margins? How will you know if you've priced a drink appropriately if you don't know how to figure the item's cost percentage?

"if you can't measure it, you can't manage it."

The answers to these questions and more can only be found through mathematics. So dust off the calculator and sharpen a few pencils, the following material covers the essential mathematical formulas necessary to manage a beverage operation profitably.

1 **Cost Per Ounce** — This financial relationship is used to identify how much a certain liquor, beer and wine costs. For example, if the product you're analyzing is sold in a liter, dividing the item's whole-sale bottle cost by 33.8 ounces will equal the products cost per ounce. To calculate the cost per ounce for a 750ml bottle, divide the bottle cost by 25.4 ounces.

2 **Portion Cost** — When pricing a specific drink, it is necessary to first determine the cost of what you will be serving. For example, the drink being priced is Ketel One Vodka on-the-rocks and at your bar you pour an ounce and a half portion for rock drinks. To determine the portion cost, you will need to multiply the vodka's cost per ounce by 1.5. If a liter of Ketel One Vodka costs $19.07, it costs $.56 per ounce. The drink's portion cost then is $.84. If a 750ml bottle of the vodka costs $15.00, its cost per ounce is $.59, or a portion cost of $.89.

3 Cost Percentage — Cost percentage is perhaps the most often used financial indicator in the beverage management. It establishes the relationship between cost of goods sold and margin of profit. One of the reasons cost percentage is such a revealing indicator is the inverse of cost percentage is profit margin. So as cost percentage increases, profit margin decreases. Cost percentage is used to analyze everything from drink pricing to the profitability of liquor sales.

Cost percentage is derived by dividing an item's cost (or portion cost) by its sales price and then multiplying it by 100 to convert it into a percentage.

4 Gross Profit — There is no more revealing or significant financial indicator for any business than gross profit. It is the monetary difference between a product's cost (or portion cost in this example) and its sales price.

To derive a drink's gross profit, subtract its portion cost from the drink's sales price.

5 Gross Profit Margin — This financial indicator is used to express in percent the amount of profit realized on a sale. It is figured by dividing the amount of profit by the sales price and then multiplying it by 100 to convert it to a percentage.

The following example shows how to calculate gross profit margin for the same drink selling at two different sales prices. To determine the amount of gross profit, subtract the drink's portion cost from its sales price. The drink's gross profit is then divided by the selling price to reveal its gross margin.

6 Cost Multipliers — This is a measure used to determine the target selling price of a product based on its portion cost. A cost multiplier is obtained by dividing the cost percentage you want to obtain into 100 and then multiplying the result by the product's portion cost.

7 Prime Ingredient Cost Method — The prime ingredient method of pricing is used to determine the target sales price for a mixed drink when there is only one principle ingredient. For example, this is the method used to determine the target selling price for such drinks as a Tanqueray & Tonic, or Scotch on-the-rocks.

To figure the target sales price for a drink using the prime ingredient cost method, divide the item's portion cost by the desired cost percentage.

8 Percentage of Profit on Sales — To arrive at the selling price based on the amount of gross profit margin desired divide the portion cost by the gross profit margin percentage reciprocal (the result of subtracting the gross margin desired from 1.00). In the examples below, to receive an 83% gross margin on a drink with a portion cost of $.55, the selling price needs to be $3.23 ($2.68 profit ÷ $3.24 = 83%); a selling price of $3.67 will yield an 85% gross margin.

9 Beverage Cost Method — A cost method of pricing used to determine the target sales price for mixed drinks prepared with multiple ingredients. The combined cost of products is totaled and then divided by the desired cost percentage.

Long Island Iced Tea

½ oz. gin	$.16
½ oz. vodka	$.14
½ oz. rum	$.14
½ oz. tequila	$.16
½ oz. triple sec	$.09
2 oz. sweet 'n' sour	$.05
2 oz. cola	$.01
Beverage Cost	$.75

a. $.75 beverage cost ÷ .20 (desired cost percentage) = $3.75 target sales price
b. $.75 beverage cost ÷ .18 (desired cost percentage) = $4.17 target sales price

Mathematics of Profit Examples

1. **Cost Per Ounce**

   a. $12.55 liter cost ÷ 33.8 ounces = $.37/oz.

   b. $12.55 750ml cost ÷ 25.4 ounces = $.49/oz.

2. **Portion Cost**

   a. $19.07 liter cost ÷ 33.8 oz. = $.56/oz. X 1½ oz. = $.84 portion cost

   b. $15.00 750ml cost ÷ 25.4 oz. = $.59/oz. X 1½ oz. = $.89 portion cost

3. **Cost Percentage**

   a. $.37/oz. X 1½ oz. = $.55 portion cost ÷ $3.50 sales price X 100 = 15.7% cost

   b. $.37/oz. X 1½ oz. = $.55 portion cost ÷ $4.00 sales price X 100 = 13.7% cost

4. **Gross Profit**

   a. $3.50 sales price - $.55 portion cost = $2.95 gross profit

   b. $4.00 sales price - $.55 portion cost = $3.45 gross profit

5. **Gross Profit Margin**

   a. $3.50 sales price - $.55 portion cost =

   $2.95 gross profit ÷ $3.50 price X 100 = 84.3% profit margin

   b. $4.00 sales price - $.55 portion cost =

   $3.45 gross profit ÷ $4.00 price X 100 = 86.2% profit margin

6. **Cost Multipliers**

   a. 100 ÷ 18% (desired cost percentage) =

   5.56 X $.55 portion cost = $3.06 target sales price

   b. 100 ÷ 16% (desired cost percentage) =

   6.25 X $.55 portion cost = $3.44 target sales price

7. **Prime Ingredient Cost Method**

   a. $.55 portion cost ÷ .18 (desired cost percentage) = $3.27 target sales price

   b. $.55 portion cost ÷ .16 (desired cost percentage) = $3.44 target sales price

8. **Percentage of Profit on Sales**

   a. $.55 portion cost ÷ .17 (1.00 - .83 gross margin) = $3.24 sales price

   b. $.55 portion cost ÷ .16 (1.00 - .83 gross margin) = $3.44 sales price

   c. $.55 portion cost ÷ .15 (1.00 - .85 gross margin) = $3.67 sales price

9. **Beverage Cost Method**

   a. $.75 beverage cost ÷ .20 (desired cost percentage) = $3.75 target sales price

   b. $.75 beverage cost ÷ .18 (desired cost percentage) = $4.17 target sales price

Illustration 6.1

COST PER OUNCE — LITERS

The table below shows the cost per ounce for liter bottles ranging in price between $1.00 and $34.14. To figure the cost per ounce for liters that cost more than $34.14 divide the bottle cost by 33.8 oz.

Liter Cost	$/oz.	Liter Cost	$/oz.	Liter Cost	$/oz.
$1.00 - 1.35	.03	$12.17 - 12.50	.36	$23.33 - 23.65	.69
$1.36 - 1.68	.04	$12.51 - 12.84	.37	$23.66 - 23.99	.70
$1.69 - 2.02	.05	$12.85 - 13.18	.38	$24.00 - 24.33	.71
$2.03 - 2.36	.06	$13.19 - 13.51	.39	$24.34 - 24.67	.72
$2.37 - 2.70	.07	$13.52 - 13.85	.40	$24.68 - 25.01	.73
$2.71 - 3.04	.08	$13.86 - 14.19	.41	$25.02 - 25.34	.74
$3.05 - 3.37	.09	$14.20 - 14.53	.42	$25.35 - 25.68	.75
$3.38 - 3.71	.10	$14.54 - 14.87	.43	$25.69 - 26.02	.76
$3.72 - 4.05	.11	$14.88 - 15.20	.44	$26.03 - 26.36	.77
$4.06 - 4.39	.12	$15.21 - 15.54	.45	$26.37 - 26.70	.78
$4.40 - 4.73	.13	$15.55 - 15.88	.46	$26.71 - 27.03	.79
$4.74 - 5.06	.14	$15.89 - 16.22	.47	$27.04 - 27.37	.80
$5.07 - 5.40	.15	$16.23 - 16.56	.48	$27.38 - 27.71	.81
$5.41 - 5.74	.16	$16.57 - 16.89	.49	$27.72 - 28.05	.82
$5.75 - 6.08	.17	$16.90 - 17.23	.50	$28.06 - 28.39	.83
$6.09 - 6.42	.18	$17.24 - 17.57	.51	$28.40 - 28.72	.84
$6.43 - 6.75	.19	$17.58 - 17.91	.52	$28.73 - 29.06	.85
$6.76 - 7.09	.20	$17.92 - 18.25	.53	$29.07 - 29.40	.86
$7.10 - 7.43	.21	$18.26 - 18.58	.54	$29.41 - 29.74	.87
$7.44 - 7.77	.22	$18.59 - 18.92	.55	$29.75 - 30.08	.88
$7.78 - 8.11	.23	$18.93 - 19.26	.56	$30.09 - 30.41	.89
$8.12 - 8.44	.24	$19.27 - 19.60	.57	$30.42 - 30.75	.90
$8.45 - 8.78	.25	$19.61 - 19.94	.58	$30.76 - 31.09	.91
$8.79 - 9.12	.26	$19.95 - 20.27	.59	$31.10 - 31.43	.92
$9.13 - 9.46	.27	$20.28 - 20.61	.60	$31.44 - 31.77	.93
$9.47 - 9.80	.28	$20.62 - 20.95	.61	$31.78 - 32.10	.94
$9.81 - 10.13	.29	$20.96 - 21.29	.62	$32.11 - 32.44	.95
$10.14 - 10.47	.30	$21.30 - 21.63	.63	$32.45 - 32.78	.96
$10.48 - 10.81	.31	$21.64 - 21.96	.64	$32.79 - 33.12	.97
$10.82 - 11.15	.32	$21.97 - 22.30	.65	$33.13 - 33.46	.98
$11.16 - 11.49	.33	$22.31 - 22.64	.66	$33.47 - 33.79	.99
$11.50 - 11.82	.34	$22.65 - 22.98	.67	$33.80 - 34.14	1.00
$11.83 - 12.16	.35	$22.99 - 23.32	.68		

Illustration 6.2

COST PER OUNCE — 750ML

The table below shows the cost per ounce for 750ml bottles ranging in price between $1.02 and $25.65. To figure the cost per ounce for 750ml bottles that cost more than $25.65 divide the bottle cost by 25.4 oz.

750ml Cost		$/oz.	750ml Cost		$/oz.	750ml Cost		$/oz.
$1.02 -	1.26	.04	$9.40 -	9.65	.37	$17.78 -	18.03	.70
$1.27 -	1.52	.05	$9.66 -	9.90	.38	$18.04 -	18.28	.71
$1.53 -	1.77	.06	$9.91 -	10.15	.39	$18.29 -	18.54	.72
$1.78 -	2.03	.07	$10.16 -	10.41	.40	$18.55 -	18.79	.73
$2.04 -	2.28	.08	$10.42 -	10.66	41	$18.80 -	19.04	.74
$2.29 -	2.53	.09	$10.67 -	10.92	.42	$19.05 -	19.30	.75
$2.54 -	2.79	.10	$10.93 -	11.17	.43	$19.31 -	19.55	.76
$2.80 -	3.04	.11	$11.18 -	11.42	.44	$19.56 -	19.81	.77
$3.05 -	3.30	.12	$11.43 -	11.68	.45	$19.82 -	20.06	.78
$3.31 -	3.55	.13	$11.69 -	11.93	.46	$20.07 -	20.31	.79
$3.56 -	3.80	.14	$11.94 -	12.19	.47	$20.32 -	20.57	.80
$3.81 -	4.06	.15	$12.20 -	12.44	.48	$20.58 -	20.82	.81
$4.07 -	4.31	.16	$12.45 -	12.69	.49	$20.83 -	21.08	.82
$4.32 -	4.57	.17	$12.70 -	12.95	.50	$21.09 -	21.33	.83
$4.58 -	4.82	.18	$12.96 -	13.20	.51	$21.34 -	21.58	.84
$4.83 -	5.07	.19	$13.21 -	13.46	.52	$21.59 -	21.84	.85
$5.08 -	5.33	.20	$13.47 -	13.72	.53	$21.85 -	22.09	.86
$5.34 -	5.58	.21	$13.73 -	13.97	.54	$22.10 -	22.35	.87
$5.59 -	5.84	.22	$13.98 -	14.22	.55	$22.36 -	22.60	.88
$5.85 -	6.09	.23	$14.23 -	14.47	.56	$22.61 -	22.85	.89
$6.10 -	6.34	.24	$14.48 -	14.73	.57	$22.86 -	23.11	.90
$6.35 -	6.60	.25	$14.74 -	14.98	.58	$23.12 -	23.36	.91
$6.61 -	6.85	.26	$14.99 -	15.23	.59	$23.37 -	23.62	.92
$6.86 -	7.11	.27	$15.24 -	15.49	.60	$23.63 -	23.87	.93
$7.12 -	7.36	.28	$15.50 -	15.74	.61	$23.88 -	24.12	.94
$7.37 -	7.61	.29	$15.75 -	16.00	.62	$24.13 -	24.38	.95
$7.62 -	7.87	.30	$16.01 -	16.25	.63	$24.39 -	24.63	.96
$7.88 -	8.12	.31	$16.26 -	16.50	.64	$24.64 -	24.89	.97
$8.13 -	8.38	.32	$16.51 -	16.75	.65	$24.90 -	25.14	.98
$8.39 -	8.63	.33	$16.76 -	17.01	.66	$25.15 -	25.39	.99
$8.64 -	8.88	.34	$17.02 -	17.27	.67	$25.40 -	25.65	1.00
$8.89 -	9.14	.35	$17.28 -	17.52	.68			
$9.15 -	9.39	.36	$17.53 -	17.77	.69			

Illustration 6.3

Section Two
Developing a Profitable
Beverage Operation

Chapter 7

Drink Recipes:
Establishing Your Profit Margins

The drink recipes you decide to feature create your beverage operation's bill of fare. They are your bar's product, and as such, they deserve thoughtful consideration. Naturally the first variable is taste, and one aspect of taste is alcoholic potency. A drink that tastes weak is usually grounds for complaint, while one that tastes too strong is likely too liability-laden to serve.

Providing bartenders with complete information regarding drink making is vitally important. Problems may arise when a recipe is not prepared in the prescribed manner. The resulting drink may taste weak and cause the bartender to add alcohol to bring about the proper taste. The same may occur if the drink is not served in the proper glass.

Once the house drink recipes have been decided, the bartenders need access to those recipes behind the bar. Recipes are frequently put into card files or on a Rolodex. It is important that the recipes be accessible, in a usable format, and continually updated. The recipes should be formatted to include a list of ingredients, measurements, method of preparation, and glassware options.

The drink recipes you decide to feature deserve thoughtful consideration.

The following information covers the nine types of mixed drinks. The material includes portioning, glassware requirements, mixing instructions and cost factors.

1. Highball Drinks

Highball drinks are identified by the combination of a requested liquor or liqueur and a specified mixer (water, tonic, soda, juice, etc.). For most beverage operations highballs comprise 50-60% of all mixed drinks served. Nearly every type of customer orders these drinks anytime of the day or night. The majority will be made from the well, about a third more will be ordered with call liquor, and a small percentage with premium products.

Highballs are most frequently made with a 1 to 1¼ ounce portion of liquor. These drinks are typically prepared using one part liquor to two-parts mixer, or a proportion of 1:2. A proportion of 1:1, or equal parts of liquor and mixer, will produce a drink that is overly potent and tastes too strong. Conversely, a proportion of 1:3 or 1:4 will render a drink that is over-diluted and weak tasting.

The standard highball glass has a capacity of nine-ounces. Fully iced, a 9-ounce highball glass is reduced in capacity to approximately three fluid ounces. Using 1 to 1¼ ounces of requested product leaves room for a free-pour fill of mixer (approximately 2 oz.), achieving the standard recipe ratio quickly and efficiently.

Aside from switched mixers, the most common complaint among highball drinkers is that the drink is "weak." One reason a highball may taste weak is that the glass is not filled to capacity with ice. This will result in the use of too much mixer and an over-diluted drink.

In addition to the standard highball, the drink may be ordered in four other size/potency variations listed below:

a. **A Double Highball** is prepared with a double portion of the requested liquor or liqueur and served in a standard 9 oz. highball glass. This will yield a relatively potent 2:1 proportion, or two-parts of alcohol to one-part mixer. Drinking a double highball is more alcoholically potent than consuming two regularly prepared highballs.

b. **A Tall Highball** is prepared with a standard portion of requested liquor or liqueur and served in a tall highball or bucket (double old fashion) glass, ranging in volume from 10-12 ounces. The remaining capacity of the glass is filled with the requested mixer. This combination will produce a relatively weak tasting drink; an approximate 1:4 or 1:5 proportion.

c. **A Short Highball** is prepared with a standard portion of requested liquor or liqueur and served in a 7-ounce rocks glass. The remaining capacity of the glass is filled with the requested mixer. This combination will yield a strong tasting drink: a proportion of 1:1 or equal-parts liquor to mix.

d. **A Double Tall Highball** is prepared with a double portion of requested liquor or liqueur and served in a tall highball or bucket (double old fashion) glass. The remaining capacity of the glass is filled with the requested mixer. This combination will create a standard 1:2 proportion. Essentially a double tall highball is the same as preparing two regular highballs drinks in the same glass.

2. Martinis, Rob Roys and Manhattans

Martinis and Manhattans are prepared with between 1½ and 2-ounces of requested liquor. They are typically ordered on-the-rocks or straight-up. When ordered on the rocks, the drink is prepared directly into an iced rocks glass. A martini or Manhattan requested straight-up is prepared in an iced mixing glass, then stirred gently and strained into a chilled cocktail glass.

The rocks glass should be a minimum of seven ounces in capacity; any smaller and the drink will not fit into the glass. To market martinis straight-up you should select a cocktail glass with a minimum capacity of 4 ounces. If you opt to promote over-sized martinis, those prepared with over 2-ounces of liquor, it is advisable to select a larger cocktail glass.

Each recipe in this category is prepared with sweet and/or dry vermouth. Sweet vermouth is an Italian fortified aperitif wine, meaning that alcohol has been added to raise the alcoholic content to approximately 16% by volume. Dry vermouth is a pale, dry, French fortified aperitif wine with an alcohol content of 19% by volume.

Vermouth is put into these drinks to soften any edge to the liquor, and should be poured before adding the liquor. In the event too much vermouth or the wrong type of vermouth is used, the drink may be remade without wasting the more expensive liquor.

3. Rock Drinks

Rock drinks, such as the Black Russian, Stinger and Rusty Nail, are among the most popular mixed drinks. These drinks, also referred to as "two liquor drinks," are typically prepared at a 3:1 ratio (3-parts liquor to 1-part liqueur); generally 1½ oz. of base liquor and ½ oz. of a liqueur. The key to success for these drinks is that the liqueur component compliments the flavor of the base liquor.

Nearly all of these drinks are built directly into an iced rocks glass. The liquor portion is always poured first before adding the liqueur. The liqueur, being the heavier product, will settle through the layer of liquor, making any further mixing of the products unnecessary.

When a customer orders a certain liquor or liqueur on-the-rocks, he or she is requesting the product served over ice. A jigger (1½ oz.) is a standard serving portion for an on-the-rocks product, although this may vary between establishments.

These drinks are most frequently served in a 7-8 ounce rocks glass. If you anticipate serving more liquor on-the-rocks than rock drinks, it is advisable to select a 7-ounce rocks glass. The larger 8-ounce glass will often make a jigger portion of liquor appear insufficient.

4. Classic Cocktails

The majority of these cocktails, drinks such as the daiquiri, margarita and side car, are composed of a base liquor or liqueur, one or two fruit juices, and a cordial or syrup. Most recipes require the use of sweetened lemon juice (also known as sweet 'n' sour, tavern mix, sour mix, or margarita mix). The recipes in this category traditionally contain 3 fluid ounces. One ounce of the recipe is typically reserved for the main liquor or liqueur portion.

These cocktails are served straight-up, on-the-rocks, or blended ("frozen"). Each of these methods may require a different glassware choice. A cocktail requested straight-up is prepared in a mixing glass, hand shaken, and strained into a chilled cocktail glass.

A cocktail ordered on-the-rocks is also prepared in a mixing glass and hand shaken, and then strained into an iced snifter or house specialty glass. Margaritas served on-the-rocks are sometimes served in an iced bucket glass. A cocktail ordered frozen or blended is prepared in a blender with either crushed or cubed ice and served in a house specialty glass.

5. Tropical & Tall Drinks

The drinks in this category include such classics as the mai tai, planter's punch, Long Island iced tea and Singapore sling. Tropical and tall drinks share a collective reputation for being potent concoctions. This reputation is definitely warranted. These drink recipes, therefore, must be adapted for commercial use so that they are less potent and more cost-effective.

With few exceptions, the Tropical and tall drinks are hand shaken and served in tall, iced glassware. In many instances, these recipes are finished with a fill of club soda or a float of a dark rum or liqueur.

6. Coffee & Hot Drinks

Its warmth and rich flavor make coffee an excellent vehicle for serving alcoholic products. Liqueurs and cordials work especially well with hot coffee. The heat will thin the liqueur and disperse it throughout the drink. Many of the flavoring agents used to produce liqueurs are complimented by the taste of coffee.

Liquors are also used in coffee drink recipes. Dark liquors such as bourbon, Scotch, Irish whiskey and Jamaican rum compliment the flavor of coffee particularly well and are frequently used in hot coffee drinks.

These drinks are built directly into coffee mugs or insulated glasses. A ten-ounce coffee mug or glass is the standard capacity. The alcohol ingredients are poured before the hot coffee. Leave about a ½" to ¾" between the drink level and the rim of the coffee mug. This will prevent over diluting the drink and leave plenty of room for the traditional whipped cream garnish.

7. Wine & Champagne Drinks

The increasing popularity of wine has brought about a predictable increase in wine-based drinks. Drinks such as the Kir, spritzer and wine cooler are light and refreshing concoctions and they appeal to a large segment of the drinking public.

Perhaps no other product enjoys such a reputation for outstanding quality as does champagne, the classic sparkling white wine from France. It is easy to understand why the popular demand for champagne drinks continues to increase.

Drinks such as the champagne cocktail, mimosa and French 75 are all light, effervescent and delicious. With the advent of the reusable bottle-stopper that keeps champagne carbonated overnight, bars and restaurants can pour champagne by the glass without being overly concerned that the unused portion will go flat and be wasted.

There are a number of different styles, shapes and sizes of champagne glasses that will adequately accommodate single portions of champagne as well as champagne-based cocktails. Most operators select a 9-12 ounce champagne glass due to its utility.

8. Cream & Ice Cream Drinks

These sweet, creamy cocktails are most often ordered after dinner or late in the evening, something of a liquid dessert. They have excellent customer appeal, usually sell at high profit margins, and are normally low in alcoholic potency - all excellent commercial attributes.

The base ingredient in almost all of these drink recipes is half & half cream. It is the preferred ingredient in these drinks. Using whole milk will produce a drink with a thin consistency, while fresh cream causes the drink to be too sweet and heavy.

Any of these cocktails can be turned into something of a milkshake by substituting 1-2 scoops of ice cream for the half & half. The drink is then blended in the electric blender and presented in a house specialty glass.

When these cocktails are ordered straight-up, you will use either a traditional hand mixing set or an electric up-mixer. Either method will produce a frothy mixture that is served in a chilled cocktail glass.

When a cream drink is ordered on-the-rocks, it is mixed in either manner above and then strained into a snifter or house specialty glass filled with ice.

The taste and potency of these recipes can be adjusted by decreasing the portion of half & half and increasing each liquor or liqueur portion from ½ oz. to ¾ oz.

9. Shooters & Cordial Drinks

Pousse cafés are layered cordial drinks that are comprised of 3 or more layers.

Shooters are a large and diverse body of drink recipes, ranging from the elegant and sophisticated to the radically bizarre. Shooters are anything but one-dimensional. They have evolved into complex drinks with improved flavor and presentation. If any one recipe can be credited for relaunching the popularity of these drinks, it is the B-52, the layered combination of Kahlúa, Bailey's Irish Cream and Grand Marnier.

Shooters are fun, interesting and contemporary drinks. Since most are served neat or straight-up, the quality of their ingredients can be more fully appreciated. With a vast array of recipes at your disposal, shooters can also be made with slower moving inventory. And should these benefits prove insufficient incentives, shooters are exceptionally profitable.

Drink presentation is another marketing consideration. When appropriate, shooters should be served in chilled glasses. This will help keep the ingredients at their proper serving temperature and enhances the drink's presentation. Experiment with alternative glassware, such as sherry, cordial or presentation shot glasses. Match each specialty shooter with the most appropriate glass.

Pousse cafés are layered cordial drinks that are comprised of 3 or more layers. In French, *pousse café* literally translates to "push coffee", a reference to its reputation as an after-dinner drink. Technically, shooters such as a B-52 are also *pousse cafés*.

When prepared properly, the ingredients of a *pousse café* or layered shooter will form distinctive tiers or "stripes" within the glass. This occurs as a result of using liqueurs with different specific gravities or densities. The effect achieved is similar to the way oil will float on water or vinegar, creating two visible layers.

To accomplish this, care must be taken to prevent the various products from mixing in the glass. The ingredients should be poured from heaviest to lightest.

The fastest, most sanitary way to create these layers is to use the back of a bar spoon to slow the pour of the liqueur. The spoon is held just above the level of the first liqueur poured into the glass, and the next ingredient is poured slowly and carefully over the sloped back of the spoon. Each layer is poured using this same technique.

The same effect for a two-layer drink can be obtained by first tilting the glass so that the bottom layer is almost touching the inside rim. The second product is then slowly and gently poured onto the glass surface between the first liqueur and the rim. While pouring the second layer, the glass should be carefully brought upright.

Some bartenders create this layered effect by using a maraschino cherry to slow the pour of the second and third liqueurs. The cherry is held by the stem with its bottom held just above the lower layer and the liqueurs are poured over the cherry's sloped top. This is an acceptable method if the syrupy juice is rinsed off the cherry before pouring the liqueurs.

ESTABLISHING SERVING PORTIONS

An essential aspect of attaining profitability behind the bar is to establish serving portions for each major type of mixed drink and presenting it to the bartending staff in a clear and concise manner. There must be a consensus on staff as to the amount of product to use in the preparation of all of the bar's drinks.

The following is an example of how to present portioning guidelines to the bartending staff.

Example of Drink Portioning Guidelines

1. Highballs:

Regular highball: 1¼ oz. liquor portion (9 oz. highball glass)

Double highball: 2½ oz. liquor portion (9 oz. highball glass)

Tall highball: 1¼ oz. liquor portion (12 oz. bucket glass)

Short highball: 1¼ oz. liquor portion (7 oz. rocks glass)

Double tall highball: 2 oz. liquor portion (12 oz. bucket glass)

2. Martinis, Rob Roys and Manhattans:

Martini: 2 oz. gin or vodka portion (4 oz. cocktail or 7 oz. rocks glass)

Manhattan: 1½ oz. bourbon & ½ oz. vermouth (4 oz. cocktail or 7 oz. rocks glass)

Rob Roy: 1½ oz. Scotch & ½ oz. vermouth (4 oz. cocktail or 7 oz. rocks glass)

3. Rock Drinks:

Liquor/liqueur on-the-rocks: 1½ oz. portion (7 oz. rocks glass)

Liquor/liqueur drinks: 1½ liquor & ½ oz liqueur portion (7 oz. rocks glass)

Old Fashion on-the-rocks: 1½ oz. portion (7 oz. rocks glass)

Smith & Kerns: 1½ oz. Kahlúa (9 oz. brandy snifter)

Colorado Bulldog. 1½ oz. vodka & ¾ oz. Kahlúa (12 oz. bucket glass)

4. Classic Cocktails:

Margarita, straight-up: 1¼ oz. tequila & ½ oz. Triple Sec (7 oz. coupette glass)

Margarita, on-the-rocks: 1¼ oz. tequila & ½ oz. Triple Sec (12 oz. bucket glass)

Margarita, blended: 1¼ oz. tequila & ½ oz. Triple Sec
   (13¼ oz. House Specialty Glass)

Daiquiri/Side Car, straight-up: 1¼ oz. liquor portion (7 oz. coupette glass)

Daiquiri/Side Car, on-the-rocks: 1¼ oz. liquor portion (12 oz. bucket glass)

Daiquiri, blended: 1¼ oz. rum (13¼ oz. house specialty glass)

5. Tropical & Tall Drinks:

Collins: 1¼ oz. requested liquor portion (12 oz. bucket glass)

Long Island Iced Tea: 2 oz. total liquor & ½ oz. Triple Sec
   (13¼ oz. house specialty glass)

Piña Colada, blended: 1¼ oz. light rum (13¼ oz. house specialty glass)

Piña Colada, on-the-rocks: 1¼ oz. light rum (13¼ oz. house specialty glass)

6. Coffee & Hot Drinks:

Liquor/Liqueur & coffee: 1¼ oz. requested product (10 oz. coffee mug)

Irish Coffee: 1¼ oz. Irish whiskey (10 oz. coffee mug)

Irish Coffee Royale: 1 oz. Irish whiskey & 1 oz. Kahlúa (10 oz. coffee mug)

Keoki Coffee: ½ oz. brandy, Kahlúa, crème de cacao (10 oz. coffee mug)

7. Wine & Champagne Drinks:

House/Varietal white wine by-the-glass: 6 oz. wine portion
   (8½ oz. white wine glass)

House/Varietal blush wine by-the-glass: 6 oz. wine portion
   (8½ oz. white wine glass)

House/Varietal red wine by-the-glass: 6 oz. wine portion (8½ oz. red wine glass)

Spritzer/Cooler, on-the-rocks: 5 oz. wine portion

    (8½ oz. white wine glass or stemmed house specialty glass)

House champagne by-the-glass: 4 oz. champagne portion

    (5¾ oz. champagne flute)

Sherry or port, neat: 2 oz. portion (3 oz. sherry glass)

8. Cream & Ice Cream Drinks:

Cream drink, straight-up: 1½ oz. liqueur portion (7 oz. house specialty glass)

Cream drink, on-the-rocks: 1½ oz. liqueur portion (9 oz. brandy snifter)

Cream drink, blended: 1½ oz. liqueur portion (13¼ oz. house specialty glass)

Ice cream drink, blended: 1½ oz. liqueur portion (13¼ oz. house specialty glass)

9. Shooters & Cordial Drinks:

Liquor, neat/shot: 1½ oz. portion (2 oz. presentation glass)

Brandy/Armagnac, neat: 1½ oz. portion (9 oz. brandy snifter)

Shooter drink, straight-up: 2½ oz. maximum liquor portion (2¾ oz. Islande shot)

Shooter drink, rocks: 2½ oz. maximum liquor portion (7 oz. rocks glass)

CREATING SIGNATURE DRINKS

What you don't want to have happen is for guests to order your bar's specialty drinks only to find that there's nothing special about them. The natural presumption is that if the specialties in the front of the house are lacking, the specialties coming out of the kitchen must be lacking as well.

A signature drink needs three things to become an enduring classic - great taste, good production value and perceived value. Successful specialty drinks invariably have great flavor, one not easily replicated without knowing the recipe. If your guests want it again, they'll have to come back.

People buy with their eyes, making production value a critical consideration. A signature drink must look special, like something one couldn't easily make at home. Unusually colored drinks attract attention and stir the imagination. Don't discount the importance of aroma - the better a drink smells, the better it sells. Even the act of hand shaking a drink enhances its production value. The sights and sounds of a drink being masterfully prepared certainly improve its marketability.

Perceived value in a specialty drink comes down to good quality at a fair price. Sticking with quality brands and products is an unerring strategy. Likewise, people know when they're being gouged on price and rarely will they allow themselves to be consistently taken.

Garnishing drinks is a classic way to spark interest. For instance, there's a wide array of fresh fruits, vegetables, candies, pretzels, and cookies that can be used to finish the drinks. And where's it written that a Bloody Mary can only be garnished with stalk of celery? Among the other more creative options are a scallion, boiled shrimp, a crab claw, a Slim Jim or beef jerky, asparagus, cucumber spears, or a pepperocini, to name but a few. Garnishing is an art, not a burden.

Glassware is another vehicle for enhancing a cocktail's presentation. Libbey has a catalog filled with interesting, cost-effective specialty glassware. (See chapter 5 for a variety of samples from their 2000 catalog) In a world where first impressions are often the most significant, ensuring that drinks look their best is a marketing imperative.

Adding pizzazz to a drink may involve changing its presentation. For example, create a Meltdown Raspberry Margarita by serving the Chambord on the side, and letting your customers pour the liqueur themselves. The liqueur will slowly wind its way down through the drink adding the marvelous flavor of raspberries and creating a striking presentation.

> **A signature drink needs three things to become an enduring classic.**

Swirls are also a style of presentation loaded with pizzazz. Swirls involve blending two different drinks-a piña colada and strawberry daiquiri, for instance- and combining them in the same glass. The resulting drink is both delicious and visually intriguing.

USING ALCOHOL-FREE LIQUEURS

Tremendous strides have been made in the development of great tasting alcohol-free liqueurs. There are several operational benefits to using these products in drink making, the most significant being to effectively lower drink cost and alcoholic potency.

Undoubtedly the largest market penetration of these products at this time is non-alcoholic triple sec. Brands such as Rose's, D. J. Dotson, Royal and Angostura now dominate the market and outsell their alcoholic counterparts. Why have these alcohol-free triple secs caught on?

One reason for the popular acceptance of alcohol-free triple secs is that they do not have a harsh, bitter after taste like their alcoholic counterparts do. In addition, the alcohol-free versions cost a fraction of what conventional triple sec does. Perhaps the most compelling reason to use an alcohol-free triple sec is its great taste, alluring bouquet and seamless finish.

There are four popular cocktails that use triple sec in their preparation - the margarita, Long Island iced tea, kamikaze and the Lynchburg lemonade. The triple sec adds a robust orange flavor that is essential to these concoctions. What these cocktails do not need is more alcohol. The cocktails prepared with an alcohol-free triple sec will taste better and are safer to serve.

Non-alcoholic liqueurs may also be used in such exotic drinks as the rum runner, mai tai and zombie. The resulting drinks cost less, are lower in alcohol and taste every bit as good as the originals.

A WORD OF CAUTION ABOUT SERVING DOUBLES

Nearly every state has passed legislation imposing civil liability upon the server of alcohol and the liquor licensee. These statutes are referred to as the Dram Shop Acts. This subject will be covered in detail later in the book. It should stand to reason, however, that servers and managers have an obligation to do everything within reason to ensure that guests do not become intoxicated.

One advisable policy to adopt is to prohibit the service of "doubles." A double is more than twice as potent as a regularly prepared drink. For instance, a regularly prepared gin and tonic, is made in a 9-ounce highball glass using 1 ounce of gin and diluted with approximately 2 ounces of tonic, or a proportion of 1-part alcohol to 2-parts mixer. A double gin and tonic is prepared in the same size glass using 2 ounces of gin that is diluted by approximately 1 ounce of tonic, or a proportion of 2-part alcohol to 1-parts mixer.

As if to compound the situation, people typically drink doubles at about the same rate as they do a regularly prepared drink. There is nothing mandating that you have to serve a guest a double. The server could simply state that it is against house policy to serve doubles, and then inquire if he or she would care for a regularly prepared drink.

QUESTIONS LEAD TO ANSWERS WHICH LEAD TO SUCCESS

- Does your bartending staff prepare drinks according to the same recipes?
- Have you provided your staff with a comprehensive list of house recipes?
- Do you have a contemporary drink recipe guide behind the bar?
- Have you established serving portions for the major categories of mixed drinks?
- Have you solicited your bartending staff's input regarding the drink recipes you pour?
- What is your clientele's reaction to the drinks you pour?
- Are your drinks too potent? Do they taste strong? Do they taste weak?
- How do your house recipes compare with those poured by your direct competitors?
- Do you utilize non-alcoholic liqueurs and other non-alcoholic beverages in your drink recipes?
- Do you allow your staff to prepare and serve doubles?

Portion Control:
Protecting Your Profit Margins

Since the sales price of a drink is hinged to the serving portion of alcohol, if the portion size fluctuates, so will the drink's profit margin. Implementing an effective strategy to strictly control portioning is crucial to protecting your profit margins.

To demonstrate the importance of portioning control, consider the following illustration. According to your bar's policy, a Tanqueray and tonic is prepared with 1¼ ounces of gin (at a cost of $.55 per ounce) and sells at a retail price of $4.50. The Tanqueray and tonic therefore yields a gross profit of $3.81 ($4.50 - $.69) and sells at a cost percentage of 15.3% ($.69 ÷ $4.50). If a bartender overpours the portion of Tanqueray by half an ounce, the resulting drink's portion cost will jump 39% (from $.69 to $.96), which in turn will cause the cost percentage to rise a whopping 6 points, an increase from 15.3% to 21.3%.

If the portion size fluctuates, so will the drink's profit margin.

If this same bartender were to nightly overpour 20 drinks by a half a shot, the house would lose approximately 50 ounces of liquor, or nearly a liter and a half over the course of a week. If the average shot of call brand liquor costs $.50 per ounce, this one employee would be responsible for wasting roughly $25 of liquor a week. Were this situation to continue unchecked, the house would lose $1,300 in liquor over a year. Keep in mind that for many high-volume beverage operations limiting losses due to over-portioning to 50 ounces a week would be a considerable improvement.

There is also an opportunity cost associated with over-portioning. In today's society, most people are acutely aware of how much alcohol they can safely consume. They set limits for themselves. Serving potent drinks will have a negative impact on revenue by reducing the number of drinks people can safely order.

In addition, over-portioning alcohol in drinks places the public at risk and increases an operator's legal liability. The steady rise in alcohol-related litigation practically requires that operators implement measures to reduce their exposure to liquor liability.

IMPLEMENTING A PORTION CONTROL PROGRAM

Between steadily rising state and federal taxes, and climbing manufacturer costs, the cost of distilled spirits will continue to increase. Perhaps now more than any time previous, bartenders who play fast and loose with liquor pose a monumental problem for beverage operators. The solution is portion control.

There are essentially four different methods of portioning distilled spirits at a bar. The first method is called free pouring, a technique in which a bartender portions liquor through an uncontrolled pour spout, relying on an internal count or cadence to estimate the rate of flow. Hand-held measuring involves the use of such measuring devices as a jigger or shot glass.

There are essentially four different methods of portioning. The third method of portioning liquor is the use of bottle-attached control devices such as the Precision Pour, a highly effective control spout that is capable of delivering precise measurements of distilled spirits. The final means of portion control involves the use of electronic dispensers. Pioneered and perfected by the Berg Company, electronic dispensers utilize advanced microchip technology to precisely portion and accurately track the usage of liquor.

There are advantages and disadvantages to each method and it is important to assess the viability of each for your concept, clientele and operation.

FREE POURING VS. HAND-HELD MEASURING

• **Free Pouring** — Free pouring is the method of pouring in which the bartender hand pours liquor portions without the use of a jigger, relying rather on an internal count or cadence to meter the rate of flow. Free pouring is a stylish, professional technique. Its enhanced flair and panache makes it a popular method with bartenders.

Free pouring is most advantageous in high-volume beverage operations. It is an extremely fast method of preparing mixed drinks, since only one hand is engaged holding the bottle, the other is free to dispense the mixer simultaneously. There is no possibility of residual or holdover flavors. Free pouring requires little training to attain proficiency.

Free pouring does have its shortcomings though. It is far more difficult to ensure consistency of portioning when the bartenders free pour. Inconsistency of portioning will negatively affect the operation's drink recipes and cost control efforts. In addition, it is easier for bartenders to inadvertently or purposely underpour or overpour liquor when free pouring, and it is far more difficult for supervisors and guests seated at the bar to accurately gauge a correct pour.

Free pouring also requires a greater amount of concentration to maintain consistent measurements. It is especially challenging for bartenders to free pour accurate measurements when they are tired or during peak hours of business.

While a popular method of pouring with bartenders, it is the most costly method of dispensing spirits at a bar. Should you choose to allow your bartenders to free pour, it is advisable to routinely test their abilities. Set half a dozen empty glasses on the bar rail, and require them to quickly pour a series of measurements. Pour the contents of each glass into a graduated cylinder or measuring glass to gauge their accuracy. Many operators will establish minimum standards for pouring accuracy, and if a bartender cannot meet those standards, he or she is compelled to use a jigger or shot glass until able to free pour consistently accurate measurements.

Free pouring is the most costly method of dispensing spirits.

Hand-Held Measuring — Hand-held measuring is the traditional method of portioning liquor. It entails using one of a number of different hand-held shot glasses and jiggers.

There are several advantages to requiring a bartender to use a hand-held jigger. Supervisors and guests seated at the bar can more easily perceive how much liquor the person is pouring with a jigger. The use of a jigger dramatically decreases the possibility of inadvertently overpouring or underpouring liquor, making it easier for the bartending staff to achieve consistent proper portioning.

The best way to use a hand-held measure is to use a technique called "hinging." It involves imagining that there is an actual hinge between the lip of the glass and the jigger. Prior to measuring out the liquor, the jigger is brought ("hinged") to the side of the glass. At the moment the correct measure is reached, the jigger is tipped into the glass and the liquor bottle is returned to its upright position. The four separate motions—1. readying the measure, 2. the pour, 3. ending the pour, and 4. emptying the measure—should be accomplished in one smooth motion performed as quickly as possible.

The measuring device should stay in the bartender's hand until all liquor portions are poured, and then returned to the pour mat in the square space intended for that purpose. This will ensure that time isn't wasted searching for the measure.

While highly accurate, hand measuring is the slowest means of dispensing liquor. It requires two hands to pour a shot of liquor—one to hold the bottle and the other to hold the jigger. In contrast, free pouring requires only one hand to hold the bottle, the other is free to pour in the mixer or another ingredient.

Hand measuring requires training and practice before a bartender can master proper technique and the necessary wrist speed. Jiggers may retain the residual holdover flavor of the previously poured product, thereby affecting the taste of subsequent drinks.

Finally, there are beverage concepts in which the use of a jigger behind the bar might be considered inappropriate. One example would be a country & western bar, where a free-wielding, free-pouring bartender more closely follows concept.

Hand measuring requires training and practice before a bartender can master proper technique and the necessary wrist speed.

BOTTLE-ATTACHED CONTROL DEVICES

These innovative control devices offer a cost-effective method of ensuring strict portion control and accuracy without intruding on the server-guest relationship. The industry leader, Precision Pours, has created a device that is capable of precisely portioning liquor. It relies on a unique, three-ball bearing assembly in which the ball bearings work together to cut off the flow of fluid at the prescribed measure. The spouts are available in seven portion sizes ranging from ⅝ ounce to 1½ ounces.

These relatively uncomplicated, unobtrusive devices represent a significant advancement in beverage control. The control spouts, called Precision 3 Ball Pours, greatly decrease the possibility of inadvertent underpouring or overpouring, and are extremely effective at deterring fraudulent practices behind the bar. Since the device works like a regular pour spout, no specialized staff training is required to achieve consistent, optimum results.

Another advantage to these ingenious devices is they are universally applicable and concept-friendly. They can be used at any type of beverage operation without negatively impacting concept or public perception. While Precision 3 Ball Pours are more expensive than conventional, open flow spouts, they are far less capital intensive than other, more technologically advanced control systems. Incorporating Precision 3 Ball Pours into a comprehensive cost control strategy is highly advisable.

These spouts must be clean to function properly. When the spouts are dirty their internal ball bearings may not operate smoothly. This will cause the flow to be interrupted, delaying the delivery and adversely affecting the devices accuracy. Regular washing in hot, soapy water is sufficient to maintain these control spouts in perfect working order. Also make note of the manufacturer's recommendation to soak the spouts in warm water prior to initially putting them into service. The heat conditions the hard plastic, preparing it for use.

As far as the shortcomings of this type of device is concerned, there are several things you should consider. Some manufacturer's devices do an inadequate job portioning liqueurs. This is not an issue with the Precision 3 Ball Pours, which utilizes a patented ball bearing assembly and pours an accurate measurement regardless of the fluid's viscosity. Competitive devises, however, are manufactured using only two ball bearings to control the flow of liquor. This type of control spout is incapable of accurately portioning liqueurs and cordials.

Precision 3 Ball Pours utilize a patented ball bearing assembly.

Precision Pours

Precision 3 Ball Pours: Measured pours or straight pours, with or without collars.

Another consideration is that portion control spouts are designed to deliver only one measurement, thereby restricting a bartender's pouring flexibility. For drink recipes requiring more or less than a standard portion of liquor, the simple solution is for the bartenders to manually modify the pour. Training and supervision will be required to ensure that the staff doesn't abuse or take liberties with this modification in the system, which would have the cumulative effect of undermining the control features of these devices.

As is the case with most things, the control function of these devices can be purposely cheated. A bartender intent on overpouring or underpouring can hold the bottle at an acute angle, keeping the bottle nearly level. This will cause the spout to continue to pour. Of course, this breaks down if the bartender is observed committing such an obvious indiscretion.

LIQUOR CONTROL SYSTEMS (LCS)

One area where technology has made a significant impact on the on-premise trade is in making the dispensing of liquor more precise and less vulnerable to theft. At the forefront of these technological advancements are a new generation of liquor control systems (LCS). Produced by several manufacturers, these systems are so effective at controlling liquor costs and eliminating fraudulent practices behind the bar that their return on investment is typically one year or less.

The Berg Company: All-Bottle Liquor Control System

The origin of the technology can be traced back to 1975 when the Berg Company of Madison, Wisconsin, introduced the All-Bottle Liquor Control System. After 25 years of non-stop research and development, the state-of-the-art system has been installed in roughly half of all food and beverage operations around the world that have invested in LCS technology.

The revolutionary Berg All-Bottle System is capable of dispensing an unlimited number of liquors and liqueurs using a unique ring attachment, a collar-like device that couples with specially designed pour spouts that deliver multiple portion sizes with computer accuracy. Unless the activator ring is attached, the spouts won't pour, making overpouring or short pouring liquor a considerable challenge. It is especially beneficial for operations with extensive liquor inventories.

The All-Bottle System requires no complicated installations or pressurized lines. The compact control monitor and activator ring are easily mounted under-bar by each bartender's workstation. It uses tamper-evident strips attached to the pour spouts, which eliminates the possibility of employees circumventing the control features of the system without detection.

Another benefit of the system is the immediate access you'll have to point-of-sale information. The system is capable of interfacing with

your electronic cash register or point-of-sale system so every drink poured is registered immediately, making the bartender accountable for the sale. At the end of a shift, all the operational data from each system downloads to your computer, providing you with a series of

management reports detailing exactly what was poured and at what price, or you can get real-time information at a keystroke.

While attaining strict portion control is certainly a key management objective, if the operation's guests find the technology off-putting or inhospitable, the cost savings will seem inconsequential compared to the loss of good will and damage done to the business's public image.

The Berg All-Bottle System is completely unobtrusive to the operation.

One of the principle advantages an LCS such as the Berg All-Bottle System is that it is completely unobtrusive to the operation. The system doesn't impede speed of service and bartenders make drinks in the same manner using the same pouring motion. It allows your guests seated at the bar to visually confirm that what they ordered is actually being poured. The system is fast and requires little training to use.

There are several different versions of liquor control systems on the market, including towers, under-counter systems and freestanding countertop configurations. Some systems are capable of dispensing up to 250 liquors in different portion sizes and any type of beverage or drink. The systems can interface with a POS such that whenever a product is poured it is automatically registered.

Operators looking for a comprehensive LCS should consider the Berg Laser Liquor System, an efficient and highly cost-effective system that dispenses liquor through a specially designed beverage gun. It operates simultaneously with various price lists and portion sizes and can accommodate up to 128 brands of liquor stored in a secure, remote location as much as 500 feet away. While any size bottle can be used to supply the system, typically economical 1.75 liter bottles are used. The bottles are inverted into the system and allowed to drain completely, increasing the potential savings. The Laser System can also dispense up to 48 pre-programmed cocktails, each prepared precisely according to your specified recipes.

This type of LCS provides the height of efficiency and accountability. Because the inventory is dispensed through on-demand pressurized lines, liquor portions are dispensed extremely fast as well as accurately. Each product dispensed is immediately registered into a point-of-sale system. The system increases bartender productivity while greatly reducing shrinkage attributable to waste, spillage, underpouring and overpouring.

The Laser system is entirely programmable and does not require a dedicated computer. The system is capable of tracking inventory from delivery to sale, computing cost percentages and determining gross profit. The software works with numerous pricing structures for special events, such as happy hour, or promotional events, and will even shut-off the system's dispenser at a pre-programmed time.

The Berg All-Bottle System is virtually concept proof.

It should be noted that many beverage operations use both a Laser-type LCS and an All-Bottle System, with the latter used for products not poured frequently enough to dispense from the beverage gun.

The price tag for this technology, equipping a single station with a liquor control system can cost upwards of $13,000, multiple stations cost roughly $35,000 and up. Variables include difficulty of installation, number of stations and the amount of hardware required. Despite being highly reliable equipment, some servicing and maintenance will be required at an additional cost. However, these systems typically lower costs and increase profits to such a degree that the initial investment is recouped within one to two years.

There are several factors to consider prior to investing in a liquor control system. The first is to assess the company's ability to service and maintain the system. If the equipment does breakdown or for some reason becomes inoperative, it will be highly disruptive to the operation. Some manufacturers direct market their equipment through national sales representatives. Others companies have opted to establish a national network of local distributors. These distributors are then responsible for providing service and technical support to their local customer base. At the risk of stating the obvious, it is most advantageous to invest in a system and company with a dealer-based organization.

Another factor to consider prior to purchase is whether installing a liquor control system will somehow clash or conflict with the establishment's concept. For example, some people find a liquor control system behind the bar at a small neighborhood place something of a contradiction.

On the other hand, liquor control systems have been nothing short of a technological windfall for a number of food and beverage concepts. Most notable on the list are high-volume operations (nightclubs, restaurants, bars and hotel lounges), server dedicated outlets (bowling center bars, service bars and catering venues) or at operations with a high rate of customer turnover (airport lounges, dance clubs and convention centers).

To a large extent the Berg All-Bottle System is virtually concept proof. The system is almost universally applicable because it doesn't change how bartenders make drinks or prevent guests from visually confirming that what they ordered is actually what is being poured.

Do liquor control systems seem too corporate and mercenary?

Another concept-related consideration involves the growing trend of flair bartending, the skilled art of flipping bottles, glasses and mixing tins. The showmanship and enhanced professionalism exhibited by these talented bartenders keep people in their stools longer.

Flair bartending notwithstanding, liquor control systems are a foreshadowing technology, a sign of things to come. Between the growing concern over DWI issues and steadily rising liquor costs, strict liquor control will more likely be the standard than the exception, and may even someday become a licensing requirement.

DO GUESTS OBJECT TO LIQUOR CONTROL SYSTEMS?

It's a valid question, isn't it? Does the sight of liquor being portioned out by a machine somehow turn off people seated at the bar? Is it contrary to our primary mission, which is to have clientele feel like guests in our home? Do liquor control systems seem too corporate and mercenary?

These were some of the questions posed by Professor Carl Borchgrevink, Ph.D., CFBE, of the prestigious School of Hospitality Business at Michigan State University. In a study published in a recent issue of the Journal of Hospitality & Leisure Marketing (Volume 6 (3) 1999), Professor Borchgrevink looked to answer three questions. Are guests less satisfied when a visible automated beverage control system is used during a cocktail reception (chosen as a controlled point of reference) compared to when such a system is not used?

Second, do guests perceive the speed of service to be less when a visible automated beverage control system is used during a cocktail reception compared to when such a system is not used? And third, do guests perceive the quality, amount, or portion size of beverage served to be less when a visible automated beverage control system is used during a cocktail reception compared to when such a system is not used?

For the research experiment, Borchgrevink invited staff and faculty of a major mid-western university to attend a free cocktail reception. Invitations were extended until 60 guests had committed to attend to the experimental group reception and the control group reception. The experimental group session and the control group session were held in the same room, at the same time of day, with the same type and quality of food and beverages available at both events. The same bartender and food servers were used in both settings. The employees were not aware that they were participating in a study.

Borchgrevink made sure all the variables were taken into consideration, including ensuring that every drink was prepared precisely the same. The only variable was that the bartenders prepared drinks for the control group using a hand-held jigger, while the bartenders serving the experimental group were set-up with the Berg All-Bottle System.

As the guests left the reception they were asked to fill out a questionnaire regarding their perceptions of the event. The results were conclusive. Borchgrevink found that the liquor control system had no impact on public perception. None of the test subjects had any negative thought or impression of the automated system.

Professor Borchgrevink concludes that operators have little reason to be concerned about the potential that guests may respond negatively. This is particularly true with systems that allow guests to see exactly what brand is being used in a drink and how much liquor was poured into the drink.

Operators have little reason to be concerned about guests responding negatively.

QUESTIONS LEAD TO ANSWERS WHICH LEAD TO SUCCESS

- What methods of measuring and portioning liquor do your direct competitors use?
- What criteria did you use to choose the method of dispensing alcohol you currently employ?
- What advantages does the method you chose afford your operation?
- What are the disadvantages of the method?

- **If you free pour:**
    a. Do you test the accuracy of your bartenders pouring abilities on a regular basis?
    b. Do you focus on free pouring abilities in your bartending training program?
    c. Have you switched to using a hand-held measuring device for a week and compared the resulting cost percentages with those obtained by free pouring?
    d. Are there operational factors present at your bar that preclude the use of a measuring device?

- **If you use a hand-held measure:**
    a. Do you test the accuracy of your bartenders pouring abilities with a jigger on a regular basis?
    b. Do you focus on the ability to measure quickly and accurately using a hand-held jigger in your bartending training program?
    c. Have you switched to another method of dispensing alcohol for a week and compared the resulting costs with those obtained using a hand-held measure?
    d. Are there operational factors present at your bar that discourage other methods of measuring and portioning?

- **If you use bottle-attached measures:**
    a. Do you have bottle-attached measures on every product in your inventory? If not, what method of portioning do you use for those products?
    b. Do you use the same bottle-attached measuring device on liqueurs as well as liquors?

c. How frequently are the bottle-attached measuring devices cleaned?

d. What factors prompted you to choose the measuring device you are currently using?

e. How do your bartenders compensate for the lack of portioning flexibility with the bottle-attached devices?

f. How does your staff and clientele react to these devices?

• **If you use an electronic liquor dispenser:**

a. What criteria did you use when deciding to install an electronic liquor dispenser (LCS)?

b. How much portioning flexibility does your system afford you?

c. How do you portion products not contained in the system?

d. Do you have a contingency plan if your LCS breaks down?

Chapter 9

Drink Pricing
For Optimum Profits

You needn't be reminded how critically important establishing appropriate pricing for goods and services is to your eventual success. We are consumers. We all make purchasing decisions on a daily basis. It's likely we all consider ourselves savvy consumers, not ready to be taken advantage of or to needlessly overspend our hard-earned money.

The objective when developing the various price lists for your beverage operation is to establish a set of prices that will yield the highest potential profit margins and cause the products to sell at their optimum sales volume. If you raise the sales price substantially past that point, you can anticipate the sales volume to drop, thereby decreasing the amount of profit realized. After all, how many people will be willing to pay $20 for an Absolut Vodka and tonic?

On the other hand, if you price that drink well under a dollar, you can expect the drink to sell fairly vigorously, but you'll make virtually no profit on the many transactions.

> **Establishing the various price lists for your operation is dependent on the knowledge of your business, the marketplace and pricing considerations.**

Establishing the various price lists for your operation is as much an art as it is a science. The process is dependent on the knowledge of your business, the marketplace and the following four pricing considerations:

1. **Portion Costs** — The first consideration when establishing the retail liquor, beer or wine prices is portion cost. It stands to reason that the more an item costs to serve, the higher the retail price must be to realize the desired profit margin. Portion cost is determined by multiplying the product's cost per ounce by the quantity poured.

2. **Direct Competition and Market Positioning** — How you position your beverage operation in relation to your competitors will have a direct bearing on the pricing structure. Market positioning inevitably renders down to the "meet, beat or play hardball" decision.

   Some beverage operators decide to "meet" the competition by featuring the same type of products, and pricing them similarly.

This strategy is most often used when the assessment that the establishment enjoys significant advantages over the competition. As a result of these advantages—such as location, concept, interior design, lighting and sound—the operator believes they will control a majority of the market, drawing large customer counts and healthy gross sales.

Finally, there's the "hardball decision." In this strategy, the operators decide that because they enjoy distinct and significant advantages over the competition, they are going to employ a strategy of charging a dollar or so more for comparable products. The reasoning being that since the establishment is so popular, people won't mind paying a little more for their drinks or food. If the reasoning is sound, and people really don't mind the higher prices because of all of the other attractions the establishment has to offer, then the "hardball" strategy will lead to enhanced profits.

The type of operation plays a significant role in establishing a pricing structure.

3 **Type of Establishment** — The type of operation plays a significant role in establishing a pricing structure. The public image and perception of your establishment will create certain expectations in people's minds. They will have expectations about what things will cost before they walk into the place. The public expects the prices at a high end nightclub or continental cuisine restaurant to be higher than those charged at a neighborhood bar or family restaurant. Likewise, adult (topless) clubs are renowned for charging exorbitant prices. College bars and country & western clubs, on the other hand, have the reputation for being more affordable. These consumer expectations should come into play when devising your operation's pricing structures.

4 **Demographics of the Clientele** — An affluent, professional clientele is in a better financial position to afford higher prices. Operations that charge above-market prices tend to attract patrons who are accustomed to paying higher drink prices in exchange for being able to enjoy the exclusivity of the establishment.

All things being equal, operations that charge lower than market prices will experience increased customer counts, thereby stimulating the volume-end of the profit equation.

ESTABLISHING PRICING STRUCTURES

When constructing the pricing structures for your operation, thought should be given to making them "user-friendly." The more involved and complicated you make the price lists, the more likely it is that your employees will charge your guests the wrong prices. Your research and hard work are negated when your employees fail to charge the right sales prices; even if those errors result in higher gross sales, treating the clientele fairly and safe-guarding the business's reputation is worth more than a few extra dollars.

Many operators believe that investing in point of sale systems will alleviate the need to train their employees on the operation's pricing. The thinking being that with a few keystrokes, servers or bartenders can find any drink, product or menu item price. The problem with relying on technology in this way is that guests frequently ask servers and bartenders about prices. If the employees can't quickly and competently answer the question, they will have to excuse themselves and check the point of sale system for the answer. Not only does this needlessly waste time and reduce the employee's productivity, it is also extremely unprofessional. Guests are left wondering if the server doesn't know the prices, what other surprises are in store for the evening.

Make your price lists easy to use.

The following are suggestions on how to make your price lists easier to use and less prone to employee pricing errors. Illustration 9.1 is an example of a liquor, beer and wine price list.

1. **Establish Major Price Categories** — Group products together based primarily on their wholesale costs. Use a standard increment such as fifty cents to separate the price categories, such that the well price plus fifty cents equals the call price, call plus fifty cents equals the premium price, etc. Often the high cost of super-premium liquors will necessitate an incremental increase of $.75 or more. The price points are commonly referred to as well liquor; call liquor; premium liquor; super-premium liquor and top shelf liquor. Grouping similarly priced products together requires the staff learning fewer prices.

2. **Keep Drink Prices Based Only on Quarters** — Prices ending in $.25, $.50, or $.75 are easier for bartenders and servers to add mentally. In addition, rounding prices up to the nearest quarter make them less sensitive to wholesale cost increases.

3. **Product Prices Hinged to a Specific Portion** — All sales prices for each product in the liquor inventory should be listed with

LIQUOR, BEER & WINE PRICE LIST

Well Liquors

.... 1 oz. $3.00
Happy Hour $2.00/$2.50 .... 1½ oz. $3.50

Bacardi Rum	Seagrams Gin
Cuervo Gold Tequila	Smirnoff Vodka
Jim Beam Bourbon	White Horse Scotch

Call Liquors

.... 1 oz. $3.50
.... 1½ oz. $4.00

Arrow Liqueurs	Malibu Rum
Bacardi Dark	Martini/Rossi Vermouth
Bacardi Limón	Seagrams 7
Blavod Black Vodka	Seagrams VO
Canadian Club	Skyy Vodka
Captain Morgan's	Southern Comfort
DeKuyper Peach	Wild Turkey 80 Bourbon
E & J Brandy	Yukon Jack

Premium Liquors

.... 1 oz. $4.00
.... 1½ oz. $4.50

Absolut 80°	Maker's Mark Bourbon
Absolut Citron	Midori
Absolut Kurant	Myers's Jamaican Rum
Beefeater	Rumple Minze
Cutty Sark	Sauza Hornitos
Jack Daniel's	Stolichnaya 80°
Jägermeister	Stolichnaya Limonnaya
Jameson Irish	Tanqueray Gin
Kahlúa	Wild Turkey 101°

Super-Premium Liquors

.... 1 oz. $4.75
.... 1½ oz. $5.50

Bailey's Irish Cream	Frangelico
Chambord	Goldschläger
Crown Royal	J & B Scotch
Cuervo 1800	J Walker Red Label
Dewars White Label	Sambuca Romana
Di Saronno Amaretto	Sauza Conmemorativo

Top Shelf Liquors I

.... 1 oz. $5.50
.... 1½ oz. $6.25

Chivas Regal Scotch	Grand Marnier
Drambuie	Hennessy VS Cognac
El Tesoro Silver	J Walker Black Label
Glenfiddich Single	Sauza Tres Generaciones
Glenlivet Single Malt	Wild Turkey Rare Breed

Top Shelf Liquors II

.... 1 oz. $6.25
.... 1½ oz. $7.00

Courvoisier VSOP	Hennessy VSOP Cognac
El Tesoro Añejo	Patron Añejo

Premium Draft Beers

10 oz. mug - $2.25 / 16 oz. - $2.75 / 23 oz. - $3.50
32 oz. pitcher - $4.50 / 60 oz. pitcher - $6.25
Happy Hour - $ 1.75 (10 oz.)

Bud Light	Miller Genuine Draft
Budweiser	Miller Genuine Light
Coors	Miller Lite
Coors Light	O'Doul's
Michelob	

Super-Premium Draft Beers

10 oz. mug - $2.75 / 16 oz. - $3.25 / 23 oz. - $4.00
32 oz. pitcher - $5.75 / 60 oz. pitcher - $8.50

Anchor Steam	Harp Lager
Bass Ale	Molson Ice
Clausthaler N/A	Pete's Summer Brew
Foster's Lager	Pete's Wicked Ale
Full Sail Ale	Red Hook ESB Pale Ale
Guinness Irish Stout	Samuel Adam's

Premium Bottled Beers

.... $3.00
.... *Happy Hour - $2.50*

Bud Light	Miller Genuine Light
Budweiser	Miller High Life
Coors	Miller Lite
Coors Light	O'Doul's
Michelob	Rolling Rock
Michelob Light	Sharp's
Miller Genuine Draft	Zima

Super-Premium Bottled Beers

.... $3.75

Amstel Light	Heineken
Anchor Steam	Labatts Blue
Bass Ale	Molson Export
Beck's Light	Molson Golden
Bohemia	Moosehead
Corona	Negra Modelo
Corona Light	Pacifico
Dos XX	Samuel Adams
Fat Tire	St. Pauli Girl Dark
Foster's Lager	St. Pauli Girl Light

Wines

Mystic Cliffs Chardonnay	$3.50/$15
Mystic Cliffs Cabernet Sauvignon	$3.50/$15
Mystic Cliffs White Zinfandel	$3.50/$15
Chardonnay, Woodbridge	$5.75/$25
Chardonnay, K. Jackson	$4.50/$20
Merlot, Vichon	$5.75/$25
Cabernet, Columbia Crest	$5.75/$25
Cabernet, Stags Leap	$8.75/$40
Champagne, White Star	xxxx /$60

Illustration 9.1

a corresponding portion. For example, the listed sales price for an Absolut and tonic, made with 1 ounce of Absolut, is $4.00. An Absolut Martini made with 1½ ounces of Absolut is listed at $4.50.

4. Pricing Doubles, Tall Highballs and Juice Drinks — A *Double Highball*, made with twice as much product as a regularly prepared highball, is extremely potent, costly and steeped in liability. It is therefore a sound business practice to charge twice the regular highball price for doubles. *Tall Highballs*, regardless of what mixer is used, are priced the same as a regularly prepared highball. While some operators charge a higher price for drinks made with fruit juice, it runs the risk of making the house appear cheap.

5. Staff Training and Avoiding Employee Pricing Errors — Regardless of the reason, employee pricing errors hurt the beverage operation's profitability and its reputation with the clientele. It is therefore important to work with the service staff on learning the bar's prices. This is best accomplished by reviewing the pricing structures with the staff, and explaining as you go, the rationale for the prices. A test should be given several days later after the staff has had a chance to study and learn the prices.

Work with the service staff on learning the bar's prices.

To reinforce the concept that knowing the bar's prices is highly important, schedule quizzes during monthly service staff meetings. Call off the names of 10-20 popular drinks, and ask the staff to write out each recipe, including measurements and garnish, the drink price and the glass it is served in. Set consequences for a poor showing on the quiz. The testing process will also reinforce your commitment to the staff knowing the operation's prices.

STRUCTURING A DRINK PRICE LIST

Considering the vast number of drink combinations possible, the simplest method of pricing drinks is to create a well structured list. This allows bartenders and servers to easily choose the most appropriate price, even if the drink isn't specifically listed.

The pricing structure should list the major categories of drinks, such as highballs, martinis and manhattans, cocktails, tropical, on-the-rocks/two liquor drinks, and coffee and hot drinks. Each drink category is then broken down by type of base liquor or liqueur used. Illustration 9.2 is an example of an effective drink price structure.

DRINK PRICE LIST

Highballs — 1 oz. portion/9 oz. highball glass
Made with well liquor $3.00
Made with call liquor $3.50
Made with premium liquor $4.00
Made with super-premium liquor... $4.75
Bloody Mary, Bloody Maria, Harvey Wallbanger $3.75

Martinis & Manhattans — 1½ oz. portion/7 oz. rocks or 4 oz. cocktail glass
Martini or Manhattan made with well liquor... $3.50
Martini or Manhattan made with call liquor $4.00
Martini or Manhattan made with premium liquor $4.50
Martini or Manhattan made with super-premium liquor.................................. $5.25

Rocks Drinks — 1½ liquor portion & ¾ oz. liqueur portion/7 oz. rocks glass
Well liquor on-the-rocks/Gimlets (add $.50 for Kamikazes)........................... $3.50
Call liquor on-the-rocks/Gimlets (add $.50 for Kamikazes) $4.00
Premium liquor on-the-rocks/Gimlets (add $.50 for Kamikazes) $4.50
Well liquor/premium liqueur (ex: Stinger, Black Russian, Godmother) $4.50
Call liquor/premium liqueur (ex: Skyy Black Russian) $5.00
Premium liquor/premium liqueur (ex: Stolichnaya Black Russian) $5.50
Well liquor/super-premium liqueur (ex: Rusty Nail)....................................... $5.00

Cream & Ice Cream Drinks — 1½ liquor & liqueur portion/specialty glass — Add $2 for ice cream
Well Liquor/domestic liqueur (ex: Brandy Alexander) $4.00
Two domestic liqueurs (ex: Grasshopper, Banshee) $4.25
Two premium liqueurs (ex: Toasted Almond) $4.50

Coffee Drinks — 1½ combined liquor & liqueur portion/coffee glass
Keoki Coffee, Irish Coffee $4.50
Made with well liquor (ex: brandy & coffee) $3.50
Made with premium liqueur (ex: Kahlúa & coffee) $4.50
Made with two premium liqueurs (ex: Italian Coffee)..................................... $5.00

Classic Cocktails — 1½ combined liquor & liqueur portion/cocktail glass
Sour, Stone Sour, Daiquiri with well liquor (add $1.00 if blended with fruit) $3.50
Sour, Stone Sour made with premium liqueur (ex: Amaretto Sour)................... $4.50
Margarita made with well liquor (add $1.00 if blended with fruit) $4.00
Margarita made with call liquor (add $1.00 if blended with fruit) $4.50
Margarita made with premium liquor (add $1.00 if blended with fruit) $5.00

Tropical/Tall Drinks — portions & glass vary with recipe
Tom Collins, Vodka Collins made with well liquor $3.50
Piña Colada, Chi-Chi with well liquor (add $1.00 if blended with fruit) $4.00
Piña Colada with well liquor/premium liqueur (ex: Kahlúa Colada) $4.50
Mai Tai, Blue Hawaiian, Planter's Punch, Singapore Sling............................ $4.50
Long Island Iced Tea, Long Beach Iced Tea $4.50
Zombie, Hurricane... $5.00

Wine & Champagne Drinks — 6-8 oz. portion/wine or Champagne glass
Spritzers, Coolers $3.00
Kir $3.50
Kir Royale, Mimosa, Champagne Cocktail $4.50
French 75, French 95 .... $5.00

Alcohol-Free/Virgin Drinks — 6-8 oz. portion/wine or Champagne glass
Carbonated beverages $1.50
Fruit juice $2.00
Virgin mixed drinks $2.50
Virgin blended drinks (add $1.00 if blended with fruit) $3.00

Illustration 9.2

ANALYZING PRICING STRUCTURES

An effective method of analyzing your price list is to calculate each product's cost percentage and list them as done in illustration 9.3. This type of analysis will graphically illustrate if there are products that are priced either too high or too low in relation to the rest of the inventory.

For example, if Johnnie Walker Red Label, an eight-year old blended Scotch that costs $.58 an ounce, and Johnnie Walker Black Label, a twelve-year old blended Scotch that costs $.86 an ounce, were priced the same, the Black Label would have a significantly higher cost percentage than the other products in that price category. The same is true for Cuervo Especial tequila ($.41 per ounce) and Cuervo 1800 tequila ($.63 per ounce).

This type of analysis will also help you decide if you're charging the right price for products that could fall within two price categories. For instance, in illustration 9.3, Kahlúa, Jägermeister and J & B Scotch all cost $.56, so why not charge the same price? Here's where intuition comes into play. In this particular case, it could be reasoned that people who order Scotch tend to be white-collar professionals who are less price-conscious than those who are likely to order Kahlúa and Jägermeister. Therefore, the J & B is priced as a super-premium along with the other eight-year old blended Scotches.

Selling call brands will result in larger gross sales and healthier profits.

UPSELLING CALL BRANDS

Is your staff familiar with suggestive sales techniques? They should be trained to consider every sale an opportunity to up-sell. For instance, when a customer orders a rum and Coke, the server could respond, "Would you like Bacardi or Myers's in that?" For gin and tonics they could inquire, "Would you prefer Beefeater or Tanqueray?" The key is to suggest two specific call brand choices.

Having your staff trained at selling call brands will result in larger gross sales and healthier profits. To begin with, considering the sizeable investment made stocking the back bar with name brand products, increasing the rate of depletion of premium liquor makes good financial sense. More importantly, selling premium liquor will increase your bar's gross profits.

LIQUOR PRICE LIST COST PERCENTAGES

Well Liquors

	$.33/ oz. average
	1 oz. $3.00/11.0%
	1½ oz. $3.50/14.1%
Seagrams Gin	.26/ 8.6%
Bacardi Light Rum	.28/ 9.3%
Smirnoff 80 Vodka	.30/10.0%
Jim Beam Bourbon	.31/10.3%
Cuervo Especial Tequila	.41/13.6%
White Horse Blended Scotch	.42/14.0%

Call Liquors

	$.34/ oz. average
	1 oz. $3.50/ 9.7%
	1½ oz. $4.00/12.8%
DeKuyper Peach Schnapps	.23/ 6.6%
Martini & Rossi Vermouth	.23/ 6.6%
Arrow Liqueurs (average)	.25/ 7.1%
E & J Brandy	.29/ 8.3%
Seagrams 7	.31/ 8.8%
Southern Comfort	.31/ 8.8%
Capt. Morgan's	.33/ 9.4%
Bacardi Dark	.37/10.6%
Bacardi Limón	.37/10.6%
Wild Turkey 80 Bourbon	.37/10.6%
Skyy Vodka	.38/10.8%
Blavod Black Vodka	.38/10.8%
Canadian Club	.40/11.4%
Seagrams VO	.40/11.4%
Malibu Rum	.41/11.7%
Yukon Jack	.45/12.8%

Premium Liquors

	$.50/oz. average
	1 oz. $4.00/12.5%
	1½ oz. $4.50/16.6%
Beefeater	.46/11.5%
Myers's Rum	.46/11.5%
Metaxa Ouzo	.47/11.7%
Jack Daniel's	.48/12.0%
Bacardi 151	.48/12.0%
Absolut 80°	.49/12.2%
Absolut Citron	.49/12.2%
Absolut Kurant	.49/12.2%
Stolichnaya 80°	.49/12.2%
Stolichnaya Limonnaya	.49/12.2%
Tanqueray	.49/12.2%
Maker's Mark Bourbon	.49/12.2%
Midori	.49/12.2%

Premium Liquors (cont)

Wild Turkey 101°	.50/12.5%
Rumple Minze	.54/13.5%
Cutty Sark	.54/13.5%
Sauza Hornitos Tequila	.55/13.7%
Jameson Irish	.55/13.7%
Jägermeister	.56/14.0%
Kahlúa	.56/14.0%

Super-Premium Liquors

	$.63/oz. average
	1 oz. $4.75/13.3%
	1½ oz. $5.50/17.2%
J & B Scotch	.56/11.8%
Dewar's White Label	.57/12.0%
Johnnie Walker Red Label	.58/12.2%
Sauza Conmemorativo	.59/12.4%
DiSaronno Amaretto	.62/13.0%
Goldschläger	.62/13.0%
Cuervo 1800	.63/13.3%
Frangelico	.65/13.7%
Crown Royal	.66/13.9%
Bailey's Irish Cream	.67/14.1%
Sambuca Romana	.68/14.3%
Chambord	.68/14.3%

Top Shelf Liquors I

	$.92/oz. average
	1 oz. $5.50/16.7%
	1½ oz. $6.25/22.1%
Chivas Regal	.85/15.5%
Johnnie Walker Black Label	.86/15.6%
Grand Marnier	.87/15.8%
Drambuie	.90/16.4%
El Tesoro Silver Tequila	.90/16.4%
Wild Turkey Rare	.94/17.1%
Glenlivet	.95/17.3%
Glenfiddich	.95/17.3%
Sauza Tres Generaciones	1.04/18.9%

Top Shelf Liquors II

	$1.23/oz. average
	1 oz. $6.25/19.7%
	1½ oz. $7.00/26.4%
El Tesoro Añejo (5.50/6.50)	1.11/17.8%
Courvoisier VSOP (5.50/6.50)	1.20/19.2%
Patrón Añejo (5.50/6.50)	1.27/20.3%
Hennessy VSOP Cognac	1.33/21.3%

Illustration 9.3

The following are two practical examples of how premium products boost profits. In Illustration 9.4, a margarita prepared with well tequila has a raw cost of roughly $.42, and usually sells for about $3.00. The drink's cost percentage is therefore 14% ($.42/$3.00), and yields a gross profit of $2.58 ($3.00 - $.42).

MARGARITA MADE WITH WELL TEQUILA

1¼ oz. well tequila	=	$ .28
½ oz. triple sec	=	$ .08
3 oz. sweet 'n' sour	=	$ .06
Drink Cost	=	$ .42
$.42 cost/$3.00 sales price	=	14.0% cost
$3.00 sales price - $.42 cost	=	$2.58 profit

MARGARITA MADE WITH PREMIUM TEQUILA

1¼ oz. Cuervo Especial	=	$ .52
½ oz. triple sec	=	$ .08
3 oz. sweet 'n' sour	=	$ .06
Drink Cost	=	$ .66
$.66 cost/$4.25 sales price	=	15.5% cost
$4.25 sales price - $.66 cost	=	$3.59 profit

MARGARITA MADE WITH SUPER-PREMIUM TEQUILA

1¼ oz. El Tesoro 100% Agave	=	$1.13
½ oz. triple sec	=	$ .08
3 oz. sweet 'n' sour	=	$ .06
Drink Cost	–	$1.27
$1.27 cost/$5.50 sales price	=	23.1% cost
$5.50 sales price - $1.27 cost	=	$4.23 profit

Illustration 9.4

A margarita made according to the same recipe using a premium tequila, such as Cuervo Especial, sells at a higher cost percentage (17.5%), yet returns a higher gross profit of $3.30. If the same drink is made with a super-premium tequila, such as El Tesoro 100% Blue Agave, the cost percentage rises to 23%, but its gross profit increases to $4.23. Illustration 9.5 portrays the impact up-selling name brand vodkas has on the profitability of the Bloody Mary.

If you're more interested in your bar's bottom line than it's cost percentages, increasing your premium liquor sales should be a high priority.

ESTABLISHING A PLAN

As with any high-ticket item, proper marketing will greatly assist your efforts to create customer brand recognition.

The necessary next step is to educate your employees. Does your staff know what call brands you carry? Do they know what the products are? Product knowledge is essential to selling premium spirits. Make sure that your bartenders and servers are well informed about the top-shelf products, about what makes them so exceptional, and why they're worth the higher price. Customers often ask what makes one brand better than another, and a clear, simple answer is usually all that's needed to close the sale.

The impact of suggestive sales can be dramatic. The same is true for offering servers sales incentives. Set weekly goals, and see who can sell the most signature margaritas, or specialty martinis. Tell your staff what you want to happen. Then reward their success. If your objective is to create a demand for your call brands, setting sales incentives is a good way to accomplish your goal.

Make sure you provide support for your staff's marketing efforts. Promote your specialty drink of the day, shooter of the day, and any food specials on large wipe-off boards or chalkboards. Place them strategically throughout your establishment. There should be no question in anyone's mind what your specials of the day are.

Consider also listing name brand spirits in your menus. Bar menus are an effective way to promote premium liquors and liqueurs, as well as house specialty drinks, draft and bottled beer, varietal wines, and bar appetizers. Many operators also have success listing their top shelf spirits in a separate section on their wine menus.

Make sure that your bartenders and servers are well informed.

Conducting horizontal tastings is fast becoming a popular way to let your customers and staff experience first-hand the differences between the various brands. Encourage your clientele to sample short-portions of several different brands of tequila or bourbon, for example, so they can compare each, and determine their favorite styles.

QUESTIONS LEAD TO ANSWERS WHICH LEAD TO SUCCESS

- Are there laminated copies of your price lists behind the bar?
- How often do you update your price lists?
- How do your prices compare with your direct competitors? Did you decide to "meet, beat or play hardball" their prices?
- Are your price lists structured to decrease employee pricing errors?
- Are your drink prices based solely on quarters?
- Do your drink prices meet your financial objectives?
- Are your price lists sequenced by drink name or type?
- What does your bartending staff think about the bar's prices?
- What does your clientele think about your drink prices?
- Are product prices listed for specific portions?

Chapter 10

Cash Control Procedures

This is a liquid business, no pun intended. The company's inventory is liquid and the revenue flow is largely cash. Ensuring that all of the cash proceeds are deposited into the cash register or point-of-sale system is an essential aspect of the beverage manager's job description. To a large extent this is accomplished by putting into effect policies and procedures regarding proper cash management. Once the staff is completely familiar with these cash handling procedures, you will be in a position to handle any violations or wrong doings.

To be effective, the cash management policies and procedures need to meet the specific requirements of your beverage operation. There are, however, basics that should be incorporated into every cash management strategy.

This chapter will also cover on-hand cash requirements, daily cash procedures, how to reconcile cash drawers, deposit and banking procedures, and policies covering cash or credit transactions.

> **Cash management policies and procedures need to meet the specific requirements of your beverage operation.**

ON-HAND CASH REQUIREMENTS

It is vital that the business keep a specified amount of cash in various denominations on-hand at all times. This cash, which is stored in the office safe, is used for cashing checks, paying small bills, and replenishing the operation's cash drawers. The general manager may at times decide that circumstances require raising the minimum on-hand cash requirements.

Count cash when you are not likely to be interrupted. Never leave the money unattended. If you are called away while in the middle of counting cash, take a moment and lock the money up. Also, avoid discussing how much cash you keep on-hand with employees, purveyors, etc.

The exact amount of cash kept on-hand will vary with the size, type and specific needs of the establishment. As time goes by, it will become evident how much cash the operation needs to keep on-hand, however, at the onset it is better to over estimate the operation's cash requirements. Two examples of how to assemble a cash reserve fund are provided in Illustration 10.1.

The cash in the reserve fund must be verified after each shift. Any shortages should be reported to the general manager immediately.

Twenties	**1**	$1,800.00		Twenties	**2**	$1,000.00
Tens		$1,000.00		Tens		$ 600.00
Fives		$ 600.00		Fives		$ 400.00
Ones		$ 600.00		Ones		$ 400.00
Quarters		$ 500.00		Quarters		$ 300.00
Dimes		$ 100.00		Dimes		$ 60.00
Nickels		$ 20.00		Nickels		$ 12.00
Pennies		$ 10.00		Pennies		$ 6.00
Total		$4,630.00		Total		$2,778.00

Illustration 10.1

CREATING OPENING BANKS

An opening bank is the amount of money initially deposited into a register's or point of sale system's cash drawer at the beginning of a shift. It is important to provide the staff with an opening bank with enough money in each denomination to make it through a shift without requiring additional change.

As was the case with the operation's on-hand cash requirements, the exact amount of money used to make up the opening banks will vary with the size, type and specific needs of the establishment. Over time it will become more apparent how much cash and in what denominations the operation's opening banks should be. Again, in the beginning it is beneficial to over estimate the amount of the opening banks.

The opening banks should be kept in bank bags and stored in the office safe. Bartenders are required to verify the amount of the bank they are issued before beginning their shift. By verifying the amount of the opening bank before the shift, any discrepancies can be immediately corrected.

Two examples of how to assemble opening banks are provided in Illustration 10.2.

	1			2	
Twenties		$ 100.00	Twenties		$ 60.00
Tens		$ 150.00	Tens		$ 120.00
Fives		$ 100.00	Fives		$ 60.00
Ones		$ 102.00	Ones		$ 100.00
Quarters		$ 40.00	Quarters		$ 40.00
Dimes		$ 5.00	Dimes		$ 5.00
Nickels		$ 2.00	Nickels		$ 2.00
Pennies		$ 1.00	Pennies		$ 1.00
Total		$ 500.00	Total		388.00

Illustration 10.2

DAILY CASH PROCEDURES

The accounting procedures for the cash on-hand will not vary on a daily basis. The cash will be dealt with the same way and in the same order. The repetitive nature of these procedures better ensures that a step in the daily cash cycle will not be overlooked or forgotten.

The sequence of these procedures will vary with the type and size of the establishment, however, there are things that must take place in the daily cash cycle regardless of the particular beverage operation in question. The following are necessary procedures to incorporate in the daily cash cycle.

1 A complete audit of the reserve cash fund must be done every day. This figure will include the money in the opening banks plus the cash reserve fund. It is advisable to audit the cash on-hand after the bank deposit has been completed. In this way, sales proceeds will already have been accounted for, placed into a bank bag, and will not be counted as part of the cash on-hand.

To take an audit, count the money in the change reserve fund and add in the monies used to assemble the opening banks. The total should equal the set amount of cash kept on-hand. If there is a discrepancy, the first places to look for the missing funds are the opening banks. If the discrepancy still exists, notify the general manager.

2 Assign registers or drawers to specific shifts and make note of which bartender will be working that particular shift. Count the opening banks before and after the assigned employee takes possession of it. This will not only protect you, it will also protect the employee in

the event of a cash shortage. Include the adding machine tape in with the opening banks so the bartenders can verify the amount of their opening till.

3 Throughout a busy night periodically remove all large bills from the cash drawer and deposit them into the safe.

4 At the end of each bartender's shift, immediately take a "z" reading of the cash register or point-of-sale system and remove the cash drawer. For reasons explained later in the book (Chapter 22 - Preventing Internal Theft), do not allow bartenders to check out their own tills. Bring the drawer and the "z" report into the office.

5 As soon as possible after closing, lock all monies in the safe. Reconciling the cash register(s) and setting up the opening till(s) are best done the next morning.

6 Do not let anyone into the operation after the business is closed. This applies to employees as well. Law enforcement officers are allowed to enter the licensed premise only after he or she produces a badge and acceptable identification identifying the individual as a law enforcement officer.

7 Make sure all funds are safely locked-up in the safe. Before you leave for the night, double check that the safe is properly secured and that the office door is locked.

RECONCILING CASH DRAWERS

Whether you are using a cash register or a point-of-sale system behind the bar, the bookkeeping procedures for reconciling the cash drawer are basically the same. It is best to review all internal bookkeeping procedures with the company's accountant.

The following are the standard procedures on how to reconcile either a cash register or point-of-sale cash drawer. Illustration 10.3 is an example of a cash drawer reconciliation.

1 Count all of the currency in the cash drawer and enter total of each denomination in the appropriate column of the cash drawer reconciliation form.

2 Enter the total amount of coins being deposited.

3 Enter the total amount of credit card sales.

4 Enter the total amount of checks being deposited.

5 Enter the total of all other sales (such as merchandise sales) being deposited.

6 Enter the total of all "paid outs" (money taken out of the register used for various cash purchases during the course of operation).

7 Enter the subtotal of the coins, currency, credit cards, checks, other sales and paid outs.

8 Use the available funds in the cash drawer(s) to create the next shift's opening bank. Place opening bank in the safe.

9 Subtract the amount of the opening bank from subtotal. The balance is the "total accountable funds" for the shift. Enter the figure in the appropriate space on the cash drawer reconciliation form.

10 Enter the gross sales figure from each register's "z" report in the appropriate space.

11 If the resulting number is positive, the cash drawer is "over" by that amount of money. If the resulting figure is a negative number, the cash drawer is "short" by that amount of money. Enter that amount in the appropriate space on the cash drawer reconciliation form.

Cash Drawer Reconciliation

Day: _____ Date: _____ Shift: _____ Employee(s): _____
Completed by: _____ Verified by: _____

	POS ONE	POS TWO	TOTALS
NET SALES:			
Liquor	$ 796.32	$1,190.78	$2,545.09
Wine	$ 266.62	$ 88.87	$ 355.49
NABs	$ 232.26	$ 99.54	$ 331.80
Catering	$ 00.00	$ 00.00	$ 00.00
Bar Food	$ 165.55	$ 78.95	$ 244.50
Misc.: _____	$	$	$
Misc.: _____	$	$	$
Pre-tax Sales	$2,815.06	$1,799.42	$4,614.48
Sales Tax	$ 127.06	$ 55.96	$ 183.02
Total Receipts	$2,942.12	$1,855.38	$4,797.50
Subtract Adjustments:			
Credit Card Sales	($ 866.72)	($ 214.55)	($1,081.27)
Charged Tips	($ 138.67)	($ 38.62)	($ 177.29)
Pay Outs	($ 00.00)	($ 28.25)	($ 28.25)
House Charges	($ 49.95)	($ 00.00)	($ 49.95)
Over Rings	($ 00.00)	($ 00.00)	($ 00.00)
Manual Voids	($ 00.00)	($ 00.00)	($ 00.00)
Misc.: _____	$	$	$
Post-Adjustment Balance	$ 1,886.78	$1,573.96	$3,460.74
Subtract Opening Bank	($ 500.00)	($ 500.00)	($1,000.00)
Total Accountable	$ 1,386.78	$1,323.96	$2,710.74
Subtract Cash Count	($ 1,386.46)	($1,322.95)	($2,709.41)
Cash (Short)/Over	($ .32)	($ 1.01)	($ 1.33)
DEPOSIT:			
Cash Count	$1,386.46	$1,322.95	$2,859.41
Add Credit Cards	$ 866.72	$ 214.55	$1,081.27
Add Charged Tips	$ 138.67	$ 38.62	$ 177.29
Total Deposit	$2,541.85	$ 1,576.12	$4,117.97

Illustration 10.3

DEPOSIT AND BANKING PROCEDURES

Your accountant will set up the company's bookkeeping systems. Included in these systems will be how fill out bank deposits. For example, many beverage operations will make a separate checking account deposit for the net sales for each shift. Other operators take the net sales proceeds from each shift and combine them into one daily checking deposit.

The process of entering a bank deposit typically requires the following five steps:

1. Enter the amount of currency and coins in the appropriate spaces on the checking deposit slip.

2. Enter the total amount of checks being deposited in the appropriate spaces on the checking deposit slip.

Security is always a consideration.

3. Enter in the checking account register the amount of credit cards already processed and deposited into the checking account via the credit card terminal.

4. Add the checks and the total amount of cash being deposited to arrive at the amount of the bank deposit.

5. Properly date and record each deposit into the checking account register.

Security is always a consideration. Criminals know that food and beverage businesses generate a great deal of cash. As a result, there are several security-related issues involved with making bank deposits that should be considered.

1. When counting money keep the office door closed and locked. Take steps to keep interruptions to a minimum. Never count money in public view.

2. Try not to keep more than one day's gross receipts on-hand. Bank deposits should be made daily. Many banks have secure chutes that allow customers to make deposits over the weekend.

3. Make your bank deposits at different times of the day to avoid being predictable. Likewise, when ever possible make your deposits at different bank branches.

4. Do not leave the deposit unattended. If you are unable to go to the bank immediately, keep the deposit in the office safe.

5. Do not leave the establishment with the bank bag in plain view. Take precautions to conceal the bag. Do not leave a deposit unattended in your car.

POLICIES COVERING CASH OR CREDIT TRANSACTIONS

Bartenders are expected to handle the bar's sales transactions in a direct, proper manner. In some instances, these transactions may be no more involved than making change for a guest. Other transactions may be more involved-such as running customer tabs, or transferring drink charges onto a dinner check. Regardless of the task, there must be a policy in place detailing exactly how the transaction is to be handled.

The following material offers policy considerations regarding cash transactions, accepting personal checks, payment problems, walkouts, bar tabs, credit card procedures, and gratuities.

1 Cash Transactions — The cash drawer of the register or point-of-sale system must remain closed between transactions. Leaving the drawer open and unattended defeats the control functions of a cash register or point-of-sale system in the first place. If a bartender must leave the bar unattended for a moment, he or she must lock the register or point-of-sale system and remove the operating key.

When accepting cash for a sale, bartenders should state the price of the drink and the amount tendered (e.g. "That'll be $2.75 out of $10"). After ringing the sale into the register or point-of-sale system, the correct amount of change is removed before the currency is deposited into the cash drawer.

After presenting a food/drink check to a customer at a table or the bar, the bartender should give the person a minute or two to pay the bill. Once money is presented, the bartender should return the guest's change quickly. **One major customer complaint is that it takes too long to pay the check or to receive the change.** Bartenders should never ask a guest if he or she wants the change back.

When returning a customer's change, bartenders should lay the money on the bar so that the guest can see at a glance that the correct amount of change was returned. In addition, it is helpful to state how much change is being returned, by saying something along the lines of, "$5.50 is your change. Thank you."

2 Accepting Personal Checks — It is advisable to accept only local checks for goods and services, and only if the guest also presents an in-state driver's license as a form of identification. The driver's license number should be recorded onto the check. The server should make sure the check is imprinted with guest's name, address and telephone number, and that the check is filled out correctly and for the proper amount. If the person has no home telephone, request a work telephone number. The server should print his or her name in the left-hand corner of the check. If the check is returned for any reason, management can hold the particular bartender or server accountable.

If a traveler's check is used, the server should handle it as if it were a personal check. The employee should request to see the guest's driver's license and record the license number on the traveler's check. The server should also make sure that the traveler's check is signed and countersigned. In addition, the server should verify that the traveler's check is printed with anti-fraud devices-such as watermarks and micro-printing.

3 **Problems in Payment** — If a guest's check is returned for "insufficient funds" and the server who accepted the check did not follow the correct procedures for accepting a personal or business check, the server may be held responsible for the full amount of the check. Requiring servers to compensate the business in this situation is a policy decision left up to management. Servers are never to comment on a guest's returned check to other customers.

Should a guest's credit card be declined, the matter should be dealt with carefully so as to not embarrass the individual. The server should speak softly and inform the cardholder that there seems to be a problem with the credit card, and that the card could not be processed. The guest should be asked if he or she would like to submit another credit card, or would rather pay in cash or with a check.

4 **Walkouts** — "Walkouts" usually occur when a bartender or server isn't paying close attention to the clientele. Should a customer leave without paying the food/drink ticket, the bartender or server involved may be required to pay for the amount of the ticket. Occasionally there are circumstances, such as a fight, that required the immediate attention of the employee(s) involved, allowing the individual in question to leave the restaurant unnoticed. Management should always inquire as to the circumstances surrounding the "walkout" incident before making the determination whether the server should be required to compensate the business for the bad debt.

5 **Bar Tabs** — It is advisable to require a guest to use a major credit card prior to opening a running drink tab for the person. The credit card is typically held behind the bar until the guest clears his or her account. The imprinted voucher is then totaled and signed when the customer prepares to leave.

A guest may prefer to pay for the tab with a personal check. In that case, the bartender is to request the person's driver's license and hold it until the person is closing out the tab. It should be company policy to not advance an individual cash on his or her credit card.

6 Credit Card Procedures — A properly handled credit card transaction is as secure as accepting cash payment. The following general procedures should be followed when accepting a credit card for payment of a customer's tab. Before presenting the voucher for signature, the bartender is to check that the necessary information has been clearly imprinted on all copies of the draft. The date and amount of sale, the expiration date and the cardholder's complete name must be legible.

The majority of beverage operators use a credit card approval machine that is connected to a processing center via the telephone lines. The credit card is run through the machine and the magnetic strip on the card automatically transmits account data to the center. The amount of the sale is then entered. If approved, an authorization code number will appear on the sales voucher.

When presenting the completed voucher to the cardholder for his or her approval, the bartender or server should compare the person's signature with the signature on the back of the credit card. If the signatures are not similar, the employee should request the guest present another piece of identification for confirmation. After verifying the signature, the customer should be given the appropriate "customer" copy of the voucher. The remaining copy of the sales voucher should be attached to and turned in with the drink check.

7 Gratuities — At no time are bartenders permitted to put tips directly into their pocket. Gratuities are put immediately into a tip jar behind the bar. Converting tips into larger denomination bills out of the cash register drawer is also not permitted.

When two or more bartenders are working during the same shift, it is typically policy to pool all of the bar's tips to be divided at the end of the night. If the bartenders worked different numbers of hours during the night, the number of hours each bartender worked is added together. The amount of the gratuities are then divided by the total number of hours worked, the result is the tips-per-hour generated at the bar. The number of hours worked by each bartender is then multiplied by this tips-per-hour figure and the gratuities divided accordingly.

Frequently bartenders are required to prepare drinks for food servers and cocktail waitresses. Because these servers will themselves be tipped by the guest on the cost of the drinks, they are obliged to tip a percentage of their gratuities. Servers are almost always required to "tip-out" to the bar 10% of their gross tips or 1% of their gross sales at the end of the shift. Management should make the determination whether servers are required to tip the bar 10% of their gross tips or 1% of their gross sales.

Employees who receive income from customer gratuities are required to report those earnings to the applicable taxing authorities. Management should provide servers with the appropriate forms to report their tips. Employees should be required to report their tipped income honestly. While few people actually enjoy paying taxes, it is legally mandated that as citizens of the United States we do so. If it is determined that a server under-reported his or her tipped income to the business and the Internal Revenue Service, it may be grounds for immediately terminating the person's employment.

QUESTIONS LEAD TO ANSWERS WHICH LEAD TO SUCCESS

- Do you maintain a reserve cash fund comprised of a set amount of money in pre-determined denominations?
- How often is the reserve cash fund audited to confirm that there are no discrepancies?
- Is the amount of money used to make up the bar's opening banks sufficient in amount and in the proper denominations to meet the demands of the operation?
- Do you periodically remove the large denomination bills from the bar's cash drawer?
- Do you allow your bartenders to reconcile their own cash drawers?
- Do you keep the office door closed and locked when counting money?
- Do you keep more than one day's gross receipts on-hand before making a bank deposit?
- Do you vary what time of day you make bank deposits and the bank branch at which you make the deposit?
- Do you have a written policy governing accepting personal checks as payment? Traveler's checks?
- Do you have a written policy covering "walk-outs" and returned checks?
- Do you have a written policy detailing the procedures for opening a drink tab?
- Do you have a written policy outlining the amount servers are required to tip-out to the bar?

Chapter 11

Marketing
Non-Alcoholic Beverages

What if you found out that there was a large and growing segment of the population that you weren't catering to? These are people who want to enjoy the vitality and ambiance of your establishment, and are primed and ready to spend some of their hard-earned income. However, since you haven't identified their particular wants and needs, they go and spend their money at someone else's business.

Well, that's essentially what's happening if you don't actively market non-alcoholic beverages (NABs). More than a passing fad, NABs are now part of the dynamics of our industry. Today, more people are socializing without alcohol. There are many reasons why, including stricter DWI laws, health concerns, calorie content, and, of course, personal preference. This trend has propelled alcohol-free products into a multi-billion dollar industry, and the fastest growing category of beverages in the country.

More than a passing fad, NABs are now part of the dynamics of our industry.

In addition to increased consumer demand, another reason to market non-alcoholic products is that the profit margins are higher than their more potent counterparts. Also, marketing NABs incurs no third-party liability, and creates no service-related problems. From a management standpoint, incentives for selling non-alcoholic beverages are widespread.

Attitudes are changing toward the marketing of non-alcoholic beverages. Long gone are the old stigmas and stereotypes surrounding NABs, and the people who order them in bars.

Even though everyone from cowboys to yuppies seem to be drinking NABs, taking advantage of the trend requires establishing an objective. For example, current thinking suggests that non-alcoholic beverage sales should account for 10-14% of gross sales. For many mainstream nightclubs and bars that would mean doubling their NAB sales.

Developing a marketing strategy is the necessary first step to achieving your sales objective. To be effective, your strategy requires two essential elements: you need to decide what non-alcoholic drinks and beverages you're going to market, and how you're going to market them.

Never before has there been such an availability of interesting, high quality non-alcoholic products to choose from. The key is to create an alcohol-free menu that is as varied as your clientele. Here's a quick glance at some of what's available:

1. **Energy Drinks** — Popular for a long time in Europe, energy drinks have hit our shores in a big way. These products are specially formulated with ingredients such as herbal extracts, vitamins, minerals, and pharmaceutical grade amino acids-in a great tasting beverage. They are not to be confused with sport drinks or isotonic beverages that merely replenish the body's fluids; these products stimulate the metabolism and rejuvenate by replenishing the mind and body with energy.

> **Energy drinks are ideal for revelers dancing into the night.**

While the leading name brands in the energy drink category-namely Hype, Energy 2000, Red Bull, XTC, and Hansen's Functionals-all contain caffeine, don't dismiss their physiological effect too quickly. The caffeine, while a stimulant, is used primarily as a catalyst for the absorption of the B vitamins. Most of these beverages contain guarana, a berry from South America that acts as a subtle stimulant, ginseng, an aromatic root associated with the relief of stress and the cleansing of toxins, amino acids, which stimulate the metabolism and boosts energy, and vitamins, to enhance stamina and strengthen the immune system.

So why market energy drinks at your bar? For starters, their surging popularity and great taste make them highly desirable beverages. They are also fabulously creative ingredients in specialty drinks. For clubs and bars that cater to a late-night crowd, energy drinks are ideal for revelers dancing into the night.

2. **Smoothies** — Popular with the health-conscious crowd for years, fruit-based smoothies or slushes can generate hefty profits, particularly in warm weather. Several companies offer pre-made mixes and machines that will help you crank out these tempting drinks all day long. The mixes are generally made with fresh fruit juices, so they are long on flavor. And if a guest wants a high-test version, just add rum to the mix.

3. **Non-Alcoholic Liqueurs** — These liqueurs are produced with all of the characteristics of the more recognizable brand names, with one obvious exception, they don't contain alcohol. One of the leading brand names, D. J. Dotson Triple Sec, has a rich, savory flavor

and an enticing aroma that makes it excellent in margaritas, kamikazes, and Long Island iced teas. Non-alcoholic liqueurs cost a fraction of regular cordials, and make an invaluable contribution behind the bar.

4 Non-Alcoholic Beers — Few bars today are successful marketing only one label of non-alcoholic beer. Personal preferences are such that people have come to expect a selection of non-alcoholic beers to choose from. Non-alcoholic brews have ascended in quality to the point where, in many instances, they are indistinguishable from the alcoholic versions. American category leaders are O'Doul's (Anheuser-Busch), Sharp's (Miller), and Coors Cutter. Leading imports include Clausthaler and Haake Beck (Germany), Moussy (Switzerland), Kaliber (Ireland), and Buckler (Holland).

5 Iced Tea — A singularly American institution, over 35 million gallons of iced tea are consumed in this country each year, which equates to about 7 glasses per adult. Its tremendous appeal is only surpassed by its exceptionally high profit margins. There are now numerous specialty teas on the market ideal for making flavorful and distinctive iced teas.

> **People have come to expect a selection of non-alcoholic beers to choose from.**

6 Ready-to-Drink Iced Teas — The leaders in this rapidly growing, $340 million market are Snapple and Lipton, with Nestea and AriZona brands running close behind. While these ready-to-drink beverages have a higher cost percentage than freshly brewed iced teas, they are convenient, require no preparation, and have built-in consumer brand loyalty.

7 Bottled Waters — Bottled waters are skyrocketing in popularity. People are becoming increasingly more familiar with the many different types and brands of bottled waters, and as a result, savvy operators are today stocking more than just Perrier for their customers. Water is bottled both sparkling (carbonated), and still (non-carbonated). Sparkling waters vary greatly in the amount of carbonation they contain. There are those with light effervescence (Bartlett and Ty Nant), medium effervescence (Ramlösa and San Pellegrino), and high effervescence (Perrier). Still waters vary in the amount of minerals they contain, which affects how they taste. For example, Evian has a low mineral content, while Vittel has a medium to high mineral content.

8 Lemonade — This great American beverage has become a fixture in many nightclubs and bars. In addition to being a delicious, thirst-satisfying beverage, it has scores of drink-making applications. While some operators prefer to make it the traditional way by freshly squeezing the lemons, others opt to market one of the high-quality, ready-to-drink brands of lemonade, such as Snapple or AriZona, or use a powdered mix. Flavored lemonades, such as raspberry and kiwi, are also gaining in popularity.

9 **Coffee** — To best capitalize on the enormous popularity of Java, start by selecting a quality house blend of freshly roasted coffee beans. To ensure freshness, and to derive the most flavor out of the coffee, grind the beans just prior to brewing. Also, brew smaller pots of coffee more frequently to prevent the coffee from sitting too long on the burner. Once you've mastered regular coffee, consider branching off into specialty coffees, iced coffees, espresso, cappuccino, and Café Au Lait.

10 **Adult Sodas** — Believe it or not, Dr. Pepper, root beer, and Squirt are making a furious comeback, and now are popularly requested at bars. In addition to drinking them straight, they also make excellent mixers. Then there are Skeleteens, a line of adult sodas produced in Southern California. With names such as Brain Wash, Love Potion #69, and Black Lemonade, Skeleteens are herbal-based sodas with a singular, spicy flavor that boggles the imagination.

> **Lemonade has become a fixture in many nightclubs and bars.**

MARKETING ALCOHOL-FREE SPECIALTIES

Alcohol-free specialty drinks have the potential to be as delicious and sophisticated as those that contain alcohol do. To be successful, however, they should be presented with the same appeal and flair as your bar's other house specialties. Consideration also needs to be given to glassware selection and garnishing. Every effort should be made so that your alcohol-free signature drinks look and taste exceptional.

A drink menu is an excellent means of marketing NABs and non-alcoholic specialty drinks. In it you should present a balanced, broad selection of alcohol-free products. Price your alcohol-free specialties in-line with the bar's other signature drinks. If priced too low, service personnel will be hesitant to market them; if priced too high, your clientele will react negatively as if they are being gouged.

Some operators devote an entire menu to marketing alcohol-free specialties and non-alcoholic beverages. The menus should be developed with the same production value as your regular specialty drink menu. A poorly conceived menu will undermine your efforts and make it appear to both the staff and clientele that you're merely going through the motions.

Table tents are also particularly effective at marketing NABs. A well designed, graphically appealing table tent has an immediate effect on customers, as it's often the first marketing piece they see. In addition, table tents promoting non-alcoholic drinks and beverages reemphasize your marketing commitment to the service staff.

Getting your employees to fully support any beverage program is essential to its success. As the people who will be marketing the non-alcoholic beverages, they need to rid themselves of any lingering negative attitudes they may have towards NABs and the people who drink them. Secondly, they need to look for opportunities to market NABs. For example, upselling a bottled water to someone who orders a club soda, or an alcohol-free cocktail to a person who is reluctant to order another alcoholic drink. Servers need to believe in the quality and basic appeal of NABs in order to be successful selling them.

Table tents are particularly effective at marketing NABs.

High profits and no liability make these no octane products one of the most significant mega-trends to hit the nightclub and bar business. Stock up and ride the wave.

MARKETING SPECIALTY DRINKS FOR KIDS

Why would a restaurant develop a beverage campaign directed exclusively to kids? A restaurant that puts forth a concerted effort to make the dining experience special for kids has got loyal customers in their parents. Special to kids means being served a great looking, great tasting drink in a sensational looking glass that mom and dad wouldn't let them drink from at home.

If generating good will isn't motivation enough, there's also the little matter of generating more profits. While most of these small fry specialties will retail for less than their adult counterparts, they deliver relatively the same amount of gross profit. All things considered, marketing signature drinks to the minor leagues makes good sense.

The realm of possibilities has expanded greatly since the days of the kiddie cocktails and Shirley Temples. The philosophical orientation is to create a specialty drink that knocks their socks off.

Take the Chocolate/PB/Nana Shake, for example. Start with a tall specialty glass, between 16 and 20 ounces in capacity. Paint the inside of the glass with ribbons of chocolate and caramel syrups. Into your bar's blender place two #10 scoops of vanilla ice cream, 4 oz. whole milk, a half of a ripe, large banana, 1 oz. chocolate syrup and 2 tablespoons of creamy peanut butter. Blend the ingredients until they agree to get along, pour into the painted specialty glass and garnish with whipped cream. There isn't a person under the legal voting age who can resist it.

So where to start? Here are some pointers that should help you create a dynamic beverage program geared to kids.

1 **Lemonade** — This great American beverage is a good starting point. Using Monin or Torani syrups you can feature such flavorful combinations as raspberry or kiwi lemonades. Another option is to take lemonade and blend it with ice cream and fresh fruit into a slushy specialty.

2 **Smoothies** — Kids generally love smoothies as long as they don't know that they're drinking something borderline healthy. Smoothies need not be more complicated than blending juice, fruit, honey and yogurt together. For fun, blend in a few Oreo cookies as well. The creative possibilities are boundless.

> **The blender is a moneymaking machine.**

3 **The Spin Doctor of Drinks** — The blender is a moneymaking machine. For example, take an alcohol-free strawberry daiquiri or piña colada, add a banana, some vanilla ice cream, a few sweet strawberries and a healthy dash of chocolate syrup to create something they'll talk about in school. Nearly anything kids like to eat can be blended into a specialty drink.

4 **The Power of Presentation** — Sure these drinks need to taste great, but they also have to look spectacular. Always market your drinks in tall, yet durable specialty glasses. Paint the inside of the glasses with chocolate and caramel syrup. Frozen blueberries (slightly thawed) or grenadine are great sources for color, and a few dashes of vanilla extract creates an irresistible aroma. The coup de grace is using red vine licorice instead of straws.

Have fun, think like a kid and you'll succeed with the kids, and their parents.

QUESTIONS LEAD TO ANSWERS WHICH LEAD TO SUCCESS

- Is your bar doing an adequate job catering to the wants of those who do not drink alcohol?
- Is there a call to increase the number of non-alcoholic beverages you stock at the bar?
- Do non-alcoholic beverage sales account for 10-14% of your operation's gross sales?
- Do you market alcohol-free specialty drinks? Are they presented in the same manner and with the same production value as their counterparts containing alcohol?
- Do you incorporate alcohol-free specialty drinks and non-alcoholic beverages in your bar's menus?
- Do you market alcohol-free specialty drinks for kids?

Chapter 12

Maintaining Health Standards Behind the Bar

Bar and restaurant health codes are written to protect the public health. They are strictly enforced through unannounced health code inspections. A failed health report can result in the immediate closing of your business. As if to add insult to injury, the results of an unsatisfactory health inspection are frequently published in the newspaper. The damage to the reputation of a business from this kind of bad publicity is massive.

Keeping a commercial bar sanitary is a difficult assignment. It is a management responsibility. It is extremely important that management use carefully supervised sanitation procedures throughout the operation. Assuming that employees will take it upon themselves to maintain the facility to the standards of the health department is an invitation for trouble.

> **It is extremely important that management use carefully supervised sanitation procedures throughout the operation.**

FOOD-BORNE ILLNESSES

One of the basic objectives of health codes is to reduce the incidence of food-borne illnesses and the transmittal of communicable diseases. Food-borne illnesses are a major concern in the food and beverage industry. Each year, enormous amounts of money are spent industry-wide on sanitation and pest control.

There are four major strains of bacteria that make up the largest source of food contamination:

1. **Staphylococcus** — A bacterium transmitted through direct contact with the skin, mouth or nose and a contaminated food source (including ice). This contamination leads to the growth of the staphylococcus infection, which in turn produces a poison harmful to human health. Staphylococcus is killed by heat.

2. **Salmonellosis** — A bacterium most closely associated with poultry products. Similar to staphylococcus, salmonellosis is transmitted through direct contact and is also killed by heat.

3 **Clostridium Perfringens** — This particular strain of bacteria requires the presence of protein in order to grow. The bacterium creates spores that are resistant to cooking. These spores thrive at room temperature. Heating the food upwards of 160°F is necessary to kill the spores. Under the right conditions, clostridium perfringens needs only four hours to grow to the stage where human health may be seriously threatened.

4 **Escherichia Coli (015:H7)** — Better known as E. coli, is an emerging cause of foodborne illness. The bacterium produces a powerful toxin. Although the number of organisms required to cause disease is currently unknown, it is suspected to be very small. An estimated 10,000 to 20,000 (1999) cases of infection occur in the United States each year. Most illness has been associated with eating undercooked, contaminated ground beef (contaminated meat looks and smells normal). Infection can also occur through drinking water and raw milk. E. coli infection is also spread through human contact as a result of poor hygiene and inadequate handwashing habits

The majority of health codes are directed at preventing food products from becoming contaminated.

The majority of health codes are directed at preventing food products from becoming contaminated by these and other strains of bacteria. To a large degree, this is accomplished by eliminating the conditions under which bacteria thrive. Bacteria require a warm environment, the presence of moisture, a sufficient amount of time to develop, and the virtual absence of acid.

Other factors contributing to bacterial contamination include using food products obtained from an unapproved or contaminated source, insufficient or inadequate food storage, cross-contamination (raw food contaminating cooked or prepared foods), and poor employee sanitation procedures.

HEALTH INSPECTIONS

Food and beverage operations are required by law to have a valid health permit to conduct business. Health permits are issued only after a health official has conducted a thorough on-site inspection of the operation's premises. These inspections are conducted on an unannounced basis. Since the inspector can show up at any time, without warning, you must ensure that the sanitary conditions behind the bar are continually maintained.

Health inspectors use a form issued by the Health, Education, and Welfare Department of the Food and Drug Administration. This form, the "Food Service Establishment Inspection Report," contains 45 itemized violations. Each cited violation is assigned a penalty of 1 to 5 points. At the end of the physical inspection, the point values of the cited violations are deducted from 100 and a rated Health Permit is issued based on the result. A score of 60 points or less can result in the immediate closure of an establishment.

The major health code violations (4- and 5-point deduction) affecting the bar:

- Personnel with infections unrestricted and handling food products
- Unacceptable employee hygiene
- Inadequate washing of glassware and utensils, insufficient sanitation, cleaning, rinse, temperature, concentration, or exposure time
- Plumbing violations; cross-connections, back siphonage, or back flow
- Presence of insect or rodent infestation; outer openings unprotected
- Toxic items unlabeled or improperly stored

The following is a list of the most frequently violated health codes behind the bar:

- Improper refrigerator or walk-in cooler temperatures
- No thermometers present and conspicuous in refrigerators
- Dirty stainless steel, three-compartment sinks
- Employees handling round garnishes (must be speared)
- Employees handling ice (ice is considered a food substance)
- Employees scooping ice with glassware
- Ice scoop handle left in contact with the ice
- Poor employee personal hygiene
- Employees handling top of glassware
- Non-approved bar equipment; the N.S.F. or UL seal must be present and visible
- Dirty beverage gun nozzle or receptacle
- Dirty ice buckets or ice bins
- Uncovered/exposed cold plate in ice bin
- Dirty draft beer spigot or drain
- No sanitizer test paper (litmus paper) behind bar
- Insufficient detergent concentration in wash water or improper temperature

- Dirty rinse water, improper temperature
- Glassware not allowed to air dry
- Bar surfaces and equipment not clean and free of spills
- Single-service items (napkins, straws, sip stirs) not stored at least six inches above the floor
- Reuse of single-service items
- Hanging glassware racks positioned over the public portion of the bar
- Glassware stored on uncovered steel racks in the cooler or refrigerator
- Presence of insect or rodent infestation
- Sanitizer solution not maintained at sufficient concentration
- Glassware left in contact with sanitizer solution for less than sixty seconds
- Employees drying the insides of glasses with towels or linen
- Glassware left to dry on towel or linen
- Dirty or scummy floor drains
- Dirty bar mats on floor
- Unsealed light source behind the bar
- Toxic substances unlabeled or improperly stored
- Reuse of bar towels or linen

OPENING AND CLOSING SHIFT BAR PROCEDURES

The opening and closing bar procedures assign specific tasks to each shift so that bartenders know what is required to properly open and close the bar. It is management's responsibility to ensure that the staff follows the opening and closing procedures, many of these affect the sanitary conditions behind the bar.

The majority of the opening shift responsibilities involve making sure that the bar is adequately stocked. Since the level of business during the day is usually slower than at night, there are normally more cleaning and maintenance chores assigned to the opening bartending shift.

The night shift experiences a completely different set of dynamics. Arriving in the late afternoon or early evening, the night crew is frequently busy immediately upon stepping behind the bar and often stays busy throughout the evening. The closing duties primarily involve making sure supplies are put away and the bar is cleaned for the night. Liquor, beer and wine stock is replenished and sales proceeds are deposited.

OPENING

• **Opening Bartending Shift Procedures** — The peak demand on the day bartender is usually at lunch time and again at "Happy Hour." The time before lunch is spent stocking and getting the bar ready for business. During the one- to two-hour "lunch crunch," the bartender will be expected to keep up with the sales demand. Once lunch is over and the bar area is cleaned, the day bartender should return to the process of "prepping" the bar.

The following are responsibilities typically assigned to the day bartending shift:

- Check to make sure all closing duties were performed from the preceding day.
- Open the bar by filling the ice bin with fresh ice, placing the start-up fruit juices and prepared mixes from the reach-in cooler into jockey boxes and setting up the station's mixing equipment and electric blender(s); open additional stations if needed.
- Check CO_2 tanks and lines, soda tanks, draft beer kegs and lines are connected correctly; try to anticipate depletions or breakdowns.
- Make coffee and check that there are sufficient clean cups available.
- Clean the bar top and set out cocktail napkins, clean ashtrays and match books.
- Scour and rinse the three-compartment sink. Fill each compartment with the correct solution. Determine the proper balance in sanitizer/rinse solution by testing with litmus paper.
- Requisition clean bar towels; fold and dampen several and place at regular intervals under the front bar rail.
- Fill the garnish tray with fresh cut limes, lemon twists, maraschino cherries, green stuffed olives, orange slices and cocktail onions; cut additional supplies of fruit to meet the needs for the day and night shifts.
- Fill all paper and plastic items, such as cocktail napkins, sipsticks, long straws, sword picks and matchbooks.
- Check for a sufficient supply of glassware behind the bar to meet the needs of both shifts.

- Examine house specialty drink menus and food menus for cleanliness and presentability.
- Count opening bank, verify its dollar amount, and place money into the cash drawer; notify manager-on-duty of any discrepancies between expected and actual cash count.
- Check the par on all bottled beers, wines, liquors, liqueurs, cordials, etc., using par checklists; notify manager-on-duty of any discrepancies between bar par and actual count.
- Open house wine and varietal wines offered by-the-glass.
- Stock or prepare fruit juices, bar mixes and dairy products to meet par levels.
- Stock bottled waters, flavored seltzers and other non-alcoholic beverages.
- Check the temperature of the bottle cooler and adjust if necessary (ideal is 42°F).

• Closing Bartending Shift Procedures — Bartenders report to work for the night shift about the time the bar is starting to get busy and often have to start their shift "on the fly." The night bartender(s) often only has time to switch out cash drawers, run a "z" report of the cash register or point-of-sale system, and start making drinks.

The closing duties at the end of the shift require replacing emptied bottles and thoroughly cleaning the work station(s), the bar facility and all of the beverage equipment.

The following responsibilities are typically assigned to the night bartending shift:

- "Last Call" is usually announced 15-30 minutes before closing. The staff should proceed to clear customers from the premise, thanking them as they leave.
- The bar top, bar rail, all work surfaces and the back bar should be wiped clean. The work station and ice bin must be thoroughly cleaned.
- All mixing equipment, blenders, bar pour mats and other bar matting must be cleaned.
- Store all fruit juices and prepared mixes in the reach-in coolers.
- All glassware should be cleared from the tables and the bar top. The bar's glassware must be washed and restocked. Scour the stainless steel sinks and rinse thoroughly.
- Clean the draft beer taps drain by flushing it with bleach diluted with hot water.

- Empty and wash coffee pots.
- Deposit used bar towels in the linen return bag.
- Restock the house wines and bottles of varietal wines, bringing stock up to par levels.
- Rotate and stock the bottled beer up to par levels.
- Check the bar par sheet to make sure all products are stocked in the appropriate quantities.
- Account for products emptied during both bartending shifts ("breakage") and enter the items on the bar's liquor requisition form.
- Place all of the used bar checks, food tickets, charge slips, and the cash proceeds into the night shift's bank bag, which should then be turned over to the manager-on-duty. In addition, return all unused bar and food checks to the manager-on-duty. Leave the empty register or POS cash drawer open.
- Secure all of the bar's liquor, beer, and wine inventory.
- Turn off the bar lights after double-checking that all is secure behind the bar.

WEEKLY CLEANING SCHEDULES

There are sanitation-related items behind the bar that require daily attention, and there are some things that can be adequately dealt with on a weekly basis. A complete listing of daily opening and closing responsibilities should be posted behind the bar.

The weekly cleaning schedule covers items not normally associated with standard opening and closing procedures. The entire bartending staff shares equal responsibility for seeing that these sanitation-related items are carried out on a consistent basis. To create staff accountability, each shift is delegated its share of the weekly cleaning schedule.

Items to incorporate on the weekly cleaning schedule may include:
- Wash the glassware shelves and netting and rotate the glasses on a regular basis. This will lessen the chances of the glasses sticking to the shelf matting.
- Clean the back bar liquor displays.
- Clean all of the bottles behind the bar.

The weekly cleaning schedule covers items not associated with standard opening and closing procedures.

- Check the water level in the condensation trays of the refrigeration units. Drain water if necessary.
- Switch off the refrigeration units and clean the side grills. Ensure that air is able to circulate freely around units.
- Clean the automatic glass washer, including the jets, filters, scrap traps, and wash arms. Service glass washer if necessary.
- Check gas bottles for gas levels and leaks. Report any equipment problems to the appropriate service.
- Check the gasket seals on each reach-in cooler behind the bar. Check the seals to be sure they are not cracked, or worn out and cooler door closes properly.
- De-scale the bar sinks.
- Clean all of the equipment and area around cash register.
- Remove and thoroughly clean all liquor pourers.

GLASS WASHING PROCEDURES

There are several glass washing options available.

A bartender spends the majority of his or her time washing glasses. Knowing how to properly wash, sanitize and dry glassware, is mandatory for a bartender. When a drink is returned to the bar because the glass is dirty or the lip is chipped, the establishment's reputation suffers, the bartender is embarrassed, and the cost of the drink is lost down the drain.

Washing glassware behind the bar is a challenging task. More glasses are chipped, cracked and broken while being washed, however, than at nearly any other time. The objective behind requiring standard procedures detailing how to properly wash glassware is to ensure the bar's glasses are spotlessly clean without paying too high of a price. One method of quickly checking the cleanliness of the bar's glasses is to fill a glass with club soda. A perfectly clean glass will have no streams of bubbles rising from the bottom up the sides of the glass. Carbon dioxide bubble streams indicate the presence of dirt, grease, oil or film.

There are several glass washing options available. The operation's procedures will need to conform to whatever methods are used.

The following material details the procedures for both four-compartment sinks and automatic glass washing machines. The advantages and disadvantages of each method are also discussed.

FOUR-COMPARTMENT SINKS

The traditional method of washing glassware at the bar involves the use of a four-compartment sink. The dump, wash, rinse, and sanitize procedure will meet the needs of nearly all beverage operations. In some states, bars must be equipped with a four-compartment stainless steel sink.

The four-compartment sink contains, from left to right, a dump sink, the wash water, clear rinse water, and a sanitizing solution. These units are outfitted with corrugated drain boards for air-drying glassware. It is advisable to scour each of the stainless steel sink compartments before use. A dirty sink will undo much of the effectiveness of the solutions. As a result, the bartenders may add more solution to the sink to achieve relatively the same effect.

The first of the four sink compartments is used as a dump sink for the contents of dirty glassware and returned drinks. It is advisable to regularly empty the remains from the sink. The ice in the dump sink should regularly be melted with hot water.

The second compartment of the sink contains a detergent solution and hot water. It will usually be equipped with submerged brushes designed to scrub all surfaces of a glass that is plunged and raised over its bristles. A motorized brush is more effective at cleaning glassware than stationary mounted brushes, hand held brushes, cloths or sponges.

The detergent used should be a low suds, non-fat and non petroleum-based soap.

The detergent used in the second sink should be a low suds, non-fat and non petroleum-based soap. If possible, rinse all beer glasses before washing. This will remove any foam or remaining beer that could cause the cleaning solution to break down and lose its effectiveness.

The third compartment contains hot, clear rinse water. A trickle of hot water running into the sink will not only help maintain the proper temperature, but it will also keep the water clean. Slowly adding water to the sink will cause any residual soap accumulating on the water's surface from rinsing glassware to drain down the standpipe.

The warm water and sanitizer solution in the fourth compartment is to sanitize the glassware. Besides containing a sterilizing agent, which is mandatory under health codes, the solution in the fourth sink compartment may also contain a solution to prevent spotting while the glassware dries.

When using a powdered sanitizer/rinse agent, it is helpful to dissolve it first in a glass of warm water before adding it to the fourth sink. This will better ensure that all of the powder will go into solution. The effective strength of the sanitizer solution should be regularly monitored using a litmus paper testing kit. If the sanitizer/rinse solution is too weak, the glasses will spot and not rinse completely; if the solution is too strong, it may be toxic and possibly affect your customers' health. Using extremely hot water in the fourth sink will cause the sanitizer/rinse agent to dissipate too quickly.

The water in the sinks should be changed regularly or whenever the solutions become weak or the temperature becomes too cool. The time and effort saved by ignoring dirty or depleted sink solutions is not worth running the risk of drinks being returned by guests.

• **Advantages of the Four-Compartment Sink** — In some states, bars must be equipped with a four-compartment stainless steel sinks. Four-compartment stainless steel sinks are easy to install, easily maintained and relatively inexpensive. When used properly, glasses can be washed quickly and effectively. Because the water temperatures used in the sinks are significantly lower than that used in an automatic glass washer, glasses can be recycled back into use more quickly. Hand washing also allows for bartenders to closely exam the glassware, which should result in fewer dirty or chipped glasses being served to the clientele. Four-compartment sinks require little regular maintenance and use far less water and chemicals than automatic glass washers.

• **Disadvantages of the Four-Compartment Sink** — Management must train the staff on how to properly hand wash glassware. Managers must also regularly check the cleanliness of the bar's glassware, far more frequently if the glasses are hand washed than if they are cleaned in an automatic glass washer. Additionally, sink solutions and temperatures must be continually monitored and maintained at correct levels. Hand washing glassware is a labor and time intensive operation. It's hard on the back and hands. Washing an individual glass in a four-compartment sink may take only a few moments, but washing an entire shift's worth of glassware can seem like an endless chore.

AUTOMATIC GLASS WASHING MACHINES

High volume bars are sometimes equipped with an automatic glass washing machine. Tremendous strides have been made in designing automatic glass washing machines to be smaller, more affordable, energy efficient and more cost-effective to operate. Volume is the largest determining factor. If a bar uses 300-500 glasses a night, an automatic glass washer may be a sound investment. While the machine does the dirty work, your bartenders are fulfilling the income-generating portion of their job description.

• **Advantages of Glass Washing Machines** — The majority of these machines are capable of washing a rack of glasses every few minutes. Automatic glass washers are easy to use and require little training and supervision. When operated properly, these machines clean glassware more thoroughly and consistently than when done by hand. These machines meter out the exact right amount of solutions per load and operate with water temperatures of 180°F, far exceeding what is tolerable washing by hand. Far and away the chief advantage is that these machines allow the staff to perform more profitable activities.

• **Disadvantages of Glass Washing Machines** — Cost is the major downside to glass washing machines. They are capital intensive to purchase and install. These machines are more costly to operate and maintain, and consume more water than the hand washing method. With many machines, the glassware comes out prohibitively hot, requiring a "cool-down" period. If possible, invest in a machine that uses a cool rinse, allowing glasses to be used immediately out of the machine. Glass washers also require regular attention and service to properly operate. If the soap and sanitizer mechanisms are not periodically inspected, the machine may wash and rinse glasses using hot water alone. To be convenient, these machines need to be behind the bar where they will occupy a significant amount of space in an already confined area. They often generate heat, steam and a fair amount of noise, all of which might prove distracting to the operation. The water temperature in the dishwasher must be checked twice daily.

QUESTIONS LEAD TO ANSWERS WHICH LEAD TO SUCCESS

- Has the staff been trained on health codes, proper sanitation and how to prevent food-borne illnesses?
- Are the sanitary conditions behind the bar maintained to the strict standards of the health department? Could the operation pass an unannounced health inspection at any time?
- Is the staff aware of what acts constitute health code violations?
- Are the opening and closing procedures posted behind the bar?
- Is there a weekly cleaning schedule posted behind the bar?
- Has the staff received training on how to properly wash glassware?
- Are your bartenders first-rate at washing glasses? Do the bar's glasses meet an exacting standard of cleanliness?
- Do bartenders use plastic (Lexan) or metal ice scoops?
- Do your bartenders periodically rotate the glassware inventory and wash the shelf netting?
- Is there a need to install an automatic glass washer behind your bar?

Chapter 13

Getting the Most Out of
Your Drink Mixes

Often in a team effort the contributions of a few go unheralded. Such is the case with the drink mixes you'll be using at the bar. Drink mixes play a vital role in the success of your beverage operation while remaining in the background and serving only a supporting role.

Take for example, sweetened lemon juice. Better known as sweet 'n' sour, it is easily the most frequently used drink mix at any bar and is the base ingredient for scores of cocktails. A good sweet 'n' sour mix should taste delicious by itself when sampled over a few ice cubes. It should taste similar to lemonade, although slightly less sweet. Few operators still make sweet 'n' sour from scratch, opting rather for the convenience of a bottled mix. It is important to taste test various mixes before making a final selection.

Drink mixes play a vital role in the success of your beverage operation.

While most operators like the idea of serving made-from scratch drink mixes, the idea frequently breaks down in execution. For one thing, there's the question of time. Preparing scratch drink mixes is a labor-and time-intensive process. There's also the issue of consistency. Even a detailed recipe doesn't ensure that your employees will prepare scratch mixes consistently. Or necessary fresh ingredients may not always be available. For whatever reason, scratch drink mixes don't always measure up to expectations.

So the question remains. If a prepared drink mix used high quality ingredients, tasted great, required little or no time to prepare and cost less than making the mix from scratch, would you use it in your beverage program?

There are many prepared drink mixes that meet the above criteria. Selecting drink mixes requires sampling and comparing each available brand to choose the one best suited for your operation. Since there is a vast difference in quality and taste between these products, a side-by-side comparison is a must. While you may decide to prepare all of your mixes by scratch, the potential cost- and time-savings make it best to weigh all of your options.

If you use scratch recipes, create detailed recipes complete with exact measurements and specific instructions on how the mixes are prepared. The drink mix recipes should be laminated and posted behind the bar. Par levels for each mix should be set so that there is always a sufficient supply to meet demand, but not so much it runs the risk of spoiling. Refrigerated mixes should be dated on the outside of the container and rotated so that those with the earliest dates are used first. Bartenders should taste test the mixes for freshness at the beginning of each shift and discard those that are questionable.

PREPARED VS. SCRATCH - BLOODY MARYS

As every bartender knows, the secret to a world class Bloody Mary is the mix. The vodka may be the fuel, but the mix is the delivery system. There is something satisfying about building a classic Bloody Mary from the ground up, skillfully adding a few dashes of this and a healthy pinch of that. At a busy bar, however, preparing the mix in small batches better ensures freshness, consistency and quality.

If you use scratch recipes, create detailed recipes complete with exact measurements and specific instructions on how the mixes are prepared.

Most scratch recipes start with a base of tomato juice. The next step is to add the modifiers. Worcestershire sauce, horseradish, and Tabasco sauce are generally considered a must. The true creative artistry comes into play when adding the seasonings. Like most works of art, you'll probably have to taste-test and sample several batches until you find a mix recipe that best captures the flavor of your establishment.

One pitfall to avoid is making your Bloody Mary mix too hot. One option is to provide customers with the spicy condiments on the side and allow them to doctor their own Bloody Marys. If they make it too hot, the bartender can add some more toned-down mix.

For many operators, however, making Bloody Mary mix from scratch is not practical. In growing numbers, operators are turning to a new breed of small batch Bloody Mary mixes as an alternative. In most cases these mixes are produced in small batches to assure quality and sold in local or regional markets. Others have caught-on nationally.

Many bottled Bloody Mary mixes rival the most delicious scratch recipes. Possessing thick, rich bodies, great seasonings and well-balanced flavor, bottled Bloody Mary mixes offer a great, cost-effective alternative to making the mix from scratch.

Should you select a bottled product for your bar, consider transferring the mix from it's bottle into reusable quart containers. There is no reason why you can't make a few modifications to a bottled Bloody Mary mix to make it better suited to your particular tastes or beverage concept. Splash in some olive juice, add a little crushed roasted garlic or a heaping tablespoon of fresh salsa. It's your house specialty, after all.

PREPARED VS. SCRATCH - MARGARITAS

If your mix is less than wonderful, what chance do your margaritas have? Starting with a great margarita mix will greatly increase your odds for success. It should be delicious and completely without any bitter or artificial aftertaste. Your sweet 'n' sour should have a light, fresh quality and be well balanced, not too sweet or tart.

Starting with a great margarita mix will greatly increase your odds for success.

Making sweet 'n' sour mix from scratch is easier than it might sound. The basic ingredients are lime or lemon juice (or both), sugar and a little water. You may have noticed that these are also the ingredients for making limeade and lemonade. For this purpose, we're looking for something not quite as sweet as limeade and lemonade.

As for the taste profile, there are different directions you can take your sweet 'n' sour mix. The traditional slant is to use fresh lime juice. Most bars and restaurants use a lemon-based sweet 'n' sour in their margaritas, primarily because it's also the base ingredient in other standard drinks, such as the daiquiri, Collins and sour. The final taste profile is attained by using both lime and lemon juice.

While there is a quality image associated with using fresh squeezed juice in a scratch mix, there are also frozen products already sweetened and far more convenient. If you use a frozen concentrate as a base, it is advisable to use less water than called for in the product directions.

As mentioned, the finished margarita mix should taste delicious on its own. If you have an urge to improve on perfection, splash in orange juice and Rose's Lime Juice for added dimension and character.

On the other end of the spectrum, there is a large number of bottled margarita mixes to choose from, many of which are excellent. Keep in mind that you can use a sweet 'n' sour and modify it to better suit your tastes. Bottled mixes do have the advantage of being stabilized for a longer shelf life. So keep your options open and don't disregard using a bottled mix.

PREPARED VS. SCRATCH - PIÑA COLADAS

Ask any bartender, piña coladas are about the messiest, most hassle-ridden drink made behind the bar. Conventional coconut syrups necessary in their preparation are oily, difficult to measure and even harder to pour. For scratch recipes, consider blending the coconut syrup with a portion of pineapple juice or half & half cream to increase its ease of use. Coconut syrup darkens and develops a brownish hue when it's turning bad. Bartenders should taste test to ensure freshness at the beginning of each shift.

If searching for the perfect scratch piña colada recipe sounds more involved than time at-hand permits, there are a number of outstanding bottled mixes to choose from.

FRESH JUICE VS. FRUIT JUICE CONCENTRATES

Rinsing fruit under hot water before juicing will yield more juice.

Using freshly squeezed juice behind the bar may yield the best tasting drinks. However, the down-side to relying on fresh juices and the seasonal availability, is inconsistent quality, increased prep time and expense. Then there are the pulp-stained glasses to cope with. Bartenders should taste each batch of fresh squeezed juice to make sure it tastes good. A good commercial juicer will dramatically reduce preparation time. Rinsing fruit under hot water before juicing will also yield more juice.

One advantage to using freshly squeezed juice versus frozen concentrate is that with fresh juice, you have more control on how much you prepare; with a concentrate, you have to prepare a quart or half-gallon. Par levels should be set to avoid preparing too much juice, which if set too high, will result in increased waste due to spoilage.

There are many operational advantages to using fruit juice made from concentrates; consistency of taste, ease of preparation, cost-effectiveness and uninterrupted supply. Since most juice concentrates yield a quart or half-gallon, setting par levels, dating the containers and rotating the stock are necessary to reduce spoilage.

Consider using the single-portion, six ounce cans of infrequently poured juices, trading higher cost per ounce for convenience and reduced waste. Prior to pouring, bartenders should check that the juice is still good. When juice begins to spoil it develops a natural carbonation, or "spritz" that will be visible on the inside of the container.

HOW TO REDUCE GARNISH WASTE

You don't have to garnish drinks with fresh, exotic flowers to be concerned about the amount of money you're spending on fruit garnishes. If typical, your service staff will devour their weight in orange slices, pimento-stuffed green olives, lemon twists, celery stalks, shaved chocolate, peppermint sticks, pretzels and oreo cookies. Find a way to stem their foraging and you'll have taken a big step toward reducing bar costs.

Garnishes not immediately needed for the garnish tray should be stored in air-tight glass containers in the cooler. Lime wedges (and wheels) and lemon twists, wedges and wheels stay fresher, longer in the garnish tray on top of a cocktail napkin saturated with club soda. Likewise, olives and cherries last longer if kept in the tray in their own juices. Because they are infrequently used, cocktail onions should be stored in the jar and speared as needed. For Bloody Marys, use only the hearts of the celery stalk - they taste and look better than the outer, more fibrous stalks, and leave the leafy foliage on. To keep the celery fresher longer, cut the bottom of the stalks on an angle and store them in water.

Establish par levels for fruit garnish preparation.

Establish par levels for fruit garnish preparation, with the emphasis placed on cutting only what will likely be used during that shift. Bartenders should check garnishes prior to service. As lime wedges and wheels become old and spoiled, their peels darken and get leathery and stringy membranes begin to fray from the fruit. When in contact with other fruit, spoiled limes, lemons and oranges become slimy to the touch. The white, inner side of the lemon twist gets soft and pasty as they spoil. Celery stalks become soft and limp, and the leaves shrivel and turn brown when they spoil. Cut garnishes should be stored overnight in the cooler and kept sealed in glass containers with a clean, damp napkin.

QUESTIONS LEAD TO ANSWERS
WHICH LEAD TO SUCCESS

- Are there specific recipes for all of the bar's scratch drink mixes?
- Have all of the bar's drink mixes been evaluated for taste, cost and consistency?
- Have bottled mixes been considered for the bar?
- If you use commercial pre-mixes, did you taste numerous products before selecting the brand you currently use?
- Have par levels been established for the drink mixes and fruit juices behind the bar?
- Are the containers of drink mixes and fruit juices marked with the date of preparation to simplify rotating stock?
- Do your bartenders check the freshness of a mix or juice before committing it to a drink?
- Is your Bloody Mary mix too spicy hot?
- Do you have a quality bottled Bloody Mary mix behind the bar as a back-up?
- Have you weighed the advantages and disadvantages of using fresh fruit juice versus juice concentrates behind the bar? Do the time-savings of concentrates outweigh the quality difference of fresh-squeezed?
- Do you have established par levels for how much fresh fruit garnishes are prepared on a nightly basis?
- Are there specific instructions on how to properly prepare cut garnishes? Are there procedures for your bartenders to follow outlining how to properly store, cut garnishes?

Chapter 14

Pouring Practices and Procedures

Keeping the lid on cost of sales behind the bar need not adversely affect the quality or image of your operation's product. The objective behind putting cost controls into effect is to prevent the waste of invested capital. Bars and restaurants often suffer losses as a result of inadequate pouring policies and procedures.

The following cost controls are designed to not only safeguard the operation's inventory, but also to improve your establishment's efficiency and consistency of product.

USING A WRITTEN CALL ORDER

There are many benefits associated with using a written call order.

Call orders are used to provide cocktail waitresses and food servers with an exact method for sequencing drinks within an order in a logical and systematic manner. This will allow the bartender to work as effectively as possible.

There are many benefits associated with using a written call order. In addition to the increased control gained by requiring all orders to be written onto drink checks, the bartender can make the drinks quickly and efficiently by reading the order off the ticket. This will greatly reduce, if not eliminate, liquor waste and spillage due to miscommunication. Another benefit is that little training is required to implement a written call order.

Written drink orders are sequenced by type:

1st — Virgin blended drinks	7th — Plain sodas and juice
2nd — Blended drinks	8th — Cream or ice cream drinks
3rd — Cocktails, straight-up	9th — Mixed or shaken drinks
4th — Highballs	10th — Coffee and hot drinks
5th — Rocks/on-the-rocks	11th — Wine
6th — Shots and neat drinks	12th — Beer

The following is the reasoning behind the sequencing of each written call order.

1st & 2nd: Blended drinks — These drinks appear first in the order so that while they are blending, the bartender can make the other drinks in the order. The reason virgin drinks are first is best illustrated by a drink order containing both a strawberry daiquiri and a virgin strawberry daiquiri. In this instance, the bartender would be well advised to make two virgin strawberry daiquiris, pour one and then add a shot of rum to the drink remaining in the blender. The bartender then only has to flash blend and the order is complete.

3rd: Cocktails, straight-up — Cocktails are prepared in a mixing glass and then strained into a chilled cocktail glass. While the drink is chilling in the mixing glass, the bartender can be making the other drinks in the order.

4th, 5th, 6th & 7th: Highballs, rocks, shots and sodas — These drinks are prepared directly into the same glass as they are served and require no special preparation.

8th: Cream or ice cream drinks — By their very nature, cream and ice cream drinks need to be served shortly after being prepared and therefore need to be among the last drinks prepared in an order.

9th: Mixed or hand shaken drinks — Because of the mixing techniques involved, these drinks are frequently served with a frothy foam on top. The froth, not unlike the head on a draft beer, will vanish quickly and should be served shortly after being prepared.

10th: Coffee or hot drinks — Being temperature sensitive, coffee and hot drinks should be served shortly after being prepared. Do not add the whipped cream garnish until the server is actually ready to take the drinks.

11th & 12th: Wine and beer — Both beverages need to be served within a specific temperature range and should be the last items in the call order.

USING DRINK CHECKS

Drink checks (a.k.a. drink tickets) are used by the bartending staff in the same way and for the same reasons that food checks are used by waiters and waitresses. Each drink sold should be recorded onto a drink check. This will provide an accurate record of every transaction over the course of a shift. Should any discrepancies arise, the drink checks are invaluable documentation as to what actually happened.

Drink checks are an effective means of controlling costs behind a bar by reducing the frequency of unrecorded sales. If a ticket must be rung-up each time a drink is sold, a bartender who gives out free drinks runs the risk of not having an accompanying drink check. If a manager or another employee observes this in standard operating procedure, it will be obvious that the bartender is stealing.

From an operational standpoint, the following are procedures that need to be used for drink checks to be effective.

Drink checks are an effective means of controlling costs behind a bar.

1. **Maintain Accurate Records** — A ledger should be maintained to keep track of the serial numbers of the drink checks issued to the bar. This register is used at the end of the shift to make sure that every bar check- used or unused - is accounted for. This procedure should also be used for the food guest checks issued to waiters and waitresses. All checks given out to service employees should be accounted for at the end of the shift. If an immoral employee learns that a ledger tracking the numbers of checks issued is not being maintained, he or she could then steal from the operation by selling drinks or food to customers and pocketing both the sales proceeds and the used drink check.

2. **Use of a Drop Box** — A drop box is intended to prevent bartenders from reusing drink checks. Once a ticket has been imprinted, it cannot be reused. The best means of implementing this is through the use of a lockable box with a hinged top and a slot large enough to deposit a drink check through. Bartenders could reuse the imprinted drink tickets to defraud the clientele and steal from the business. With a drop box, a bartender caught in possession of a previously rung-in drink check would be suspect.

3. **Red Lining** — After a drink order has been prepared, the bartender should underline the order to signify that the drinks have been prepared and delivered. Red lining also means that the bartender has verified the prices being charged as accurate. Each drink order written on the same ticket should be red lined

in this manner. Red lining will prevent servers from claiming a drink was never made, when in fact, it was sold and the sales proceeds pocketed.

4. **Ordering Mistakes** — If a drink order is written incorrectly, either in pricing, abbreviating, or in call order, the bartender should attempt to make the order despite the mistake(s) only if it is clear what is being ordered. If the mistake(s) on the check make it difficult to know for sure what is being ordered, the bartender should not proceed with the order until it can be made clear, and should go on to the next ticket.

STANDARDIZED DRINK AND PRODUCT ABBREVIATIONS

Standardized abbreviations are an effective way in reducing waste.

Liquor waste and spillage resulting from miscommunication is unnecessary. Servers have been known to hurriedly abbreviate Margarita as "*Marg*" and Jack Daniel's as "*JD*" only to have the bartender read their scrawl and make a "*Mary*" and pour a "*JB*." While mistakes happen, these types of losses are avoidable. Standardized abbreviations are an effective way in reducing this type of waste. Another benefit is that they make it easier and faster for servers to write drink orders and for bartenders to read them.

The following are examples of abbreviated drink orders. Slashes are used as spacers between the abbreviations, making it easier to read and understand the order.

1.)	Perfect Chivas Regal Rob Roy straight-up	= Perf/Chivas/Rob/Up
2.)	Jim Beam Manhattan on-the-rocks	= Beam/Man/R
3.)	Tanqueray and tonic water	= Tanq/T
4.)	Stolichnaya vodka and orange juice	= Stoli/OJ
5.)	Kahlúa and coffee	= Kah/Cof
6.)	Dry Bombay Martini straight-up, twist	= Dry/Bom/Marti/Up/Tw
7.)	Double Seagram's Seven and Seven-up	= Dbl/7/7
8.)	Tall Bacardi Rum and Coke	= Tall/Bac/C
9.)	Johnnie Walker Black Label and water	= Black/W
10.)	Jack Daniel's on-the-rocks splash soda	= Jack/R/Spl/S
11.)	Virgin Blended Strawberry Daiquiri	= Virg/Straw/Daiq/Blend

Illustration 14.1 is a list containing the standard abbreviations of name brand liquors, liqueurs, mixers, pouring instructions and drink names.

Standardized Drink and Product Abbreviations

Well Liquor Abbreviations
Bourbon = B/
Blended = Bl/
Brandy = Br/
Gin = G/
Rum = R/
Scotch = S/
Tequila = T/
Vodka = V/

Name Brand Liquor Abbreviations
Absolut 80° = Abso/
Absolut Citron = Citron/
Absolut Kurant = Kurant/
Absolut Mandarin = Mandarin/
Absolut Peppar = Peppar/
Bacardi Light Rum = Bac/
Bacardi Limon = Limon/
Bacardi Select = Bac Select/
Beefeater = Beef/
Belvedere Vodka = Belvedere/
Bombay = Bom/
Bombay Sapphire = Sapph/
Booker Noe Bourbon = Booker/
Bushmill's Irish = Bush/
Canadian Club = CC/
Chivas Regal = Chivas/
Chivas Regal 18 = Chivas 18/
Chivas Royal Salute = Salute/
Chopin Vodka = Chopin/
Courvoisier VS = Cour VS/
Courvoisier VSOP = Cour VSOP/
Courvoisier Napoleon = Cour Nap/
Crown Royal = Crown/
Cuervo Esp. Tequila = Gold/
Cuervo 1800 = 1800/
Cutty Sark = Cutty/
Dewar's White = Dewars/
E & J Brandy = E&J/
El Tesoro Añejo Tequila = ETAñejo/
Gentleman Jack = Gentleman/
Glenfiddich = Fiddich/
Glenlivet = Livet/
Glenmorangie = Moran/
Herradura Tequila = Herradura/
J & B = JB/
Jack Daniel's = Jack/

Jameson Irish = Jameson/
Jameson 1780 = James 1780/
Jim Beam Bourbon = Beam/
J. Walker Black Label = Black/
J. Walker Blue Label = Blue/
J. Walker Gold Label = Gold Label/
J. Walker Red Label = Red/
Leyden Gin = Leyden/
Maker's Mark = Makers/
Mount Gay Eclipse Rum = Gay/
Myers's Jamaican = Myers/
Patrón Tequila = Patron/
Pinch 12 yr. Scotch = Pinch/
Sauza Conmemorativo = Conmem/
Sauza Hornitos = Horny/
Sauza Tres Generaciones = 3G/
Sauza Triada = Triada/
Seagram's Seven = 7/
Seagram's V.O. = VO/
Skyy = Sky/
Smirnoff = Smirnoff/
Smirnoff Black = Smir Black/
Stolichnaya 80° = Stoli/
Stolichnaya Gold = Stoli Gold/
Stolichnaya Kafya = Kafya/
Stolichnaya Limonnaya = Limonnaya/
Stolichnaya Ohranj = Ohranj/
Stolichnaya Pertsovka = Pertsovka/
Tanqueray Gin = Tanq/
Tanqueray Malacca = Malacca/
Tanqueray Ten = Tanq 10/
Van Gogh Gin = Van Gogh/
Wild Turkey 80 = Turk 80/
Wild Turkey 101 = Turk 101/
Wild Turkey Rare Breed = Rare/

Name Brand Liqueurs
Bailey's Irish Cream = Baileys/
Benedictine = Bene/
Benedictine & Brandy = B&B/
Chambord = Chambord/
Cointreau = Coin/
Di Saronno Amaretto = Amo/
Drambuie = Dram/
Frangelico = Fran/
Galliano = Gall/
Godiva Chocolate = Godiva/

Illustration 14.1

Standardized Drink and Product Abbreviations (Cont.)

Name Brand Liqueurs (cont.)

Goldschlager = Schlager/
Grand Marnier = Marnier/
Irish Mist = Mist/
Jägermeister = Jäger/
Kahlúa = Kahlua/
Midori = Midori/
Ouzo = Ouzo/
Peppermint Schnapps = Peppermint/
Rumple Minze = Rumple/
Sambuca = Sambuca/
Southern Comfort = Comfort/
Tia Maria = Tia/
Yukon Jack = Yukon/

Mixer Abbreviations

Branch water = /Branch
Coffee = /Cof
Cola = /C
Cranberry juice = /Cran
Diet cola = /Diet or /DC
Ginger ale = /Ginger
Grapefruit juice = /Grape
Half & half = /Cream or /Cr
Orange juice = /OJ
Pineapple juice = /Pine or /PJ
Soda water or seltzer = /S
Seven-up = /7
Sweet 'n' sour = /SS
Strawberry puree = /Straw/
Tomato juice = /Tom or /TJ
Water = /W

Pouring Instructions

Back = /Bk
Blended = Blend
Double = Dbl/
Dry = Dry/
Extra Dry = XDry/
Mist = /Mist
Neat = /Neat
Olive = /Olive
Perfect = Perf/
Presbyterian = /Press
Rocks = /R or /X
Shot = Shot/
Splash = Spl/
Straight-up = /Up
Tall = Tall/
Twist = /Twist
Virgin = Virgin/
With = /With

Drink Name Abbreviations

Black Russian = Bl Russ
Bloody Maria = Maria
Bloody Mary = Mary
Bocci Ball = Bocci
Brandy Alexander = Alex
Brandy Manhattan = Br/Man
Cape Codder = Cod or V/Cran
Colorado Bulldog = Bulldog
Cosmopolitan = Cosmo/
Cuba Libre = Cuba
Daiquiri = Daiq/
Dry Manhattan = Dry/Man
Dry Martini = Dry/Marti
Fuzzy Navel = Fuzzy
Golden Cadillac = Caddy
Grasshopper = Grass
Greyhound = Grey or V/Grape
Harvey Wallbanger = Harvey
Irish Coffee = Irish
John Collins = John
Kamikaze = Kami/
Keoki Coffee = Keoki
Kir = Kir
Lemon Drop = Lemon/
Long Island Iced Tea = Tea
Manhattan = Man/
Margarita = Marg/ or Rita/
Martini = Marti/
Old Fashion = OF or Old Fash
Piña Colada = Piña
Pink Lady = Lady
Pink Squirrel = Squirrel
Presbyterian = /Press
Rob Roy = Rob
Russian Quaalude = Lude
Rusty Nail = Nail
Screwdriver = Driver or V/OJ
Seabreeze = Breeze
Singapore Sling = Sling
Sombrero = Kah/Cr
Stinger = Sting
Tequila Sunrise = Sunrise
Toasted Almond = TA
Tom Collins = Tom
Vodka Gimlet = V/Gim/
Vodka Martini = V/Marti/
White Russian = Wh/Russ

Illustration 14.1 (Cont.)

INTERNATIONAL CALL ORDER

The *International Call Order* (ICO) is the most widely used spoken call order. It allows cocktail waitresses and food servers to quickly and efficiently place drink orders with the bartender. Verbally calling orders does have its disadvantages though. It increases the likelihood of errors due to miscommunication, errors that could result in liquor spillage and waste. Spoken orders require the bartender and server to concentrate. Fatigue, distractions and normal stress and strain can all disrupt an employee's concentration, again increasing the probability of costly errors. The ICO also requires training and continued use before the staff will master it.

The ICO eliminates as many extra words as possible. It is structured so that the order is sequenced depending on the type of glass required, then by the liquor needed, and lastly by the mixers used.

In the International Call Order, glassware is sequenced as follows. Cocktails such as the martini and Manhattan are made straight-up unless specified on-the-rocks.

1st — Shots and pony glasses	7th — Cocktail
2nd — Brandy snifter	8th — Sour
3rd — Rocks	9th — Specialty
4th — Highballs	10th — Beverage
5th — Bucket	11th — Beer
6th — Collins/chimney	12th — Wine

In the International Call Order, the various liquors are sequenced as follows. Unless otherwise specified, bourbon is used automatically.

1st — Bourbon	5th — Rum
2nd — Scotch	6th — Brandy
3rd — Gin	7th — Tequila
4th — Vodka	

In the International Call Order, the various mixers and fruit juices are sequenced as follows:

1st — Water	8th — Soda water/seltzer
2nd — Seven-up	9th — Cola
3rd — Ginger ale	10th — Collins mix
4th — Tonic water	11th — Sweet 'n' sour
5th — Orange juice	12th — Grapefruit juice
6th — Bloody Mary mix	13th — Pineapple juice
7th — Cream (half & half)	14th — Cranberry juice

Here's how it works. A group of six guests place their drink order with a server. The guests order a margarita, straight-up, Scotch, rocks, Manhattan, rocks, a Tom Collins, a screwdriver and a bottle of Budweiser with a mug. When the server places the order at the bar according to the International Call Order, the drinks would be sequenced, "Order, 2 rocks, Man, Scotch, Driver, Tom, Marg, Bud with."

The following are several other examples of how a drink order would be sequenced according to the International Call Order.

1 **If the drink order is:** a V.O. and water, a plain Coke, bourbon and water, bourbon and Seven-up, vodka, rocks, martini, rocks, bocci ball, using the ICO the drink order would be sequenced, "Order, 2 rocks, Marti, vodka, 2 waters, one is VO, Seven-up, bocci, plain Coke."

2 **If the drink order is:** a white wine, gin and tonic, Bloody Mary, tall bourbon and water, whiskey sour, a rum and Coke, and a bourbon, rocks, using the ICO the drink order would be sequenced, "Order, rocks, tall water, gin tonic, rum Coke, Mary, Sour, white wine."

3 **If the drink order is:** a martini, frozen daiquiri, tall Scotch and soda, vodka and soda, tequila sunrise, plain Seven-up, brandy, rocks, using the ICO the drink order would be sequenced, "Order, rocks brandy, vodka soda, tall Scotch water, sunrise, martini, frozen daiquiri, plain Seven."

QUESTIONS LEAD TO ANSWERS WHICH LEAD TO SUCCESS

- Do your servers and cocktail waitresses call out their drink orders at the bar or do they write them onto drink checks?
- Do your servers and cocktail waitresses place drink orders at the bar in a prescribed call order?
- Do bartenders record every sales transaction onto a drink check?
- Is a ledger maintained listing the serial numbers of the checks issued to the bartender, cocktail waitresses and food servers?
- Do you use a drop box to prevent bartenders from reusing drink checks?
- After a drink order has been prepared, is the drink check red lined?
- Does your staff have access to a list of the operation's standardized abbreviations?

Chapter 15

Developing a Successful Beer Program

Beer remains one of this country's favorite drinks, and often accounts for a large percentage of an operation's sales revenues. Having a dynamic beer program is crucial to nearly every beverage operation's long term success.

The principal areas of concern with bottled beer are pricing and reducing waste due to improper storage. With draft beer, the problem areas are portioning control and reducing losses due to theft, improper head, over-pouring and spillage.

In a perfect world, every ounce of draft beer you purchased would be poured and sold. As it is, one industry survey estimates that on average losses of draft beer due to overpouring, giveaways, and theft is roughly 20%, which translates to one out of every five kegs purchased. For an operation depleting twenty kegs per week at an average $47.50 per keg, that equates to nearly $10,000 in lost profits per year.

Having a dynamic beer program is crucial to nearly every beverage operation's long term success.

PRICING AMERICAN AND IMPORTED DRAFT BEER

Two significant factors in pricing draft beer are the amount of foamy head and the shape and size of the glass. Both combine to determine the exact serving portion, as well the number of servings obtained from a half-barrel keg of beer. Because of the shape of certain glasses, an inch of foamy head at the top of the glass will displace a larger volume in some than in others, which will result in more servings per keg.

Illustration 15.1 provides the approximate number of servings obtained from a half-barrel keg for three different size heads for the following glasses:

Draft Beer Servings Per Keg				
Type of Glass	Size	1" Head	¾" Head	½" Head
Heavy Goblet	10 oz.	330	296	264
	12 oz.	248	220	204
Hourglass	10 oz.	264	248	233
	12 oz.	220	204	189
Pilsner	8 oz.	325	292	280
	10 oz.	250	233	215
Schooner	10 oz.	330	293	256
	12 oz.	256	214	198
Sham Pilsner	10 oz.	265	245	223
	12 oz.	221	204	186
Shell	8 oz.	315	292	275
	10 oz.	245	236	220
Stein	10 oz.	248	233	223
	12 oz.	203	189	176
Tulip Goblet	10 oz.	248	230	207
	12 oz.	210	191	167

Illustration 15.1

Estimating the number of servings per half barrel will allow you to arrive at an accurate portion cost. Most American half-barrel kegs contain 1,984 ounces of beer; many imported kegs contain less. For example, there are 1728 ounces in a keg of Heineken or Guinness Stout, while a keg of Moosehead and Beck's contains 1690 ounces. A half-barrel of Whitbread Ale only contains 1536 ounces.

Illustration 15.2 is an example of how to calculate a draft beer's cost per ounce and gross profit margin. Presuming a keg cost of $38, a 12-ounce serving portion of draft beer costs $.24. Once the portion cost is known, the gross profit, cost percentage and profit margin can then be determined. The example goes on to illustrate how gross profit, cost percentage and profit margin are affected based on what retail price is charged.

The size and shape of the beer glass and the amount of foamy head served will affect the gross profit, cost percentage and profit margin of draft beer. In illustration 15.3 the assumption is being made that the draft beer analyzed above is being served in a 12 oz. schooner with a ¾" foamy head. The example details the impact the serving per keg estimate will have on the gross profit equation at the different retail price points.

Per Keg Draft Beer Profits

Keg Cost					$38		
Divide: Cost per Ounce ($38 ÷ 1,984 oz.)					$.02/oz.		
Multiply: Serving Portion Cost (12 oz.)					$.24		
(A) Retail Price	$1.00	$1.25	$1.50	$1.75	$2.00	$2.25	$2.50
(B) Portion Cost	$ .24	$ .24	$ .24	$ .24	$ .24	$ .24	$ .24
(C) Gross Profit (A - B)	$ .76	$1.01	$1.26	$1.51	$1.76	$2.01	$2.26
(D) Cost Percentage (B ÷ A)	24%	19.2%	16%	13.7%	12%	10.7%	9.6%
(E) Profit Margin (C ÷ A)	76%	80.8%	84%	86.3%	88%	89.3%	90.4%

Illustration 15.2

(A) Retail Price	$1.00	$1.25	$1.50	$1.75	$2.00	$2.25	$2.50
(B) Approx. Servings	214	214	214	214	214	214	214
(C) Gross Sales (A x B)	$214	$267	$321	$374	$428	$481	$535
(D) Keg Cost	$ 38	$ 38	$ 38	$ 38	$ 38	$ 38	$ 38
(E) Gross Profit (C - D)	$176	$229	$283	$336	$390	$443	$497
(F) Cost Percentage (D ÷ C)	17.8%	14.2%	11.8%	10.2%	8.9%	7.9%	7.1%
(G) Profit Margin (E ÷ C)	82.2%	85.8%	88.2%	89.8%	91.1%	92.1%	92.9%

Illustration 15.3

Spillage and waste are more the rule than the exception with draft beer. A spillage factor should be worked into your calculations, otherwise your profit estimates will likely be somewhat inflated. While losses may exceed 20%, a more realistic spillage factor is 10%.

Illustration 15.4 shows how factoring in a spillage rate of 10% will affect the gross profit equation at different retail price points. To factor in the spillage rate factor, the estimated servings per keg should be multiplied by 90% (.9). The resulting 193 servings reflects a loss of ten percent.

Per Keg Draft Beer Profits with 10% Spillage Factor

(A) Retail Price	$1.00	$1.25	$1.50	$1.75	$2.00	$2.25	$2.50
(B) Approx. Servings	193	193	193	193	193	193	193
(C) Gross Sales (A x B)	$193	$241	$289	$338	$386	$434	$482
(D) Keg Cost	$ 38	$ 38	$ 38	$ 38	$ 38	$ 38	$ 38
(E) Gross Profit (C - D)	$155	$203	$251	$300	$348	$396	$444
(F) Cost Percentage (D ÷ C)	19.7%	15.8%	13.1%	11.2%	9.8%	8.8%	7.9%
(G) Profit Margin (E ÷ C)	80.3%	84.2%	86.9%	88.8%	90.2%	91.2%	92.1%

Illustration 15.4

Many operators feature 24 or more different brands of draft beer. With few exceptions, the draft offerings should provide the clientele with a broad selection of beers, both in type and retail price.

Illustration 15.5 is an example of an effective method for analyzing a draft beer program in terms of retail price, cost percentage and gross margin.

Brand Name Keg Cost Percentage & Gross Profit

Brand/Type	Keg Cost	Keg Size	$/oz.	12 oz. Cost	Cost Percent.	Gross Profit
Rolling Rock	$38.75	1984 oz.	$.02	$2.75	9.7%	$2.51
Budweiser	$40.00	1984 oz.	$.02	$2.75	9.7%	$2.51
Miller Lite	$42.00	1984 oz.	$.02	$2.75	9.7%	$2.51
Moosehead	$66.00	1690 oz.	$.04	$3.25	15.4%	$2.77
Foster's	$69.50	1984 oz.	$.04	$3.25	15.4%	$2.77
Anchor Steam	$81.00	1984 oz.	$.05	$3.75	16.0%	$3.15
Beck's Dark	$80.00	1690 oz.	$.05	$3.75	16.0%	$3.15
Heineken	$83.65	1728 oz.	$.05	$3.75	16.0%	$3.15
Whitbread Ale	$83.00	1536 oz.	$.05	$4.25	14.1%	$3.65
Guinness Stout	$106.00	1728 oz.	$.06	$4.75	15.2%	$4.03

Illustration 15.5

DRAFT BEER CONTROL SYSTEMS

Beverage operations that depend on draft beer sales should consider investing in a draft beer control system. These technological wonders reduce beer costs in two ways. Their portion control features effectively eliminate over- and underpouring, increasing the yield of a half-barrel keg of beer. They also decrease the opportunity for retail losses due to unrecorded sales and pilferage. These microprocessor driven systems are reliable and highly cost-effective.

The industry leader in draft beer control technology, the Berg Company has developed an innovative, cost-effective draft beer control system capable of accounting for every ounce of draft beer dispensed. The Berg TAP 1 SYSTEM relies on state-of-the-art flow meters that monitor and record the volume of draft beer flowing through each feed line. It can be programmed to dispense up to eight portion sizes-each with the prescribed amount of foamy head-then compute the appropriate sales value based on three different price levels, "regular" price, "happy hour" and "entertainment" prices. The system effectively compensates for fluctuations in line pressure and flow rates, and in no way affects the quality, taste or appearance of the beer. And in the inlikely event of a flowmeter failure, the system instantly defaults to a time-based pour, which is based on a "learned" memory.

The Tap 1 System software tracks the total amount of draft beer dispensed, including the number of complimentary drafts and those poured in error. The system issues a management report for each featured brand, detailing the number of servings at each price level. It also extends the ounce cost of the beer by the amount of beer dispensed to arrive at the shift's cost of goods sold. The cost figure is then used to arrive at the exact cost percentage, providing an invaluable and previously unavailable means of verifying the profitability of your draft beer sales.

The system is easily expanded to accommodate a nearly unlimited number of tap heads and will not interfere with regular cleaning or service procedures. The system is also capable of interfacing with an electronic cash register, point-of-sale system or of downloading its data into an IBM compatible PC.

Draft beer is one of the largest profit centers in a beverage operation.

Other types of draft beer control systems include computerized tap heads that affix to the draft standards. These types of systems rely on sensors mounted in the beer lines that monitor temperature and pressure so they will dispense accurate portions regardless of fluctuations in line pressure or flow rates. They can be programmed to dispense different portions and different prices.

The system can issue reports for each portion dispensed, and detail the number of servings at each price level. Comparing the detailed usage reports with the sales entered into the cash register provides a valuable means of verifying draft beer sales.

One disadvantage of a fully computerized system is that they are relatively capital-intensive, costing in excess of $1200 per spigot to purchase and install. Flow meters cost less than a tenth of that. Should one of these fully computerized systems malfunction or short out, the bartenders would be unable to dispense draft beer through the taps. Under similar circumstances a flow metered control system would allow you to continue serving beer.

REDUCING DRAFT BEER COSTS

Draft beer is one of the largest profit centers in a beverage operation, often yielding profit margins of 85% to 90%. However, conventional inventory controls are largely ineffective in stemming the waste and theft normally associated with draft beer. Improperly maintained systems, improper pouring practices and poor sanitary conditions are also primary areas of concern.

1. **Keep the Draft Beer Delivery System Properly Pressurized** — Maintaining a constant and uniform pressure in the draft beer feed lines is crucial. Most American beers have a natural carbonation in the keg of 12-14 pounds per square inch (p.s.i.) at a temperature of 38°F. Additional gauge pressure of 12 14 p.s.i. is required to propel the beer through the lines and dispenser, and prevent the beer from losing its natural carbonation. It requires ½ lb. of carbon dioxide (CO_2) at 12-14 p.s.i. pressure to dispense a half-barrel of beer at 38°F.

2. **Keep the Draft Beer Delivery System Properly Maintained** — If the carbon dioxide regulator or air pump is set too low, or for some reason the line pressure drops below 12 p.s.i., the draft beer will go flat. If the internal pressure in the lines exceeds 16 to 18 p.s.i. the draft beer will become over-carbonated, often referred to as "wild" beer.

> Every bar with high draft beer sales needs cool, well-ventilated storage space.

The beer feed lines and the spigot must be cleaned on a regular basis to prevent off-tastes or odors from forming, and yeast and bacteria buildup. An easy and effective way to make sure that your beer maintains its high quality is to perform regular line cleaning. Beer lines should be cleaned weekly to keep the lines free of yeast deposits, and the beer fresh as possible. Refrigerated lines from a walk-in cooler should be cleaned every week. Cleaning is a "technical" job that is best performed by a specialist. Beer is a food product. Bacteria will build up rapidly if beer lines are not cleaned on a regular basis and will affect the taste. This is a service typically performed by the draft beer distributor.

3. **Store the Beer Under Proper Conditions** — Every bar with high draft beer sales needs a cool, well-ventilated storage space where the various kegs can be kept next to each other, connected by a common dispense gas main. Because draft beer is not pasteurized it should be stored at a constant 36-38°F (8-10C) temperature to prevent spoilage. High storage temperatures are the likely cause for

beer turning cloudy, sour or otherwise unpleasant. If storage temperatures drop below 36°F beer may lose its carbonation and go flat.

The walk-in cooler should be big enough to store a three-day supply of kegs. A simple rule of thumb is to allow for 2.25 square feet in area for each keg. Using storage shelves can expand the storage capacity.

Ideally, draft beer should remain still and untapped for 24 to 36 hours after delivery. The *First In, First Out* (FIFO) inventory system should be used to achieve a consistent and high-quality product. If more than two kegs are stored at one time, each should be marked with the date of delivery to simplify rotation. Never allow draft beer to freeze, which will cause the solids to separate from the liquid.

Draft beer should not be stored near foodstuffs, such as in a restaurant's walk-in cooler. Exposure to food odors, condensation pooling on the keg top, and/or fungal growth can affect the beer in the kegs.

4 Serve Draft Beer at the Proper Temperature — Draft beer absorbs heat rapidly. If served immediately, beer drawn at 36°F will rise to 38-40° by the time it reaches the patron. The ideal serving temperature for most American and imported lagers is generally considered to be 40°F. Flat beer is often a sign the beer is too cold. On the contrary, wild, foamy beer is an indication that the beer is too warm.

5 Train Your Staff in Proper Pouring Practices — The dispensing spigot should never come in contact with the beer in the glass. To prevent the foamy head from disappearing quickly, glasses must be absolutely free of any dirt, grease, oil or soapy film.

> **Draft beer should be poured directly into a glass and never allowed to run first.**

Draft beer should be poured directly into a glass and never allowed to run first. Traditionally, draft beer is served with a head of approximately ¾ to 1 inch. Tilting the glass and letting the flow of draft beer slope off the inside of the glass will inhibit the amount of head that develops. When the glass is half-full, the beer should be allowed to pour directly into the center of the glass. This technique will produce the right amount of foamy head. Serving draft beer in a frosted or frozen glass will likely result in the foamy head quickly disappearing.

6 Avoid Losses Due to Internal Theft — As a result of the difficulty in determining how much beer is in a half-barrel, draft beer is a frequent target of internal theft. Common schemes include free "giveaways," over-pouring, serving two-for-ones and ringing beer sales into the liquor sales key of the cash register to offset previous theft.

7 FOB Detectors — If you have ever tended bar you'll recall the operational difficulties caused when a keg of beer empties. Foam begins to spray out of the spigot as the gas pressure drains the last of the beer out of the feed lines. This rush of gas causes "fobbing." Once a new keg is brought on-line, the beer displaces the considerable volume of gas from the line. This takes time and creates further beer waste.

The installation of a fob detector overcomes the problems. It is a device mounted on the wall of the walk-in cooler connected to a draft beer feed line. When the keg empties, the float in the central chamber of the fob detector cuts off the flow, pouring ceases and gas is prevented from entering the gas line. Once the chamber is recharged with beer, pouring can continue with little or no waste or disruption from gas spraying from the tap. Fob detectors are highly effective at reducing waste and lowering costs. This is especially true in operations with long draft beer feed lines because of the greater volume of beer in the lines that will be saved when the keg empties.

8 • Maintain Portioning Control — While serving draft beer in pitchers is convenient and often provides a stimulus to sales, it poses two management concerns. Pitchers range in capacity from 32-80 ounces. As a result of volume discounting, purchasing draft beer in a pitcher is a better value for patrons than buying it by the glass. However, they sell at a considerably higher cost (lower profit margin) than by the glass. At the same time, by comparison, pitchers make your by-the-glass prices appear unreasonably high. As far as profitability is concerned, it is far better to sell four glasses of draft than one pitcher of beer.

The second management concern regarding pitchers of draft beer is that there is no adequate serving control. One person can drink most or all of a pitcher of beer without a bartender or server being in a position to intervene. Serving pitchers is a practice filled with liability.

> **Fob detectors are highly effective at reducing waste and lowering costs.**

PRICING AMERICAN AND IMPORTED BOTTLED BEER

Pricing bottled beer is significantly less complicated than pricing draft beer. There are fewer details that come into play. Regardless of where a bottle is purchased, a bottle of beer is a bottle of beer. There is little an operator can do to improve the product or enhance its presentation. The largest pricing factor therefore is the marketplace. Typically, operators price bottled beer within $.50 to $.75 of their competition.

With the enormous popularity of bottled beer, many operators feature dozens of brands of American and imported beer. When putting together your bottled beer inventory, the objective should be to choose brands that will provide the clientele with a broad range of choices in terms of type and retail price.

Illustration 15.6 is an example of an effective method for analyzing the retail prices, cost percentages and gross margins of a bottled beer program.

Bottled Beer Cost & Profit Analysis						
Brand/Type	Size	Case Cost	Unit Cost	Sales Price	Cost Percent.	Gross Profit
Rolling Rock	12 oz.	$10.50	$ .44	$1.75	25.1%	$1.31
Asahi Draft	12 oz.	$12.45	$ .52	$2.25	23.1%	$1.73
Bud Light	12 oz.	$12.55	$ .52	$2.25	23.1%	$1.73
Budweiser	12 oz.	$12.55	$ .52	$2.25	23.1%	$1.73
Miller Lite	12 oz.	$12.50	$ .52	$2.25	23.1%	$1.73
Sharps N/A	12 oz.	$11.65	$ .49	$2.25	23.1%	$1.76
Asahi Dry	16 oz.	$14.25	$ .59	$2.50	23.6%	$1.91
Clausthaler N/A	12 oz.	$17.75	$ .74	$2.50	29.6%	$1.76
Corona Extra	12 oz.	$17.85	$ .74	$2.50	29.6%	$1.76
Amstel Light	12 oz.	$19.60	$ .82	$2.75	29.8%	$1.93
Bohemia	12 oz.	$21.00	$ .88	$3.00	29.3%	$2.12
Dortmunder DUB	12 oz.	$21.89	$ .91	$3.25	28.0%	$2.34
Bass Ale	12 oz.	$23.40	$ .98	$3.50	28.0%	$2.52
Chimay White	25 oz.	$46.75	$3.90	$10.50	37.1%	$6.60

Illustration 15.6

REDUCING BOTTLED BEER COST CHECKLIST

Like bottled waters and cork-finished wines, portion control isn't a serious issue with bottled beer. The chief concerns are improper storage, poor service practices and limiting losses due to internal theft.

1 Maintain Proper Inventory Levels — Some establishments carry nearly every label of beer available as part of their concept. The fact that much of the inventory will turnover at very slow rates is somewhat expected and acceptable. Unless your operation happens to fall into that category, keeping a lid on the carrying costs is important. Review your purchase records; inventory that doesn't turn over in 30-days or less, or sells much slower than the other labels should be dropped. The long-term solution may be to stock fewer labels.

2 **Store the Beer at the Proper Temperature** — Bottled beer should be stored in a dry, clean and dark environment. Ideal storage temperatures range from 40-60°F. It should always be stored upright, with the rare exception of *Biere de Garde*, an aged, "laying-down" beer. Beer should not be quick chilled in a freezer (0-5°F); a sudden drop in temperature will affect its taste. It is important to never let beer freeze. Lengthy exposures to temperatures of 28°F or colder will cause separation of the solids and liquid in the beer. If it is only slightly frozen, gradual thawing in a refrigerator may bring it back to its natural state. If the beer remains cloudy or has sediment, it should not be sold.

3 **Store the Beer Under Proper Conditions** — Bottled beer should never be stored where it is exposed to direct sunlight or fluorescent light; both will cause a photochemical reaction that will negatively affect the beer's taste and create an offensive odor known as "skunky" beer.

A bottle of beer whose seal has leaked and is no longer airtight should be discarded. Evidence of this might be a larger than normal air space (called the *ullage*) in the bottle, or if the beer is cloudy or contains sediment (with the exception of wheat-sedimented beer).

Beer should remain as still as possible. Excessive movement can lead to a decline of a beer's taste and aroma. The inventory should be rotated so that the oldest products are used first (First In, First Out system).

4 **Behind the Bar Pouring Practices** — With a top-loading cooler, the temptation is to lay bottled beer on its side to most efficiently use the space. When beer bottles are stored on their side, however, the bottle's metal cap will affect the taste and character of the beer. Keeping the bottles in six-packs not only protects the bottles and their labels it will also make it easier to rotate the stock.

Consider also providing the staff with wall mounted openers and train them to open the bottles without chipping the lip. If it is chipped, the beer must be thrown away or you run the risk of a customer becoming seriously injured on the shard of glass. Only pour beer into spotlessly clean glassware.

> Bottled beer should never be stored where it is exposed to direct sunlight or fluorescent light.

5. Avoid Losses Due to Internal Theft — Most theft involving bottled beer occurs because of its perceived low cost. Scams include free "give-aways" and entering beer sales into the cash register's liquor sales key to offset previous theft.

One effective method of detecting bottled beer theft is a post-shift bottle count. A post-shift bottle count is conducted as follows:

a. The beginning inventory is obtained either by taking a physical count of the bottled beer behind the bar before the shift, or using the ending inventory figures from the previous shift. In either case, the beginning inventory indicates how many bottles of beer were behind the bar before the shift started.

b. The requisition figure (Bar Req.) reflects the amount of bottled beer transferred from the storeroom to the bar. Adding the requisitions to the beginning inventory gives you the adjusted beginning inventory, which represents the total amount of bottled beer behind the bar during the course of the shift.

c. At the end of the shift another audit of the bottled beers is taken to determine the number of bottles remaining behind the bar. By subtracting the ending inventory figures from the adjusted beginning inventory you will know precisely how many bottles of each brand were taken from inventory during the shift.

d. The next step is to multiply the number of bottles for each brand that were taken from inventory by their retail sales price. This will show how much money should have been collected in sales for each brand of bottled beer.

e. The sales for each brand are then added together to arrive at the total estimated sales of bottled beer for the shift. The retail value of the bottled beer recorded as having been given away by management, or lost due to spillage and waste is subtracted from the total estimated sales to arrive at the adjusted estimated sales.

f. The adjusted estimated sales figure is then compared to the total bottled beer sales figure from the register or point-of-sale system sales report. A negative number represents the projected retail losses for bottled beer for the shift; a positive number represents overcharges.

Illustration 15.7 is an example of a post-shift bottle count. Notice that the result of this particular post-shift bottle count reveals that the shift is missing $18 worth of bottled beer.

> **One effective method of detecting bottled beer theft is a post-shift bottle count.**

Post-Shift Bottle Count Form

Brand	Beginning Inventory	Bar Req.		Adjusted Inventory		Ending Inventory		Sales Depletion		Price		Estimated Sales
Rolling Rock	44	+	12	=	56	-	21	=	35	X	$1.75	=	$61.25
Asahi Draft	26	+	00	=	26	-	18	=	08	X	$2.25	=	$18.00
Bud Light	50	+	24	=	74	-	16	=	58	X	$2.25	=	$130.50
Budweiser	61	+	18	=	79	-	10	=	69	X	$2.25	=	$155.25
Miller Lite	54	+	12	=	66	-	19	=	47	X	$2.25	=	$105.75
Sharps N/A	29	+	06	=	35	-	18	=	17	X	$2.25	=	$38.25
Asahi Dry	15	+	00	=	15	-	09	=	06	X	$2.50	=	$15.00
Clausthaler	36	+	00	=	36	-	22	=	14	X	$2.50	=	$35.00
Corona	39	+	00	=	39	-	15	=	24	X	$2.50	=	$60.00
Amstel Light	22	+	18	=	40	-	14	=	26	X	$2.75	=	$71.50
Bohemia	39	+	00	=	39	-	26	=	13	X	$3.00	=	$39.00
Dortmunder	17	+	00	=	17	-	12	=	05	X	$3.25	=	$16.25
Bass Ale	17	+	12	=	29	-	15	=	14	X	$3.50	=	$49.00
Chimay	06	+	00	=	06	-	06	=	00	X	$10.50	=	$00.00

TOTAL ESTIMATED SALES	$755.75
Subtract: COMPLIMENTARY SALES AT RETAIL	- $19.75
Subtract: WASTE AND SPILLAGE AT RETAIL	- $4.50
ADJUSTED ESTIMATED SALES	$731.50
Subtract: REGISTER/POS SALES	$713.50
CASH UNDER/OVER	- $18.00

Illustration 15.7

QUESTIONS LEAD TO ANSWERS WHICH LEAD TO SUCCESS

- How do your beer prices compare with those of your direct competitors?
- Have you taken into consideration the size and shape your beer glass has on the number of servings you get from a half-barrel of draft beer?
- Do you have a training program in place that covers the proper technique for pouring draft beer?
- Have you specified to the staff how much foamy head to serve on a glass of draft beer?
- Do you have any inventory controls in place on your draft beer?
- Is your draft beer dispensing system cleaned weekly? Is it regularly serviced?
- Have you researched the operational advantages of installing a draft beer control system?
- Is your draft beer poured into "beer clean" glasses to better preserve the head?
- Do you use a non-petroleum detergent and sanitizer/rinse agent in your sinks behind the bar?
- Do you have your staff take a post-shift beer bottle count and get a nightly beer pour cost?
- How frequently are your bottled beers rotated to ensure a "first in, first out" inventory system?
- How frequently do you review your beer selections?

Chapter 16

Developing a Successful Wine Program

In a recent national survey, women in America responded that white wine was the drink they most frequently requested at bars or restaurants. The same survey found that wine was the third most frequently requested by men, coming in behind beer and margaritas.

Developing a successful wine program is a process similar to creating a well-received, profitable beer program. Whether it's a dust-covered bottle of Bordeaux from the wine cellar or a gallon jug of house wine, the same business principals apply. The primary areas of concern for wines by-the-glass programs include pricing, portioning and reducing waste due to overpouring, spoilage and theft. For cork finished wines the primary areas of concern are pricing, storage, and theft.

> **White wine was the drink most frequently requested by women.**

PRICING HOUSE WINES BY-THE-GLASS

There are significant differences between the various table wines that most house wines are selected from. The necessary first step is to conduct a tasting of different labels of wines before making a final selection. If the featured wines at your bar are inferior, any lingering pricing issues will not matter much because few people will be ordering it.

After narrowing down the field to several finalists, one of the selection factors will be cost. While most table wines are available in standard sized wine bottles (25.4 ounces), others are available in magnums, which are equal to 1.5 liters, or 50.7 ounces. The advantage of buying house wine in magnums is that they are typically sold at a lower cost per ounce

Illustration 16.1 is an example of how to price a glass of wine. The first step is to determine the wine's cost per ounce and gross profit margin. The example presumes the wine is being poured from a standard, 750ml bottle of wine. Once the portion cost is known, the gross profit, cost percentage and profit margin can then be determined for various retail price points.

Wines by the Glass Profit Percentage							
Wine Bottle Cost (750ml)				$6.50			
Divide: Cost per Ounce ($6.50 ÷ 25.4 oz.)				$.26/oz.			
Multiply: Serving Portion Cost (5 oz.)				$1.30			
(A) Retail Price	$3.50	$4.00	$4.50	$5.00	$5.50	$6.00	$6.50
(B) Portion Cost	$1.30	$1.30	$1.30	$1.30	$1.30	$1.30	$1.30
(C) Gross Profit (A - B)	$2.20	$2.70	$3.20	$3.70	$4.20	$4.70	$5.20
(D) Cost Percentage (B ÷ A)	37.1%	32.5%	28.9%	26.0%	23.6%	21.7%	20.0%
(E) Profit Margin (C ÷ A)	62.9%	67.5%	71.1%	74.0%	76.3%	78.3%	80.0%

Illustration 16.1

Illustration 16.2 is an example of how to analyze the pricing for varietal wines by the glass from a 750ml bottle of house wine. The example shows how gross profit, cost percentage and profit margin are affected based on what retail price is charged.

(A) Retail Price	$3.50	$4.00	$4.50	$5.00	$5.50	$6.00	$6.50
(B) Approx. Servings	5	5	5	5	5	5	5
(C) Gross Sales (A x B)	$17.50	$20.00	$22.50	$25.00	$27.50	$30.00	$32.50
(D) Bottle Cost	$6.50	$6.50	$6.50	$6.50	$6.50	$6.50	$6.50
(E) Gross Profit (C - D)	$11.00	$13.50	$16.00	$18.50	$21.00	$23.50	$26.00
(F) Cost Percentage (D ÷ C)	37.1%	32.5%	28.9%	26.0%	23.6%	21.7%	20.0%
(G) Profit Margin (E ÷ C)	62.9%	67.5%	71.1%	74.0%	76.4%	78.3%	80.0%

Illustration 16.2

WINE DRINKING PATTERNS AND PROFIT

With few exceptions, beer will outsell wine at most beverage operations. A typical beer drinker may consume three or four glasses or bottles of beer during the same period of time that a wine drinker will have one or two. And there are considerably more people who order beer than wine.

As illustration 16.3 reveals, wine sales are capable of generating higher gross profits than bottled beer. While it is true that bottled beers typically sell at lower cost percentages than wine, across the board wine delivers more dollars in profit.

In addition, while wine drinkers tend to order fewer servings than beer drinkers do, they are more inclined to "order up," buy a more expensive wine if given the opportunity. The likely explanation for this trend is that wine drinkers are taste conscious, sometimes more so than most beers drinkers, who often develop brand loyalty to one beer and order that label almost exclusively.

When developing a wine by-the-glass program, it is best to adopt a systematic approach to analyze the cost percentages and gross profit per glass. As has been the case with spirits and beer, pricing wines by-the-glass requires knowledge of the market and a fair amount of intuition.

Illustration 16.3 analyzes the cost percentages and gross profit of six different white wines ranging in cost and quality. The illustration raises several interesting questions. For example, the Buena Vista Chardonnay sells for a dollar more than the Glass Mountain, yet it generates only $.25 more gross profit. Does the quality of the Buena Vista Chardonnay warrant a higher price? If not, should the less expensive Chardonnay be featured?

There is of course a ceiling on how much consumers will pay for a particular glass of wine. This raises the question of whether your clientele will pay $7 for a glass of Edna Valley Chardonnay regardless of its enhanced quality and taste.

Adopt a systematic approach to analyze the cost percentages and gross profit per glass.

Wine Cost Percentage & Gross Profit

Brand/Type	Bottle Cost	Bottle Size	$/oz.	Portion Cost	Sales Price	Cost Percent.	Gross Profit
Almaden Chablis	$8.74	3 lt.	$.09	$.45	$3.00	15.0%	$2.55
Taylor Chardonnay	$7.33	1.5 lt.	$.14	$.70	$3.50	20.0%	$2.80
Glen Ellen Chardonnay	$9.67	1.5 lt.	$.19	$.95	$4.00	23.7%	$3.05
Glass Mountain Chard.	$8.50	750ml	$.34	$1.70	$5.00	34.0%	$3.30
Buena Vista Chardonnay	$12.42	750ml	$.49	$2.45	$6.00	40.8%	$3.55
Edna Valley Chardonnay	$14.75	750ml	$.58	$2.90	$7.00	41.4%	$4.10

Illustration 16.3

GLASS SIZE AND PORTIONING

There are essentially only three types of wine glasses that you need to consider-red wine, white wine and champagne. While many beverage operators use the same type of glass to serve white and red wine, there are benefits to selecting different glass styles to present each wine.

The traditional red wine glass is shaped like a bowl. This shape allows the maximum surface area for the wine to be in contact with oxygen or breathe. The glass is used exclusively for the service of red wine. The classic white wine glass is taller and the rim narrows perceptively to concentrate the aroma. The glass can be used to serve both red and white wines.

The size of the wine glass is of critical importance. Wine drinkers expect enough room between the rim of the glass and the level of the wine so that they can swirl the wine and smell the bouquet. One or two inches of separation are considered the norm. Too small a glass requires pouring the wine too close to the rim. If a glass is excessively large for the portion it will likely cause the guest to think that he or she received an insufficient portion.

Beer glasses can be large and heavy, which often enhances the experience. Wine drinkers prefer the opposite; the thinner and more delicate the glass the better. While this is not practical in most commercial settings because of breakage and cost, beverage operators should consider this weight preference to some extent when selecting glassware.

The traditional red wine glass is shaped like a bowl.

The classic white wine glass is taller and the rim narrows.

REDUCING WINE COSTS

Wine is a relatively fragile product, one that is highly susceptible to waste and spoilage. It's not uncommon for bars and restaurants to lose hundreds of dollars worth of wine annually due to improper storage and handling. These are almost totally avoidable losses that add up extremely fast. As little as a $1.25 portion of wine going to waste a day equals nearly $500 in lost profits per year.

It is therefore important that management implement a program aimed at ensuring that the wine inventory is stored and portioned properly. The following are points to consider including in your wine management program.

Establishing Par Levels for Opened Bottles of Wine — Only a limited number of bottles should be opened before each bartending shift. Open bottles of wine are highly susceptible to spoilage, especially unrefrigerated bottles of red wine. Establish par levels for each label of wine stocked behind the bar. The list should include the number of bottles for each label to be opened prior to a shift.

Something as simple as not pulling a cork completely out of the bottle can help preserve wine and reduce spoilage. If a cork is pulled only ¾ of the way out, the bottle remains sealed and the wine is protected from oxygen.

2 **Wine Preservation** — For open, partially full bottles there are several proven methods to preserve the wine. One such system is the Vacu-vin® system. It can prolong the freshness and quality of wine by several days. The system is inexpensive and easy to use. It uses a rubber stopper that is inserted into the neck of the bottle. A small hand pump is then attached and the air inside the bottle is sucked out.

There are also a number of inert gas systems available. The systems use aerosol type canisters that inject nitrogen, argon, or carbon dioxide to displace the oxygen in the open bottle of wine. Carbon dioxide is not inert, but wine reacts slower to it than oxygen.

For champagne and sparkling wines there are reusable bottle stoppers with clamps that hook onto the lip of the bottle. This inexpensive, uncomplicated device keeps the champagne properly pressurized. The stopper will allow you to affordably pour champagne by-the-glass without being overly concerned that the unused portion will go flat and be wasted.

For champagne and sparkling wines there are reusable bottle stoppers.

3 **Over Portioning** — Over-pouring is a constant concern with wine served by-the-glass. Determining how many servings in a bottle and noting it at the bartender's work station is an effective technique to reemphasizing the importance of proper portioning. Another effective method is to take a wine glass and fill it with the correct portion of wine. Place the glass next to a vertical surface by the bartenders' workstation, such as the slant board (silent bartender), and make a mark on the surface where the level of the wine is. After that, the bartender can verify that a glass of wine is properly filled by comparing it to that mark.

4 **Estimating Sales Through Potentializing** — Taking a physical count of a shift's emptied bottles is advisable for two reasons. The first is that it reinforces to the staff that there is strict inventory control over the wine inventory. The second is that it allows estimating wine sales through potentializing. Multiplying the quantity of each label emptied by number of servings per bottle will give you an estimate of wine sales.

For example, if a bartender empties six 1.5 liter bottles of house wine and the specified wine serving is 5 ounces, the individual should have entered approximately 60 to 61 glasses sold.

Illustration 16.4 shows the estimated number of servings obtained from the various sized wine bottles/containers.

Portion Size	4 oz.	4½ oz.	5 oz.	5½ oz.	6 oz.
750ml (25.4 oz.)	6.4	5.6	5.1	4.6	4.2
Liter (33.8 oz.)	8.5	7.5	6.8	6.1	5.6
Magnum (50.7 oz.)	12.7	11.3	10.2	9.2	8.5
3-Liter (101.4 oz.)	25.3	22.5	20.3	18.4	16.9
18-Liter (608.4 oz.)	152.1	135.2	121.7	110.6	101.4

Illustration 16.4

IMPLEMENTING A BOTTLED WINE PROGRAM

Most food and beverage operations open for dinner offer wine by the bottle.

Most food and beverage operations open for dinner offer their clientele the option of purchasing wine by the bottle. The principle areas of concern when implementing a bottled wine program are pricing, storage and security.

▪ Pricing Bottled Wine — Many bars and restaurants establish a fixed percentage as their standard mark-up on bottled wines. This is often two to three times the wholesale cost. While establishing a fixed mark-up makes for simple calculations, it often doesn't result in the higher potential profits being realized. Sometimes taking less of a markup on a better quality wine, makes the wine even more appealing. It may also give the house higher revenues and a higher net profit.

For example, some premium wines could be discounted to give the staff an opportunity to up-sell guests from house wine. Were management to establish a selling price by tripling the wholesale cost, a $5.00 bottle of wine would yield a net profit of $10. A wine that costs $7.50, however, would yield a net profit of $11.25 were it priced at 2.5 times wholesale costs. A guest would spend $3 more per bottle for a better wine, and the business would realize the larger net profit.

This strategy also works well with "special buys," such as when wholesalers drastically reduce wholesale cost on a label of wine to blowout their stock. Passing along part of the savings to the clientele can increase sales, patron good will, and wine sales net profits.

2 Storage — Wine is extremely sensitive to temperature change, heat and light. The ideal cellar temperature is 55°F (12.8°C), or an acceptable range between 45°F to 60°F. Rapid changes in temperature are more damaging than a constant temperature at a higher range. It is a good idea to feel the bottles of newly delivered wine to see if the glass is hot to the touch. In such instances the wine delivery should be refused.

Sunlight and other bright light sources, especially fluorescent light, can rapidly damage wine. Even with its darkly tinted glass, a bottle of wine left in direct sunlight for as little as a few hours can be damaged.

Wines should be stored on their sides to keep the corks moist and maintain the seal. In addition, they should be stored with their labels facing up. This will prevent unnecessarily jostling bottles to identify them.

The wine storage room should be free of vibrations. Old red wines and Ports throw sediment as they age. Care must be taken to not agitate the sediment in the wine; which is why old bottles of wine are transported nearly horizontal and decanted into a carafe before serving.

Wines should be stored on their sides to keep the corks moist and maintain the seal.

Excessive humidity in the room will not affect the stored wine. Over long periods of time, however, humidity will cause wine labels to deteriorate, sometimes to the point of being unreadable.

A system should be used to properly rotate your wine inventory. With the exception of old red wines and Ports, the wine inventory should be rotated such that the bottles purchased earliest are sold first. Rotating inventory according to the "First In, First Out" (FIFO) system will ensure that wine doesn't remain too long on the shelf.

Many bars and restaurants use a bin card system to track the wine inventory. Bin cards are index card-sized ledgers kept in a file in the wine room or physically affixed to the actual wine bin. The bin card is used to keep track of the purchases and requisitions. The last entry on the card should correspond to the number of bottles remaining in the rack or bin.

There are several indications that a wine may have spoiled. A bottle of wine that shows evidence of leaking from the cork (a "weeper") and appears to have lost even a small amount of wine should be considered suspect. A bottle of wine with an unusually large amount of air space between the cork and the level of the fluid should also be considered unfit for guests. This space, or "ullage," is typically uniform between products bearing identical labels and the inconsistency may indicate an improperly sealed bottle.

3 **Security** — Bottles of wine are a likely target for theft. Access to wine storage areas should be strictly limited. Breakage per shift should be counted and marked off a perpetual inventory or bin card. Spot audits conducted weekly are highly advisable. Regularly conducting complete audits of the wine inventory is absolutely essential in limiting exposure to theft.

PROFESSIONAL WINE SERVICE

Wine should always be served in a spotlessly clean glass. To prevent smudges or fingerprints from marring a wine's appearance, always handle wine glasses by the stem. This practice holds true regardless of whether serving wine or removing an empty glass.

Wine should always be served in a spotlessly clean glass.

When pouring wine into a glass, care should be taken to not over-fill the glass. The size and shape of the glass will normally dictate the proper serving level. In each case, however, over-filling a glass will likely result in spillage and is therefore an unacceptable practice.

Wine should never be poured in a glass that has just been washed and is still hot and wet. Heat has a detrimental affect on wine and water still clinging to the glass likely contains sanitizer/rinse solution, an agent equally harmful to wine.

When serving a bottle of wine, the bottle should be placed on the bar or table in front of the customer who ordered it. The bottle is placed with the label facing the person who ordered the wine. Before proceeding, the server should wait for approval that it is the correct bottle of wine.

Most wine openers used in bars and restaurants have a small knife used to cut through the lead or plastic seal. The seal should be cut no less than a ¼" below the lip of the bottle so the wine may be poured without coming into contact with the foil. The lead in the seal may add a metallic taste to the wine.

The server should slowly turn the bottle clockwise with his or her free hand for one full rotation, positioning the label once again facing the customer. Unless the seal is unusually thick, one rotation will be all that is needed to cut through completely. If not, the server should repeat the procedure. The seal should be removed and discarded. If necessary, the mouth of the bottle should be wiped clean prior to removing the cork.

The most frequently used commercial wine opener is called the French waiter's wine screw. It operates on the lever principle. The corkscrew portion of the opener is extended. The tip of the index finger is placed on the second to the last spiral of the screw and positioned on the edge of the bottle's lip. The finger holding the corkscrew should then be pointed toward the center of the cork. This technique will center the corkscrew, which is important since removing a cork is always easier when the corkscrew is centered.

Once the tip of the corkscrew has touched the top of the cork, turn it a half-turn counter-clockwise. This will coil the server's wrist so that the screw can penetrate the surface of the cork cleanly and solidly. The corkscrew is turned clockwise until the screw has penetrated the flat hilt of the corkscrew. Pushing downward with the palm will force the lever-end of the screw upward so that the notched end of the lever can be placed on the lip of the bottle.

While the server is gripping the bottle with his or her free hand, pressure is applied upward on the wine screw forcing the cork to rise from the neck of the bottle. It is important that the server not yank the cork out completely, an action that often causes wine to spurt out with the releasing vacuum. In addition, the server should make sure the cork-corkscrew combination remains vertical, which will prevent the cork from breaking. When the lever is completely extended, the server should release his or her grip on the opener and grab hold of the cork. Gently move the cork back and forth until it can be removed. The server should check the mouth of the bottle to make sure it is clean. If it isn't, the mouth of the bottle should be wiped with a clean towel or napkin.

The size and shape of the glass will normally dictate the proper serving level.

The cork is then removed from the screw and handed to the host with the wet end upward. This will prevent the host from getting wet with wine. The host will inspect the cork, signifying that it was stored properly, and that it doesn't have any off-odors. The server should wait for the host's approval before proceeding.

Once approval has been given, a small amount of wine is poured into the host's glass. There should be just enough wine in the glass for one good taste. This affords the opportunity to swirl the wine, inhale its bouquet, and assess its attributes.

After approval has been given to pour, the women at the table are served first, then the men. The server should exercise care not to overfill the glasses. As the host for that particular bottle of wine, the guest who tasted the wine first is traditionally the last to be served.

When pouring wine, the server should hold the bottle by the bottom so that his or her hand won't hide the label. Care should be taken to not let the bottle touch the rim of the glass. Likewise, he or she should not let wine drip off the lip of the bottle. This can be easily avoided by giving the bottle a slight twist before raising the bottle.

After the glasses have been filled, set the wine on the bar or table with the label facing the host, and if possible, the rest of the party's guests. If placing the wine into an iced wine bucket, drape a clean napkin or towel over the edge of the bucket so the bottle can be wiped dry before pouring.

The server should make sure that customers' glasses are refilled as necessary. This should be done without asking unless given prior instructions. Wine glasses are usually placed just to the right of the water glass. If more than one type of wine is to be served with a meal, the glass farthest to the right is used first.

Women at the table are served first, then the men.

It is important to serve customers their wine immediately after it is ordered. This practice will avoid the serious mistake of the wine arriving to the table after the main course has been served.

Most establishments have an adequate supply of white wine, rosé and sparkling wines chilling at all times. This avoids having to rapidly chill the wine, a practice that may affect the wine's taste. In some instances, a wine bucket is used to keep the open bottle of wine cold. When the bottle is empty, it is placed upside down into the bucket.

As previously mentioned, old red wines and Ports throw sediment as they age. If the sediment, or crust, is disturbed in moving, allow the wine to rest and the sediment will settle. Decanting the wine into another vessel is advisable.

QUESTIONS LEAD TO ANSWERS WHICH LEAD TO SUCCESS

- Do you know the portion cost of each of your house wines?
- Have you implemented a means of visually verifying the serving portion of a glass of wine?
- Have you considered offering a selection of varietal wines by-the-glass to give your guests the opportunity to "order-up?"
- Are your wines being served in sparkling clean glasses?
- Are wines by-the-glass being served in appropriately sized glassware? Does the wine portion appear under-poured or poured too close to the rim?
- Have you established a par level for all of the wines opened for each shift?
- Do you have a system or device to preserve the freshness of opened wines and champagnes?
- Are your wine storage areas climate controlled?
- Do you physically inspect wine deliveries to make sure they have been properly handled?
- Is access to your wine storage areas strictly limited?
- Do you check breakage records against wines sales after each shift?

Inventory Control:
Implementing Safeguards

I nventory levels behind the bar change with every flick of the bartender's wrist. Controlling costs is dependent on knowing precisely what you have, where it is or when you sold it. Obtaining this information requires that you accurately monitor the inventory from the moment it comes through the back door until it's served.

In jargon it's referred to as "cradle to grave" accounting and it involves implementing a series of overlapping internal bookkeeping systems that track every product through the inventory cycle. While uncomplicated, the key to the system is making sure that all of the components are in place and being used properly.

Illustration 17.1 shows the six forms that make up the inventory control system being described in this chapter. The first form, the *Purchase Order*, is used to record the specifics of every inventory purchase. After products have been purchased, the *Perpetual Inventory Form* tracks the flow of inventory in and out of the liquor and wine storerooms, and provides a complete accounting of each product's rate of turnover. The third element, the *Requisition Form*, is used to record the transfer of inventory from the storeroom to a specific bar or outlet and provides an accounting of each outlet's breakage.

The *Bar Par Form* is used to control the quantity of each brand of liquor or liqueur stocked behind the bar. The *Depletion Allowance Forms* are used to track the amount of inventory spilled, transferred to another outlet, or given away in a complimentary drink. Completing the inventory cycle is the *Physical Inventory Form*, which is used at the end of each accounting period to record the result of a physical audit of the inventory.

Track every product through the inventory cycle.

Inventory Control Cycle

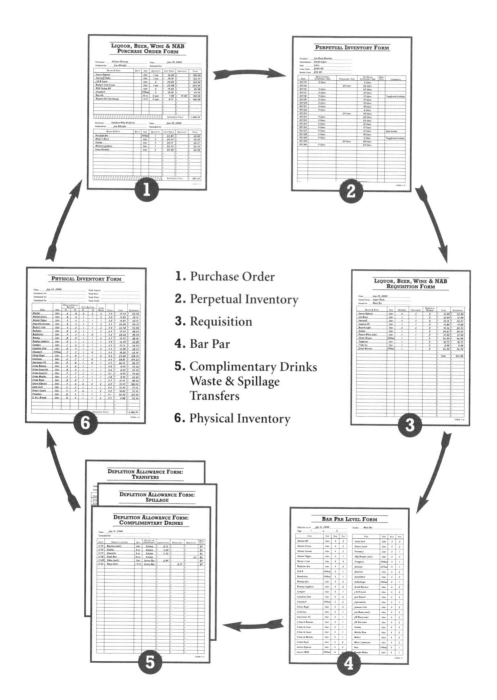

1. Purchase Order
2. Perpetual Inventory
3. Requisition
4. Bar Par
5. Complimentary Drinks
   Waste & Spillage
   Transfers
6. Physical Inventory

Illustration 17.1

LIQUOR, BEER AND WINE PURCHASING GUIDELINES

The challenge when ordering the liquor, beer and wine inventory is to purchase the right items, at the right price and in the right quantity. Ordering too much results in your working capital being unnecessarily tied-up. Failing to purchase enough inventory can lead to shortages.

To avoid costly mistakes, ordering, receiving and requisitioning inventory should be the responsibility of one, or at most, two managers. Liquor, beer and wine deliveries should all be scheduled for the same day of each week, preferably one or two days after the order is placed. You can specify to each distributor the day and time period when deliveries will be accepted. Specifying the time of delivery will ensure that the person whose responsibility it is to check-in the deliveries is present. Each delivery should be physically inspected for bottle size, quantities ordered, price, damage and to verify that seals are intact. Only after the delivery has been determined to be complete and correct should the invoice be signed, formally accepting the order. For security reasons, the delivered products should immediately be stocked into the liquor storeroom or wine room.

The faster an item is depleted the better its financial rate of return.

LIQUOR, BEER AND WINE ORDERING PROCEDURES

Products that have a short turnover rate, such as well liquor, should be ordered by the case to take advantage of case discounts. Liters are more economical than 750ml bottles. Products with a slower rate of turnover should be stocked in short supply. The faster an item is depleted the better its financial rate of return. Well vodka, the product with the fastest turnover rate behind the bar, has a better return on investment than a top-shelf liqueur that may take over a year to empty.

One rule of thumb is to order liquors or liqueurs by the case if it takes less than five weeks to sell that product. Regardless of the broken case charge it may add, if it takes more than five weeks to deplete a case of a particular brand of spirits then it should be ordered by the liter(s).

A standardized purchase order is used to record the specifics of each liquor, beer and wine order. When the delivery arrives, the purchase order provides a way to verify the shipment. For the form to be effective it should note who placed the order, who received the delivery and identify each individual distributor. In addition, the order form should contain the following specifics:

• **Liquor Orders** — Each brand of liquor or liqueur being ordered should be clearly identified, leaving no possibility that the wrong product could be mistakenly accepted. For example: Johnnie Walker *Black Label*; Jim Beam bourbon in the *square liters*; Wild Turkey *White Label 101 proof*; Glenmorangie *Port Wood Finish* Single Malt; Glenlivet *18 Year* Single Malt; Bombay *Sapphire* Gin; and Grand Marnier *Cuvee de Centenaire*. In each instance, unless clearly stated, other similar products could be mistakenly delivered and accepted. The liquor order should also clearly specify the size and quantity of each product. If any discount or quoted post-offs are anticipated, it should also be noted.

• **Beer Orders** — Each label of beer being ordered should be clearly identified leaving no room for error. For example: Miller *Genuine Draft Light*; Budweiser *Long Necks*; Heineken *Dark*; Anchor *Porter*; Miller Lite in *six-packs* and Foster's *25 ounce can*. The purchase order should clearly specify the size of the bottle and the quantity being ordered. If any discounts or quoted post-offs are anticipated, it should also be noted.

> **The liquor order should clearly specify the size and quantity of each product.**

• **Wine Orders** — House wines should be identified by the vintner, type and bottle size. There is often a volume discount or quoted post-off for purchasing a certain number of cases of wine. The quantity ordered and anticipated discount should be noted on the purchase order. When ordering varietal wines identify the vintner, the grape variety, and vintage. In some cases, the particular appellation needs to be specified, such as Rodney Strong Chardonnay *Chalkhill Estate* or Heitz Cellar Cabernet Sauvignon *Martha's Vineyard*.

Illustration 17.2 is an example of a completed Liquor, Beer and Wine Purchase Order.

IMPLEMENTING A PERPETUAL INVENTORY SYSTEM

This internal bookkeeping system is used to track the flow of inventory in and out of the liquor storeroom. Every product stocked in the liquor storeroom should have a separate page in the perpetual inventory notebook. At any point in time, the perpetual inventory should indicate the exact quantity on-hand for every product stocked. The more inventory on-hand, the more important it is that a perpetual system be used.

LIQUOR, BEER, WINE & NAB PURCHASE ORDER FORM

Purveyor: _Alliance Beverage_   Date: _June 19, 2000_

Ordered by: _Jim Albright_   Extended by: _____

BRAND & KIND	BIN #	SIZE	QUANTITY	UNIT PRICE	DISCOUNT	TOTAL
Cuervo Especial		liter	1 case	$ 16.00	$	$ 192.00
Smirnoff Vodka		liter	1 case	$ 10.19	$	$ 122.33
J & B Scotch		liter	6	$ 20.84	$	$ 125.04
Bailey's Irish Cream		liter	1 case	$ 22.08	$	$ 264.90
Wild Turkey 80°		liter	6	$ 15.83	$	$ 94.98
Chambord		750ml	3	$ 18.18	$	$ 54.54
Bass Ale		12 oz.	6 cases	$ 1.08	$ 15.00	$ 140.40
Blossom Hill Chardonnay		1.5 lt.	4 cases	$ 8.17	$	$ 196.00
				$	$	$
				$	$	$
				$	$	$
				$	$	$
					EXTENSION TOTAL	$ 1,190.19

Purveyor: _Southern Wine & Spirits_   Date: _June 19, 2000_

Ordered by: _Jim Albright_   Extended by: _____

BRAND & KIND	BIN #	SIZE	QUANTITY	UNIT PRICE	DISCOUNT	TOTAL
Van Gogh Gin		750ml	1	$ 22.83	$	$ 22.83
Maker's Mark		liter	2	$ 20.25	$	$ 40.50
Kahlua		liter	3	$ 20.17	$	$ 60.51
Molinari Jambuca		liter	1	$ 22.33	$	$ 22.33
Sauza Hornitos		liter	2	$ 20.58	$	$ 41.16
				$	$	$
				$	$	$
				$	$	$
				$	$	$
				$	$	$
				$	$	$
				$	$	$
					EXTENSION TOTAL	$ 187.33

©2000 Robert Plotkin's **BarMedia**

Illustration 17.2

When a product is requisitioned from the liquor room, the transaction is recorded on the item's *Perpetual Inventory Form* (or bin card). The requisitioned amount is subtracted from the quantity on-hand as reflected in the perpetual. All entries should be made in ink and the entries made into the *Perpetual Inventory Form* should be the responsibility of one manager. The last entry on the perpetual inventory sheet should correspond to the actual amount of product on the liquor room shelf.

Since the perpetual inventory clearly reveals a product's depletion rate, it makes ordering liquor much more precise. In illustration 17.3, Jim Beam bourbon is requisitioned to the bar(s) at an average rate of 21.5 liters per week, warranting the weekly purchases of two cases.

The perpetual inventory system also greatly assists in detecting internal theft. Should the amount of product stocked on the shelf fall below the quantity shown on the perpetual inventory, first check your math - you may have made a mistake adding or subtracting on the perpetual. Check also for any unrecorded transfers or requisitions to the bar that were not entered onto the *Perpetual Inventory Form*. Each would explain why the amount of product on the shelf doesn't match the figure on the perpetual. If that doesn't resolve the discrepancy, the only remaining explanation is internal theft.

Illustration 17.3 is an example of the *Perpetual Inventory Form* in use.

PERPETUAL INVENTORY FORM

Product: Jim Beam Bourbon
Distributor: United Liquor
Size: Liters
Case Cost: $144.00
Bottle Cost: $12.00

DATE	REQUISITIONED INVENTORY / SIZE	PURCHASES / SIZE	ON-HAND INVENTORY / SIZE	MGR. INTL.	COMMENTS
07/15	2 liters		2 liters		
07/16		24 liters	26 liters		
07/16	3 liters		23 liters		
07/17	2 liters		21 liters		
07/18	4 liters		17 liters		Transferred to kitchen
07/19	2 liters		15 liters		
07/20	3 liters		12 liters		
07/21	2 liters		10 liters		
07/22	4 liters		6 liters		
07/23		24 liters	30 liters		
07/23	4 liters		26 liters		
07/24	3 liters		23 liters		
07/25	2 liters		21 liters		
07/26	4 liters		17 liters		
07/27	4 liters		13 liters		Liter broken
07/28	3 liters		10 liters		
07/29	4 liters		6 liters		Transferred to kitchen
07/30		24 liters	30 liters		
07/30	3 liters		27 liters		

©2000 Robert Plotkin's **BarMedia**

Illustration 17.3

REQUISITIONING AND ISSUING LIQUOR, BEER AND WINE

The *Liquor, Beer, Wine and NAB Requisition Form* is used to record the transfer of inventory from the liquor room to a specific bar or outlet. Bartenders use this form to log every product emptied (a.k.a. *breakage*) during the course of a shift. Afterwards, a replacement bottle is issued for the products being requisitioned and the transfers are noted in the perpetual inventory system.

The bar requisition form should include the date and make mention of which bar or outlet is submitting the requisition. The form should allow the bartenders to identify the exact product name, size and quantity being requisitioned. Space needs to be provided for whoever issues the stock to note how much of each product was actually delivered. In some instances there may be insufficient product to fill the requisition, in which case, the requisition is marked T.O. ("temporarily out").

In some instances there may be insufficient product to fill the requisition, in which case, the requisition is marked T.O. ("temporarily out").

The following are procedures for requisitioning and issuing inventory:

1. At the end of the closing bartending shift, the bartender(s) should mark down all of the liquor bottles emptied during the course of the shift on the bar requisition form.

2. The bar manager should verify that the products being requisitioned were actually emptied. There should be an empty bottle for every item requisitioned. After the manager has verified the requisition, he or she should throw away the empty bottles.

3. To prevent bookkeeping errors, before the manager takes a product off of the liquor room shelf, he or she should first make the appropriate entry in the perpetual inventory system. Only after the perpetual inventory entry has been recorded should the manager take the product off the shelf.

4. After the liquor order has been filled, the products are taken to the bar and restocked.

5. Bottled beer is issued based on cooler shelf availability. If during the course of a shift three six-packs of a particular brand of bottled beer are sold, the three six-packs are replaced and the product is brought back to par.

6. Completed requisition forms should be kept on file for approximately a month. In the event of a discrepancy, the month's requisition forms may be used to resolve the issue.

Illustration 17.4 is an example of a completed *Liquor, Beer, Wine and NAB Requisition Form.*

LIQUOR, BEER, WINE & NAB REQUISITION FORM

Date: _____June 19, 2000_____

Issued from: __Liquor Room__

Issued to: __Main Bar__

BRAND & KIND	SIZE	ORDERED	DELIVERED	PERPETUAL MARKED	COST	EXTENSION
Cuervo Especial	liter	2	2	X	$ 16.00	$ 32.00
Jim Beam	liter	1	1	X	$ 12.00	$ 12.00
Smirnoff	liter	3	3	X	$ 10.19	$ 30.57
Seagram VO	liter	1	1	X	$ 14.89	$ 14.89
Bacardi Light	liter	2	2	X	$ 10.36	$ 20.72
Kahlúa	liter	1	1	X	$ 20.67	$ 20.67
Dewars White Label	liter	1	1	X	$ 21.00	$ 21.00
Chivas 18-year	750ml	1	1	X	$ 46.90	$ 46.90
Tanqueray	liter	1	1	X	$ 18.75	$ 18.75
Triple Sec	liter	1	1	X	$ 8.08	$ 8.08
Grand Marnier	750ml	1	1	X	$ 36.40	$ 36.40
					$	$
					$ Total	$ 261.98

©2000 Robert Plotkin's **BarMedia**

Illustration 17.4

ESTABLISHING INVENTORY PAR LEVELS

Every product behind the bar needs to be stocked in sufficient quantity to meet sales demand. The *Bar Par Level Form* maintains the inventory at set levels by listing how much of each product should be stocked behind the bar at any time. Bar par sheets should be checked daily and kept behind the bar at all times.

Establishing and maintaining par levels behind the bar is also effective in controlling theft. Any product missing from the shelves or back-ups can be detected quickly and the disappearance reported immediately. The products should be listed alphabetically and indicate how many of each brand should be open in the well or back bar and how many are to be kept as back-ups.

Illustration 17.5 is an example of a (partially) completed *Bar Par Level Form*. The column marked "Bar" indicated the number of bottles of each product that are open and in use. The column marked "Par" indicates the number of bottles of each product that are to be kept in reserve as back-ups.

BAR PAR LEVEL FORM

Effective as of _July 16, 2000_   Outlet: _Main Bar_

Page ___1___ of ___2___

ITEM	SIZE	BAR	PAR	ITEM	SIZE	BAR	PAR
Absolut 80°	liter	3	2	Cutty Sark	liter	3	2
Absolut Citron	liter	3	2	Dewars Scotch	liter	3	2
Absolut Kurant	liter	3	2	Drambuie	liter	3	1
Absolut Peppar	liter	3	1	E&J Brandy (well)	liter	3	3
Bailey's Irish	liter	3	3	Frangelico	750ml	3	1
Beefeater Gin	liter	3	2	Galliano	375ml	3	1
B & B	750ml	3	1	Glenlivet	liter	3	2
Benedictine	750ml	3	1	Glenfiddich	liter	3	2
Bombay Gin	liter	3	2	Goldschlager	750ml	3	1
Bombay Sapphire	liter	3	2	Grand Marnier	liter	3	2
Campari	liter	3	1	J & B Scotch	liter	3	2
Canadian Club	liter	3	2	Jack Daniel's	liter	3	3
Chambord	750ml	3	2	Jägermeister	liter	3	1
Chivas Regal	liter	3	2	Jameson Irish	liter	3	2
Cointreau	liter	3	1	Jim Beam (well)	liter	3	3
Courvoisier VS	liter	3	1	JW Black Label	liter	3	2
Crème de Banana	liter	3	1	JW Red Label	liter	3	2
Crème de Cacao	liter	3	1	Kahlúa	liter	3	3
Crème de Cassis	liter	3	1	Malibu Rum	liter	3	2
Crème de Menthe	liter	3	1	Midori	liter	3	2
Crown Royal	liter	3	2	Myers's Jamaican	liter	3	2
Cuervo Especial	liter	3	3	Ouzo	750ml	3	1
Cuervo 1800	750ml	3	2	Rumple Minze	liter	3	1

Illustration 17.5

TRACKING TRANSFERS, SPILLAGE AND COMPLIMENTARY DRINKS

The *Depletion Allowance Forms* are used to record cost information regarding product that was used without a corresponding sales value. There are three reasons that product can be used without being sold. Inventory can be transferred to another outlet or department, it can accidentally be wasted or spilled, or it can be given out in a complimentary drink. It is important to track the cost of this inventory as it will affect the bar's cost of goods sold, commonly referred to as pour cost.

There should be a *Depletion Allowance Form* devoted to tracking the cost associated with transfers, waste/spillage and complimentary drinks. These forms should remain behind the bar at all times and changed at the end of each inventory period.

It is important to track the cost of this inventory.

1 **Depletion Allowance Form: Transfers** — A transfer involves sending inventory from one outlet or department to another. For instance in a restaurant the chef may decide to use bourbon in a particular sauce or a liqueur like Kahlúa or Amaretto in a pastry. He or she would get the spirit or liqueur from the bar, at which time the bartender would record the amount requested by the kitchen onto the *Depletion Allowance Form*. Transfers could involve sending inventory to a catering function, or transferring inventory from one bar to another. The person receiving the transferred inventory should sign or initial the form.

2 **Depletion Allowance Form: Spillage** — Waste and spillage is a cost of doing business and cannot be avoided. Inventory that is wasted or spilled should be recorded onto the *Depletion Allowance Form* listing what was spilled, in what amount and a brief comment as to the circumstance. The form should be filled in as soon as possible or after the end of the shift. It should not take the bartender away from a more timely activity.

The bartending staff should be made to understand that there is no penalty because they spilled inventory. While it should be kept at a minimum, waste and spillage is an unavoidable aspect of bartending. The staff should understand that the intent behind the form is only to assign a cost to the spilled products and factor it into the pour cost analysis.

3 **Depletion Allowance Form: Complimentary Drinks** — There are a number of reasons why a manager might want to give

out complimentary drinks to guests. The individuals may have waited too long for their table. It could be a special occasion and the manager wants to acknowledge the event with a complimentary round of cocktails. Regardless of the exact reason, it is within management's rights to "comp." guests their drinks. Information detailing all complimentary drinks given out should be recorded onto the *Complimentary Drinks, Depletion Allowance Form*. The manager's signature should be required for any complimentary drink.

Should a bartender feel that it is in the business's best interest to "comp." a customer(s) a drink for a legitimate reason or as a means of acknowledging a special occasion, he or she must receive prior management approval.

DEPLETION ALLOWANCE FORM: TRANSFERS

Date: July 14, 2000
Extended by: _____

DATE	PRODUCT OR ITEM	QTY.	OUTLET OR DEPARTMENT	LIQUOR COST	WINE COST	BEER COST	MGR. INTL.
7/15	Bourbon (well)	liter	Kitchen	$ 8.12	$	$	RP
7/15	Kahlúa	6 oz.	Kitchen	$ 3.60	$	$	RC
7/17	Amaretto	6 oz.	Kitchen	$ 3.72	$	$	RC
7/18	Draft Beer	16 oz.	Kitchen	$	$	$ .32	RC
7/20	Vodka (well)	liter	Service Bar	$ 6.95	$	$	RP
7/21	House white	1.5 lt	Service Bar	$	$ 8.17	$	RP
				$	$	$	
				$	$	$	
				$	$	$	
				$	$	$	
				$	$	$	
				$	$	$	
				$	$	$	
				$	$	$	
				$	$	$	
				$	$	$	
				$	$	$	
				$	$	$	
				$	$	$	
				$	$	$	
				$	$	$	
				$	$	$	
				$	$	$	
				$	$	$	
				$	$	$	
				$	$	$	

©2000 Robert Plotkin's **BarMedia**

There are a number of reasons why a manager might want to give out complimentary drinks to guests.

Illustration 17.6

Illustration 17.6 is an example of a (partially) completed *Depletion Allowance Form: Transfers*. The forms used to track spillage and complimentary drinks are similar.

THE INVENTORY AUDITING PROCESS

Conducting an audit of the inventory is to determine the dollar value of the liquor, beer and wine inventory on-hand at a specified point in time. How frequently a physical inventory is conducted depends on the sales volume of your business. The higher the volume, the more control you need to maintain over the operation, and thus the shorter amount of time between physical inventories.

There are beverage operations that take a physical audit of the inventory on a daily basis. The result is that they know precisely what was depleted from inventory during the previous shift. A cost is then assigned to the depleted inventory, and when divided by the sales for that shift an exact cost percentage can be figured. If there is a problem, the management will know about it in a matter of hours after the shift. They are then in the position to take timely and appropriate measures.

Management must perform the physical audit of the inventory.

Compare that level of managerial control to an operation that analyzes their beverage costs on a monthly basis. If the bar's costs have increased sharply, an entire month will have passed before management has an opportunity to react. In some instances this lapse can prove costly.

One aspect of the physical audit involves determining the amount of product in each opened bottle behind the bar. The most frequently used method of determining the amount of liquor remaining in a bottle is the "tenthing method" - which is estimating to the nearest tenth of the bottle. For example, if the contents of a bottle is estimated to be 4/10ths-meaning that the bottle is a little less than half full-it is recorded as .4. When the product's bottle cost is extended (or multiplied) by .4, the result is the value of the remaining contents. The entries for the partial bottles are then added to the number of unopened bottles of that brand stocked behind the bar and in the storeroom.

Management must perform the physical audit of the inventory. No hourly personnel should be involved. To be effective, the result of the physical audit must be as accurate as possible.

While you will undoubtedly develop your own way of doing things, one helpful technique in taking a physical inventory behind the bar is to start each time at the same place and work clockwise from there. Care must be taken to not overlook any products or count something twice. Estimating the contents remaining for odd-shaped bottles is made considerably more reliable when the bottle is held lengthwise.

It is highly advisable to use a standardized form to help keep the results of the physical audit in an organized manner. Illustration 17.7 is an example of a (partially) completed *Physical Inventory Form*.

The extensions in illustration 17.7 will be added to the extensions for the remainder of the liquor inventory. The resulting total will reflect

PHYSICAL INVENTORY FORM

Date: _____July 23, 2000_____   Total Liquor: _____

Inventory by: _____   Total Beer: _____

Extension by: _____   Total Wine: _____

Examined by: _____   Total NABs: _____

ITEM	SIZE	OPEN OR PARTIAL BOTTLES #1	#2	FULL BOTTLES #1	#2	STORE ROOM	TOTAL	COST	EXTENSION
Absolut	liter	.6	.8	2	2	2	7.4	$ 15.33	$ 113.44
Absolut Citron	liter	.8	.2	1	1	2	5.0	15.83	79.15
Absolut Peppar	liter	.5	.3	1	1	1	3.8	15.83	60.15
Amaretto Saronno	liter	.9	.4	1	1	2	5.3	20.90	110.77
Bailey's Irish	liter	.3	.7	1	1	2	5.0	22.58	112.90
Beefeater	liter	.8	.6	1	1	3	6.4	15.35	98.24
Benedictine	liter	.5	.7	1	0	1	3.2	28.28	90.50
Bombay	liter	.8	.9	1	1	2	5.7	15.47	88.18
Bombay Sapphire	liter	.9	.1	1	1	1	4.0	16.70	66.80
Campari	liter	.1	.2	1	1	1	3.3	17.13	56.53
Canadian Club	liter	.8	.5	1	1	2	5.3	12.90	68.37
Chambord	750ml	.7	.7	1	0	1	3.4	18.29	62.19
Chivas Regal	liter	.3	.9	1	1	2	5.2	24.68	128.34
Cointreau	liter	.6	.7	1	0	1	3.3	28.91	153.22
Courvoisier VS	liter	.9	.8	1	0	1	3.7	26.15	96.75
Creme Banana	liter	.4	.6	1	1	1	4.0	8.44	33.76
Creme Cacao/wh	liter	.8	.4	1	1	1	4.2	8.44	35.45
Creme Cacao/br	liter	.4	.7	1	1	1	4.1	8.44	34.60
Creme Menthe	liter	.7	.1	1	1	1	3.8	8.44	32.07
Crown Royal	liter	.8	.9	1	1	1	4.7	21.14	99.36
Cuervo Especial	liter	.3	.6	2	2	2	6.9	14.57	100.53
Cutty Sark	liter	.7	.7	1	1	1	4.4	17.53	77.13
Dewar's Scotch	liter	.4	.5	2	1	2	5.9	18.83	111.10
Drambuie	liter	.8	.3	1	1	1	4.1	30.50	125.05
E. & J. Brandy	liter	.8	.5	1	1	2	5.3	9.88	52.36
						EXTENSION TOTAL		$	$ 2,086.94

©2000 Robert Plotkin's **BarMedia**

Illustration 17.7

the dollar amount of the ending liquor inventory for a specified period of time. The ending liquor inventory for the period just completed will become the beginning liquor inventory for the next audit.

This process is repeated for the beer, wine and non-alcoholic beverage (NABs) inventories. Every bottle, keg and magnum must be included in the audit.

AUDITING FOOD AND DRY GOODS

Conducting a physical audit of the bar's dry goods, paper products, foodstuff, juices and mixes is a tedious process. While collectively items such as margarita salt, cocktail napkins, cocktail onions, canned pineapple juice and sweet 'n' sour represent a significant cost of doing business and should be factored into the cost analysis, they are unlikely targets of abuse or theft.

Precise monitoring of the inventory leads to better control.

One quick way of assigning a dollar value to these products is to hinge the figure to gross sales. As sales increase, so does the use of cocktail napkins, straws, green olives, cherries, pineapple juice and coconut syrup. When business drops off, so does the use of lime wedges, Bloody Mary mix and tonic water. This figure is normally estimated between 2-4% of gross sales depending on the specific features of the inventory.

BEVINCO AUDITING SERVICES

The age of information has finally arrived behind the bar. Technological advances now make it possible for you to see your beverage operation from a new and fascinating perspective.

Bevinco is the Ultimate Weapon

If it's true that knowledge is power, then Bevinco is the ultimate weapon. This unique service is designed to tell you more about the profitability of your beverage operation than was ever before available, using software technology that didn't exist a few years ago. Armed with a laptop and electronic scales, a Bevinco auditor is capable of generating management reports that provide an exact representation of what transpired throughout the operation. Naturally the reports figure the cost percentages for each product. The report also analyzes each product's actual sales and profits, then compares those figures to their respective ideal figures both in units and dollars.

The working premise behind the service is that precise monitoring of the inventory by an independent third party leads to better control, which in turn, leads to lower costs and increased profits. Bevinco, like x-rays, looks beneath the surface and reveals a computer-enhanced view of the workings of your bar. The database was developed specifically to track the depletion of brand-specific

A Bevinco Auditor

products throughout the operation. It then compares each product's depletion to what was sold. The Bevinco management reports will also document exactly where and how you're losing money.

Auditor using electronic scale

The potential savings to an operator using the Bevinco auditing services on an on-going basis are considerable. They are capable of taking a physical audit faster and more accurately than most managers inventorying their own bars. The Bevinco reports show far more about what has happened behind the bar than standard auditing

The Bevinco management reports document exactly where and how you're losing money.

techniques. In addition, the system is so precise that it will catch any type of impropriety and prevent its happening again in the future.

Illustration 17.8 is an example of a *Bevinco Bar Variance Report* (partial). The report details any overages or shortages of inventory, pour costs for all categories, revenue per ounce for all depleted inventory, and the revenue potential of the lost inventory.

	Used oz/Btl	Sold oz/Btl	Over/Short Oz/Btl	0%	(Value)	Used (Value)	Onhand (Value)	Sales (Value)	Rev Per oz/btl	Pour Cost	Rev Potl (Value)
Whiskey	167.42	151.00	-16.42	-9.8%	-4.85	49.50	80.50	468.10	2.80	10.6%	
Gin	95.85	84.00	-11.85	-12.4%	-5.72	46.29	51.70	273.00	2.85	17.0%	
Rum	189.41	162.00	-27.41	-14.5%	-8.92	61.62	114.40	494.10	2.61	12.5%	
Vodka	329.43	235.00	-94.43	-28.7%	-48.97	170.84	355.30	834.25	2.53	20.5%	
Tequila	127.50	108.00	-19.50	-15.3%	-9.08	59.38	176.85	340.20	2.67	17.5%	
Brandy	57.21	49.00	-8.21	-14.4%	-4.37	30.45	95.54	213.15	3.73	14.3%	
Aperitif	22.03	20.00	-2.03	-9.2%	-0.58	6.55	32.55	30.50	1.38	20.8%	
Liqueurs	168.30	123.00	-45.30	-26.9%	-30.81	114.46	345.52	412.05	2.45	27.8%	
Total Liquor	1157.16	932.00	-225.16	-19.5%	-113.31	538.87	1252.36	3065.35	2.65	17.6%	740.55
Wine	1187.37	1002.00	-185.37	-15.6%	-29.23	187.25	160.75	517.70	0.44	36.2%	95.77
Champagne	54.67	48.00	-6.67	-12.2%	-1.44	11.84	49.42	42.40	0.78	27.9%	25.89
Beer - Bottle	736.00	633.00	-103.00	-14.0%	-61.37	438.51	0.60	1772.40	2.41	24.7%	268.40
Beer - Draft	16865.00	15088.00	-1777.00	-10.5%	-45.30	430.05	936.01	2734.70	0.16	15.7%	322.08
GRAND TOTAL					-250.66	1606.51	2399.13	8132.55		19.8%	$1452.69

Illustration 17.8

A UNIQUE OPERATIONAL BENEFIT OF BEVINCO

Bevinco offers us a glimpse into the future. In the not too distant future, all of us will be using sophisticated software packages to determine precisely what has transpired behind the bar. One aspect of the technology Bevinco has developed is an intriguing concept they call the Bevinco Efficiency Rating.

The Efficiency Rating was developed to give their clients the capability of comparing the performance of one beverage outlet to another. It compares a bar's actual cost percentages to its ideal or theoretical pour costs. The ideal or theoretical pour cost is calculated by subtracting the dollar value of the missing inventory (shortages) from the total dollar value of the inventory used, and then dividing the remainder by the gross revenue. This figure is then divided by the bar's actual cost percentage to arrive at the efficiency rating.

Bevinco offers us a glimpse into the future. For example, an audit reveals that one bar in the establishment used $900 in liquor and generated $4000 in liquor sales. The bar was short $100 in liquor. Another outlet in the same establishment used $1200 in liquor, was short $185 in liquor, and generated $5500 in gross liquor sales. Which bar performed better?

The ideal pour cost at the first bar was 20% [($900 - $100) ÷ $4000]. The ideal pour cost is then divided by the bar's actual pour cost of 22.5% [$900 ÷ $4000] to arrive at an efficiency rating of 88.8%. The ideal pour cost at the second bar was 18.5% [($1200 - $185) ÷ $5500]. The ideal pour cost is then divided by the bar's actual pour cost of 21.8% [$1200 ÷ $5500] to arrive at an efficiency rating of 84.9%. The Bevinco Efficiency Rating clearly shows that despite having slightly lower sales in liquor, the first bar was more efficient with the liquor inventory than the second outlet.

Another unique feature of the Bevinco Bar Inventory Management Service is a special report identifying the effectiveness of the services at contributing to the increased NET profit to the establishment. The Historical Analysis is a true indication of the extra profit that can be had with an effective inventory management program such as Bevinco's. Combined with Bevinco's "Rating" it is especially valuable to chain stores where volumes vary dramatically. The new Bevinco report allows owners to assess the efficiency of one store to another regardless of their individual sales volume. This is a tool no multi-unit operator should be without.

QUESTIONS LEAD TO ANSWERS WHICH LEAD TO SUCCESS

- Do you order liquor using an order form designed for that purpose? Is it kept where others can refer to it to check-in orders as they arrive?
- Is ordering, receiving and issuing liquor inventory solely a management responsibility?
- Is there a perpetual inventory system in place to track the flow of inventory in and out of the liquor storeroom?
- Is there a *Depletion Allowance Form* behind the bar on which bartenders can record inventory that was wasted or spilled?
- Is there a *Depletion Allowance Form* behind the bar on which bartenders can record inventory that was given out in complimentary drinks?
- Is there a *Depletion Allowance Form* on which bartenders can record inventory that was requisitioned to the kitchen or another outlet?
- Are bartenders required to take a bar par reading before the opening shift and again at closing?
- Are bartenders required to record their breakage for a shift onto a bar requisition form?
- Do bartenders use a requisition form to record the transfer of inventory from one bar to another?
- How frequently do you conduct a physical audit of the liquor, beer and wine inventory? How did you determine the frequency between audits?
- Do you work from a form developed specifically for recording the results of a physical inventory audit?
- Do you allow hourly employees to assist in the physical inventory process?
- Is there a manager(s) solely responsible for conducting the physical inventory?
- What method do you use to determine how much product is left in a bottle?
- Is the time it takes to conduct a physical inventory of your operation growing into a hardship?

- Is the task of extending the inventory lengthy and riddled with errors?
- Does the process of conducting a physical inventory becoming more of an obstruction than opportunity?
- Do the managers currently responsible for auditing the inventory have a vested interested in how the cost percentage numbers turn out?
- Have you researched the feature/benefits of using the auditing services of Bevinco for your business?

Bevinco's Palm Pilot data
collection device improves
the efficiency and accuracy
of the stocktaking service.

Chapter 18

**Beverage Operation
Analysis**

A beverage operation is comprised of numerous components. Making sure that the operation is performing up to its fullest potential in terms of efficiency and profitability is not always clear. Yet, for a food and beverage operation, efficiency and profitability are essential. The analytical devices detailed in this section are designed to provide you with the information necessary to assess your operation's performance in several critical areas.

POUR COST ANALYSIS

Keeping a finger on your bar's financial pulse is best accomplished through analyzing your cost percentages, or what in jargon is referred to as pour cost. It accurately reflects the direct relationship between cost of goods and gross profit margin. Because liquor, beer, wine and non-alcoholic beverages sell at substantially different cost percentages each category must be calculated separately for the process to have significance; the method of figuring pour cost percentage is the same for all four types of products. Perhaps the single constant in the beverage business is that every operator would like to see their pour cost lower.

> **Pour cost accurately reflects the relationship between cost of goods and gross profit margin.**

Pour cost is figured by dividing the cost of depleted inventory (cost of goods sold) by the gross sales generated over a given period of time. A liquor pour cost of 18.3%, for example, means that it cost a little more than 18 cents to generate a dollar of liquor sales. It also means that the gross profit margin is 81.7%, or just under 82 cents per dollar of sales. Every percentage point it decreases, gross profit increases by the same amount.

How often you calculate the bar's pour cost is an important decision. There are establishments that take physical inventories and formulate pour cost daily. Others do so on a weekly, biweekly, or monthly basis. The shorter the amount of time between physical audits, the more insight you'll have into your business. The higher the operation's sales volume, the more frequently you should take physical audits. If a problem does exist, the sooner it is uncovered, the sooner it can be dealt with.

Knowing your bar's cost percentages, however, is only half of the information that you'll need to make informed decisions. The direction pour cost is heading is as important as the actual percentage itself. A pour cost of 18.3% could be cause for elation or alarm depending on its relationship to the bar's previous performance.

Large fluctuations in pour cost percentage signal trouble. A swing of one or two points in either direction should trip an alarm. Costs typically shouldn't vary more than a point between inventory periods. However, when pour cost increases, an attempt should be made to determine why.

Unless your bar has attained peak performance and efficiency, adopt the attitude that there's always room for improvement. Determine what your optimum pour costs should be. Use those as your target percentages and don't be content until you hit your mark. The result will be a more profitable operation.

Large fluctuations in pour cost percentage signal trouble.

Illustration 18.1 is an example of how to figure the cost percentage for liquor. In the example, the value of the bar's beginning liquor inventory is $9,814. (The previous month's ending inventory becomes the current month's beginning inventory.) During the course of the month the bar purchased $2,580 in liquor purchases. The adjusted beginning inventory equals the cost of the beginning inventory and the purchases. The sum of $12,394 represents the total cost of the liquor inventory over the course of the month.

An audit is conducted at the end of the month and the cost of the liquor inventory was determined to be $8,946. The cost of the month's spillage ($18), complimentary drinks ($136) and transfers ($46) are added to the ending liquor inventory to arrive at an adjusted inventory of $7,146. Spillage, complimentary drinks and transfers represent product that was depleted from inventory without a corresponding sale.

Subtracting the adjusted ending liquor inventory from the adjusted beginning liquor inventory will establish the cost of the liquor taken from the bar's inventory. In the example, the liquor cost of $5,248 is divided by the month's gross liquor sales of $31,720. The result is multiplied by 100 to convert it to a percentage. The liquor pour cost for the month is 16.5%.

Liquor, Beer & Wine Pour Cost Percentage

	Beginning Liquor Inventory	$ 9,814
Add:	Liquor Purchases	$ 2,580
	Adjusted Beginning Liquor Inventory	$ 12,394
	Ending Liquor Inventory	$ 6,946
Add:	Cost of Spillage	$ 18
Add:	Cost of Complimentary Drinks	$ 136
Add:	Cost of Transfers	$ 46
Subtract:	Adjusted Ending Liquor Inventory	$ 7,146
	Liquor Cost (Cost of Goods Sold)	$ 5,248
Divide by:	Gross Liquor Sales	$ 31,720
	Cost Percentage	16.5%

Illustration 18.1

While it's natural to want to see your bar's cost percentages as low as possible, there is a point where cost percentages are too low. In other words, a liquor pour cost in the low teens suggests that prices are too high, serving portions are too small, or both. In either case there's little value for the clientele.

Bars will operate with different pour costs.

Bars located in the same general vicinity, with the same concept and appealing to the same clientele will operate with different pour costs. There are, however, industry standards that can be used as a basis of comparison. These cost percentage targets are presented in illustration 18.2.

For the ranges in cost percentages presented in illustration 18.2 to have meaning, there are operational factors that should be taken into consideration.

1. The grade or relative quality of well liquor you choose will be the largest contributing factor to the range in cost percentages you will experience. Should you opt for pouring brands in the well, you may expect the well liquor to sell in the 7% - 10% range. On the other hand, if you select premium brands for the well, you can expect them to sell in the 10% - 15% range. Since all of the bar's prices are based on the well, the grade of the well liquor will greatly affect the bar's pour costs.

2. For both bottled and draft beer, there is a wide range in the quality of American, imported and microbrew beers, which explains the large swing in cost percentages. The cost percentages will be greatly affected by the bar's beer sales mix percentages, which is the relationship in sales between the various products. For example, if you sell far more low cost bottled beers than those that are more

Category	Cost Percentage Range
Liquor	
Well Liquor	9% - 10%
Call Liquor	12% - 14%
Premium Liquor	16% - 18%
Super-Premium	18% - 20%
Top-Shelf Liquor	20% - 24%
Overall Liquor Pour Cost	16% - 20%
Beer	
American Bottled Beer	17% - 33%
Imported Bottled Beer	20% - 37%
Microbrews Bottled	25% - 35%
Overall Bottled Beer Pour Cost	18% - 28%
American Draft Beer	10% - 20%
Imported Draft Beer	14% - 35%
Microbrews Draft	22% - 33%
Overall Draft Beer Pour Cost	16% - 28%
Wine	
House Wine By The Glass	12% - 18%
Varietals By The Glass	20% - 25%
Varietal Bottled Wine (750ml)	33% - 60%
Overall Wine Pour Cost	16% - 33%

Illustration 18.2

expensive, the bar's pour cost will be lower than if the reverse were true. The same holds true for draft beer.

The principal factors affecting the pour cost of wines by the glass are cost per ounce and portion size. Most operators look to obtain four to five glasses per 750ml bottle of varietal wine. This will yield wine cost percentages of between 20% - 25%.

TROUBLESHOOTING A RISING POUR COST

As pour cost increases, profit margins decrease. Rectifying the situation depends on finding the source(s) of the problem. The following eight items are factors that cause pour costs to rise. No one factor is more or less likely to occur, so it is best to overlook nothing and rely on the process of elimination.

Physical Inventory Inaccuracies — Errors in the physical inventory process will provide misleading results. Common mistakes include conducting inaccurate audits; products being overlooked and not included in the audit; arithmetic errors;

understating liquor inventory wholesale costs; and using inaccurate (understated) liquor sales figures. Any error that causes the ending inventory figure to be understated (making it appear as if more inventory was depleted than actually occurred) will make pour cost rise.

2 **Lagging Sales Prices** — Rising wholesale costs will steadily push pour cost upward. At some point rising costs will require raising drink prices.

3 **Poor Ordering and Receiving Procedures** — Poor ordering and receiving procedures can drive up pour cost; such as not carefully inspecting liquor shipments, or accepting products in the wrong quantity, wrong size package or at the wrong price.

4 **Promotional Discounting** — Promotions and special drink offers such as "two-for-ones" or serving doubles at regular prices during Happy Hour will effectively double the pour cost for each drink served during the promotion.

5 **Shift in Sales Mix Percentage** — A significant shift in your sales mix percentages can cause pour cost to increase. With few exceptions, premium and super-premium liquor sell at a much higher cost percentage than do well brands. Premium and super-premium liquors may sell at higher cost percentages, but they also generate higher profits.

As pour cost increases, profit margins decrease.

6 **Drink Portioning** — The staff may be over-portioning drinks, which negatively affects pour cost. Increasing the liquor portion in a drink from 1¼ ounce to 1¾ ounces raises its cost and alcoholic potency 40%.

7 **Unrecorded Spillage, Transfers & Complimentary Drinks** — Unrecorded spillage, transfers and complimentary drinks will make the beverage operation appear less efficient and profitable than it actually is. Each result in inventory being depleted without an offsetting sale, which if not accounted for will cause pour cost to increase.

8 **Employee Theft** — Internal theft, practices such as selling unrecorded drinks, undercharging for drinks and giving away free drinks will cause pour cost to increase dramatically.

When faced with a rising pour cost, which is the better approach to reverse the situation—look to lower costs or increase sales? In a perfect world, the answer would be both. In reality the most effective approach is to concentrate on getting a handle on costs before devoting efforts to boosting sales.

In Illustration 18.3 the bar's liquor cost is calculated to be 22.7%. To lower the pour cost one percent down to 21.7%, there are two options. The first is to reduce the liquor cost by $250. That will cause the pour cost to drop 1%. The second option is to increase liquor sales. To achieve the same one point reduction in pour cost, liquor sales would have to increase by $1,143.

	Beginning Liquor Inventory	$ 20,594	
Add:	Liquor Purchases	$ 5,897	
	Adjusted Beginning Liquor Inventory		$ 26,491
	Ending Liquor Inventory	$ 20,519	
Add:	Cost of spillage	$ 29	
Add:	Cost of complimentary drinks	$ 168	
Add:	Cost of Transfers	$ 52	
Subtract:	Adjusted Ending Liquor Inventory		$ 20,768
	Liquor Cost (Cost of Goods Sold)		$ 5,723
Divide by:	Gross Liquor Sales		$ 25,211
	Cost Percentage		22.7%

Illustration 18.3

To lower the above pour cost by one percentage point, liquor cost needs to be reduced by $250, or liquor sales have to increase by $1143.

Reducing Cost		**Increasing Sales**	
$250		$1143	
Liquor Cost	$ 5,473	Liquor Cost	$ 5,723
Gross Liquor Sales	$ 25,211	**Gross Liquor Sales**	$ 26,355
Cost Percentage	21.7%	Cost Percentage	21.7%

BEVERAGE OPERATION COST BREAKDOWN

Once the separate cost percentages have been figured, the information is compiled in a format similar to that in Illustration 18.4. Each beverage category combines to become a component of the whole. Using this type of table simplifies the process of calculating the operation's overall cost percentages and profit margins.

Food costs are the perishable and non-perishable goods and products that make up the cost of goods sold, e.g. straws, sip-sticks, napkins, juices, mixes, limes, lemons, olives, etc. Their combined cost can be estimated to be approximately 2% of gross sales.

Beverage Operation Cost Breakdown

Category	Month Cost	Month Percent	Month Sales	Sales Mix	Gross Profit	Gross Margin
Liquor	$ 5,248	16.5%	$31,720	43%	$26,472	83.5%
Beer	$ 5,026	28.3%	$17,761	24%	$12,735	71.3%
Wine	$ 4,552	36.3%	$12,540	17%	$ 7,988	63.7%
Non-alcoholic	$ 2,591	23.6%	$10,980	15%	$ 8,389	76.4%
Food	$ 1,460	2.0%				
Month Totals	$18,877	25.8%	$73,001		$54,124	74.2%

Illustration 18.4

BAR PRODUCTIVITY

Monitoring productivity is a highly reliable method of gauging the effectiveness of your employees. Bar Productivity is measured in terms of sales per hour and is calculated by dividing gross sales by the payroll hours it took to generate those sales.

Different shifts will experience significantly different sales volume.

Different shifts will experience significantly different sales volume. For instance, sales volume will typically be lower on a Monday night than it will on a Friday or Saturday night. Likewise, the sales generated during a day bartending shift will be lower than a night shift. It's advisable to calculate the day shift's average sales per hour separately from the night staff's average. Because there is often a considerable difference between the two figures, calculating the day shift's productivity separately from the night makes the process more significant.

For example, if the night bartenders rang-in $6,935 in sales for the week, and clocked-in a combined 83 payroll hours, the staff average for the night crew works out to $83.55 per hour. During the day, the bartending staff rang-in $2,250 is sales and worked 40.5 hours for a staff average of $55.55 per hour.

Calculating an individual bartender's productivity involves dividing the gross sales for the shift by the number of hours the person worked. The higher an employee's sales per hour in relation to the staff average, the more effective the person is behind the bar. Keep a journal or use a spreadsheet to track productivity figures for each shift on an on-going basis. After several weeks patterns will emerge. It will soon become clear who your sales leaders are, and who fall consistently short of the staff average.

In Illustration 18.5, there are two bartenders—Jim and Alan—who typically work on Thursday night. On February 7th, Jim worked 6½ hours and rang-in sales of $876.35, or $134 is sales per hour. Working at the same bar on the same night, Alan registered sales of $966.50 over six hours, which translates to $161 per hour. After seven weeks, Jim bartended 7 shifts at an average productivity of $123 per hour, Alan worked five shifts at an average productivity of $152 per hour, and Neil covered two shifts with an average productivity of $153 per hour.

The staff average is the benchmark by which other productivity figures are measured. The staff average is calculated by dividing the weekly bar sales by combined bar payroll for the week. In the example provided in illustration 18.5, the bartending staff worked a combined 87.25 payroll hours over the 14 night shifts. They generated gross sales of $12,675 for the week, for a staff average of $144 per hour.

Keep a journal to track productivity for each shift on an on-going basis.

Bar Productivity

Date	Name	Day/Shift	Sales	Hrs	Sales/hr
2/07	Jim	Thurs/PM	$ 876.35	6.5	$134/hr
	Alan	Thurs/PM	$ 966.50	6.0	$161/hr
2/14	Jim	Thurs/PM	$ 799.10	6.5	$123/hr
	Alan	Thurs/PM	$ 867.38	6.0	$145/hr
2/21	Jim	Thurs/PM	$ 781.33	6.5	$120/hr
	Alan	Thurs/PM	$ 903.71	6.0	$151/hr
2/28	Jim	Thurs/PM	$ 691.85	6.5	$106/hr
	Neil	Thurs/PM	$ 875.00	6.0	$146/hr
3/07	Jim	Thurs/PM	$ 745.95	6.5	$115/hr
	Alan	Thurs/PM	$ 905.00	6.0	$151/hr
3/14	Jim	Thurs/PM	$ 809.88	6.5	$125/hr
	Alan	Thurs/PM	$ 898.90	6.0	$150/hr
3/21	Jim	Thurs/PM	$ 891.95	6.5	$137/hr
	Neil	Thurs/PM	$ 955.50	6.0	$159/hr

Average Productivity

Jim — 7 shifts at $123/hr

Alan — 5 shifts at $152/hr

Neil — 2 shifts at $153/hr

Weekly Staff Average — 14 PM shifts at $144/hr

Illustration 18.5

ANALYZING PRODUCTIVITY

If a bartender's sales per hour figures fall consistently below the staff average, five things are possible. One, the bartender may move too slowly and literally can't keep up with demand. Two, the individual could make sub-standard drinks, so guests are less inclined to stay for a second or third round. The third explanation for continued low productivity is the bartender's personality and attitude could be so off-putting that guests are more likely to leave early. The fourth explanation is the person's sales ability could be so unrefined that he or she consistently undersells. The fifth and final explanation for continued low productivity is theft. The bartender could be skimming away the sales proceeds, which would account for the low sales per hour.

How do you know which of the explanations are at the heart of the problem? Take some time and observe the person. Does the bartender move quickly and with purpose? Or is he more laid back and sluggish? If the person can't keep up behind the bar, then you've identified an area in which he needs to improve.

If that's not a problem, does it appear as if the bartender has the necessary skills for the job? Do his or her drinks look like they are being prepared up to your operation's standards? Are the bartender's drinks frequently returned? Does the bartender have a good personality for the job? Does it seem as if he or she has a positive working attitude? Does the bartender exhibit good sales ability?

If none of these things seem to be a problem, the final explanation is that the employee may be stealing.

If a bartender's sales per hour figures fall consistently below the staff average, five things are possible.

BAR PRODUCTIVITY AS AN ANTI-THEFT DEVICE

Regardless of the scam, theft takes a toll on productivity. Between pour cost and bar productivity, there isn't a scam or fraud that you can't catch.

Monitoring pour cost has long been the accepted way of analyzing the profitability of a beverage operation. It is, however, not nearly as effective at detecting bartender theft as tracking bar productivity. Most of the illicit practices used to steal cash and product from the bar won't have the slightest affect on pour cost. In fact, a clever thief can steal from your bar and actually make your pour cost percentage drop.

Pour cost analyzes the relationship between cost and sales. It does it by analyzing the change in inventory levels, which are based on liquid measurements. If a bartender serves a drink and pockets the cash proceeds, he or she is essentially depleting inventory without a corresponding sale, which will cause pour cost to rise. If the bartender then replaces the stolen ounce of liquor with an equal volume of water, pour cost will remain unaffected.

Substitutions are a type of theft that won't cause pour cost to increase. The scam involves a bartender making drinks with well liquor instead of the requested call brands. The guests are served the drinks and charged call prices. The bartender registers the sales at the well price and pockets the difference. Since the bartender poured well liquor and entered the transaction as a well sale, pour cost remains unaffected. The business, unfortunately, is out the stolen sales proceeds and the clientele have been treated fraudulently.

Pour cost analyzes the relationship between cost and sales.

Productivity will also detect short pouring scams. The intent behind short pouring is to create a surplus of inventory that the bartender can sell, pocket the cash proceeds and leave pour cost unaffected. For example, if a bartender pours one ounce instead of the specified 1¼ oz. portion in four drinks, he or she will have created a surplus ounce of liquor that can in turn be sold. The bartender could pocket the cash proceeds and pour cost would remain unaffected (5 ounces of well liquor depleted and 4 well drinks sold with the fifth sale stolen). Conversely, bar productivity would be adversely affected in as much as five drinks were served yet only four were rung into the cash register.

With all types of theft behind the bar, one thing is certain, the cash proceeds eventually wind up in the bartenders' pockets or tip jar, and not in the register. Regardless of the scam involved, bar productivity will always be negatively affected by theft, making it an invaluable management tool.

LABOR COST PERCENTAGE

After cost of goods sold, your single largest operating expense will be payroll and payroll taxes. Reducing payroll, therefore, is a major concern. Start by considering how effectively you use the bar staff. One chronic problem is understaffing, not scheduling enough people to handle busy shifts. Aside from subjecting employees to undue stress, running with a skeleton crew when it's busy will undoubtedly cost you sales, cost the bartenders gratuities, and cost the clientele the level of service they expect. Understaffing is expensive, exceeding any savings in payroll.

For shifts too busy to be handled effectively by just one bartender, but not busy enough to warrant two, consider scheduling a bar back. While the bar back gains valuable, practical experience, it affords the bartender another set of helping hands while getting to keep a larger percentage of the gratuities. You reap the benefits of an in-house training system and since bar backs are typically paid less than bartenders, labor costs will be lower.

One source of concern are employees "riding the clock," meaning that they purposely take longer to break down the bar and perform their closing duties, thereby increasing their payroll. It's advisable to supervise their duties to make sure that they are working expediently.

Labor cost percentage measures the relationship between payroll expense and gross sales. It is a means of determining how effectively your payroll dollars are being invested. To determine a shift's labor cost percentage, the payroll for the employees working the shift must first be totaled. The process requires extending the number of hours each employee worked by his or her base salary. The total payroll is then divided by the shift's gross sales and multiplied by 100 to convert the figure into a percentage. It is advisable to compare the number of hours your employees actually "clocked-in" with the number of hours they were scheduled. This process will improve your ability to forecast scheduling requirements and afford you an opportunity to investigate any inconsistencies.

One source of concern are employees "riding the clock."

What should your labor cost percentage be? While there are no industry standards, a labor cost of 6.5% may be relied upon as an initial target figure. The larger the establishment, the more employees that must be scheduled to cover the bar and the floor, and therefore the higher the labor cost percentage. Smaller operations require fewer employees per shift and typically have lower labor costs percentages.

An increasing labor cost percentage indicates that your payroll dollars are being invested less efficiently. Probable explanations include over-staffing and employees being allowed to stay "on-the-clock" longer than necessary. Conversely, a labor cost percentage well below 6.5% may suggest that there are too few employees being staffed to provide your clientele with adequate service. A stable labor cost percentage is an indication of a well-managed operation.

Illustration 18.6 is an example of how to calculate labor cost percentage.

Bartenders		Servers	
Carol	6.0 hrs. x $5.50/hr = $33.00	Hannah	4.0 hrs. x $4.00/hr = $16.00
Ron	4.5 hrs. x $4.50/hr = $20.25	Edie	4.5 hrs. x $4.00/hr = $18.00
Claude	5.0 hrs. x $5.50/hr = $27.50	Sarah	5.0 hrs. x $4.00/hr = $20.00
		Kelly	5.0 hrs. x $4.00/hr = $20.00
Total Bartending Payroll	$80.75	Total Servers Payroll	$74.00
	Total Shift Payroll	$154.75	
	Divide by: Gross Sales	$2,309.34	
	Labor Cost Percentage	6.7%	

Illustration 18.6

LIQUOR REQUISITION TRACKING

A product's usage rate can be accurately estimated by tracking how often that item is issued to the bar. Bar requisitions closely correspond to an item's actual usage. Tracking inventory requisitions is essential in analyzing what products are turning over and which are collecting dust. It will make ordering liquor a more precise process, resulting in fewer product outages. It will reveal any sudden surges in usage and allow you to investigate whether there is a legitimate reason behind the increase. Requisition tracking is also necessary in computing the operation's liquor sales mix percentages.

All of the data necessary to track each product's usage can be found in the perpetual inventory system. The number of bottles of each product issued to the bar is divided by the month's total requisitions to arrive at the product's usage percentage.

Illustration 18.7 is an example (partial) of how to track liquor requisitions.

SALES MIX PERCENTAGES

There are several different sale mix percentages that are important to monitor. The first involves determining the sales relationship between the major price categories of liquor. Since well, call, premium and

Liquor Requisition Tracking

Item	Size	January Requisitions Qty/%	February Requisitions Qty/%	March Requisitions Qty/%	April Requisitions Qty/%
WELL: Smirnoff	lt	54/22%	59/22%	50/20%	61/22%
Absolut	lt	9/ 4%	10/ 4%	9/ 4%	11/ 4%
Ketel One	lt	2/ 1%	3/ 1%	2/ 1%	1/ 1%
Stolichnaya	lt	12/ 5%	15/ 6%	15/ 6%	16/ 6%
Stoli Cristall	lt	3/ 1%	3/ 1%	2/ 1%	3/ 1%
Stoli Limonnaya	lt	5/ 2%	5/ 2%	4/ 2%	5/ 2%
WELL: Booth's	lt	18/ 7%	17/ 6%	13/ 5%	15/ 5%
Beefeater	lt	8/ 3%	9/ 3%	8/ 3%	7/ 3%
Bombay	lt	2/ 1%	2/ 1%	3/ 2%	2/ 1%
Bom/Sapphire	lt	2/ 1%	3/ 1%	2/ 1%	2/ 1%
Tanqueray	lt	6/ 2%	8/ 3%	9/ 4%	12/ 4%
WELL: Jim Beam	lt	20/ 8%	26/10%	27/11%	24/ 9%
Booker Noe	lt	3/ 1%	4/ 2%	3/ 2%	3/ 1%
Gentleman Jack	lt	2/ 1%	2/ 1%	1/ 1%	1/ 1%
Jack Daniels	lt	11/ 5%	12/ 5%	12/ 5%	14/ 5%
Maker's Mark	lt	4/ 2%	5/ 2%	5/ 2%	4/ 1%
Seagram's Seven	lt	6/ 2%	8/ 3%	8/ 3%	7/ 3%
Wild Turkey 80	lt	3/ 1%	3/ 1%	4/ 2%	4/ 1%
Wild Turkey 101	lt	2/ 1%	2/ 1%	3/ 2%	2/ 1%
Month Totals		245/100%	266/100%	254/100%	278/100%

Illustration 18.7

super-premium liquor sell at different cost percentages, the sales mix between these major price categories will have a significant impact on your operation's liquor cost percentages.

For example, if the sales of premium and super-premium liquor increase in relation to the well liquors, your operation's liquor cost percentage will likely increase. Conversely, if the sales of well liquor increases relative to the more expensive call brands, your operation's cost percentage will likely decrease.

The information necessary to calculate sales mix percentage can be found on the liquor requisition tracking form. Total all of the requisitions for each liquor category, e.g. well, call, premium, etc. The total for each category is then divided by the total amount of all liquor requisitioned and multiplied by 100 to convert the sales mix into a percentage. It is advisable to also track the total number of requisitions per inventory period. The higher the volume, the more significant any increase or decrease in sales becomes.

Illustration 18.8 is an example of a sales mix percentage tracking form.

Sales Mix Tracking Percentage

	January Requisitions	February Requisitions	March Requisitions	April Requisitions
	245 liters total	266 liters total	254 liters total	278 liters total
Well	132/ 54%	136/ 51%	142/ 56%	150/ 54%
Call	56/ 23%	69/ 26%	56/ 22%	69/ 25%
Premium	37/ 15%	32/ 12%	33/ 13%	42/ 15%
Super-Premium	20/ 8%	29/ 11%	23/ 9%	17/ 6%
Month Totals	245/100%	266/100%	254/100%	278/100%

Illustration 18.8

There are several different sale mix percentages that are important to monitor.

The sales mix between liquor, beer, wine and NABs is another important operational gauge. The sales mix percentage for the major categories of beverages will greatly simplify your marketing efforts by revealing what type of products are in highest demand. To calculate this sales mix percentage, divide the sales for each category by the operation's gross sales and multiply by 100 to convert the sales mix into a percentage.

Illustration 18.9 is an example of a beverage sales mix tracking form.

Beverage Sales Mix Tracking

	January Sales Mix	February Sales Mix	March Sales Mix
Liquor Sales	$34,128/ 48%	$40,248/ 52%	$39,909/ 53%
Beer Sales	$16,353/ 23%	$20,124/ 26%	$18,072/ 24%
Wine Sales	$10,665/ 15%	$ 7,740/ 10%	$ 9,789/ 13%
Non-Alcoholic Sales	$ 9,954/ 14%	$ 9,288/ 12%	$ 7,530/ 10%
Month Totals	$71,100/100%	$77,400/100%	$75,300/100%

Illustration 18.9

Eating establishments often identify the essential components of their business as a ratio between gross food sales and gross beverage sales. A sales mix ratio of 60:40 food-to-beverage means that 60% of the operation's gross sales is food and 40% beverage. This simple ratio goes a long way to characterize a business. For example a business whose sales are 60:40 food-to-beverage is a substantially different type of an establishment whose sales mix is 20:80 food-to-beverage.

POTENTIALIZING GROSS SALES

Potentializing is a method used to estimate potential gross liquor sales. It involves placing a sales value on every bottle of liquor depleted during the course of an inventory period. Totaling the sales values for the period's requisitions should closely correspond to the operations actual gross sales.

To establish the potential sales value for a particular product begin by estimating how many serving portions there are per bottle. For example, per liter of well gin, you may estimate that that there are eighteen 1-ounce portions and ten 1½-ounce portions. The sales price for the one-ounce portion is $3.00 and the sales for a 1½-ounce portion is $3.50. The potential sales value of a liter of well gin is estimated at $89.

Potentializing is a method used to estimate potential gross liquor sales.

18 drinks (18 oz.) @ 1.0 oz. X $3.00	=	$ 54.00 potential gross sales
10 drinks (15 oz.) @ 1.5 oz. X $3.50	=	$ 35.00 potential gross sales
33 oz.		$ 89.00 potential gross sales

If ten bottles of well gin were depleted for the inventory period, $890 in gross sales should have been generated. Every bottle of liquor requisitioned during the inventory period is extended by its potential sales value and totaled to arrive at the potential gross sales of the operation's requisitioned inventory. The potential sales figure serves as a basis for comparison for the actual gross liquor sales realized for the same period of time.

The weakness of potentializing sales is that it is based on assumptions rather than hard, factual data. In reality the assumptions you made as to the number of serving portions per product may not correspond to reality. The accuracy of your estimates will greatly affect the viability of the potential gross sales figure.

ABC AUDIT METHOD

Many of the state Alcoholic Beverage Commissions use a simple and straight-forward technique for auditing beverage operations to figure average cost per portion and average drink sales price. These formulas present another means of projecting your cost percentages between physical inventories.

The first step is to calculate the average purchase cost per ounce by totaling the number of ounces purchased during the week. Using either the wholesaler's invoices or your purchase orders, determine the number of liters and 750mls you purchased. Multiply the number of liters by 33.8 ounces and the number of 750mls by 25.4 ounces. Add the figures together and divide the sum into the dollar total of the week's purchases. The result is the cost of the average ounce of liquor purchased, which is used to represent the average cost per ounce of liquor poured behind the bar. If your standard portion size is 1¼ ounces, multiply the average cost figure by 1.25 to arrive at your average portion cost.

By reviewing your POS sales reports, register tapes or drink tickets, estimate as accurately as possible the number of drinks sold for the week. Divide that figure into the week's gross liquor sales to determine the average drink sales price. By dividing the average portion cost by the average drink sales price you will obtain your projected pour cost percentage.

For example, after reviewing your purchase orders for the week, you determine that you bought six cases (72) of liters and fourteen 750ml bottles. Extending the figures, you arrive at a total of 2,789.2 ounces purchased. Dividing the combined cost of the liquor purchases, $1,296.39, by the number of ounces purchased you arrive at an average purchase cost per ounce of $.46. With a standard pour of 1.25 ounces your average portion cost is $.57 per ounce ($.46/oz. x 1.25).

You determine that during the week the bar sold 955 drinks for gross sales of $3,476.76. Dividing the gross sales by the number of drinks, you arrive at an average drink sales price of $3.64. By dividing the average portion cost ($.57) by the average drink sales price of $3.64, you get a projected pour cost of 15.7%.

QUESTIONS LEAD TO ANSWERS WHICH LEAD TO SUCCESS

- How frequently do you calculate the bar's cost percentages?
- Do you calculate the liquor, beer and wine cost percentages separately?
- Do you track your bar productivity on an on-going basis?
- When calculating bar productivity, do you track the staff average sales per hour, each bartender's sales per hour, and productivity per day of the week (e.g. Monday day, Friday night, etc.)?
- Are payroll and payroll taxes your largest operating expenses?
- Do you calculate what percentage of your daily revenue was earmarked for payroll?
- Do you track your labor cost percentage on an ongoing basis?
- Do you use labor cost to gauge how effectively management is investing payroll dollars?
- Do you track and analyze bar requisitions?
- Do you calculate your sales mix percentages for the various liquor price categories?
- Do you calculate your beverage operation's sales mix percentages for the various types of beverages?

Chapter 19

Point of Sale Systems
by Steve Goumas

Successfully managing a food and beverage operation requires accurate point of sale (POS) information, data that affects literally every decision you make regarding your operation. POS information will answer such crucial questions as: What products are selling? What prices are being charged for goods sold? Which employees are selling those products and when are those sales occurring?

Historically, two types of sales-capture and cash control devices have been available for the hospitality industry — computerized point of sale systems (POS) and electronic cash registers (ECR). Until recently, with the advent of computer component miniaturization, and cost reduction, computerized systems were too costly for most small, independent food and beverage operations. These computerized systems were cost-justified investments for only larger restaurants, chains and hotels.

Cash registers with manual guest checks and ordering systems have been the mainstream for smaller, independent operations. But manual ECRs do not provide the types of detailed information required to effectively compete in today's competitive marketplace. Neither do they provide management reporting on labor productivity or deter employee theft. With the availability of more affordable, easier to use systems, many operations are now considering and turning to computerized point of sale systems.

> **Successfully managing a food and beverage operation requires accurate point of sale (POS) information.**

CHOOSING A POINT OF SALE SYSTEM

Since the introduction of Microsoft Windows and open-architecture P.C. computer systems, there is a greater variety of hospitality-related offerings and more new ideas on how to utilize them than ever before. Innovations in software development and programming have allowed many restaurateurs to develop software cost-effectively, and some have become POS vendors. Windows-based systems have dominated the market and are highly functional systems. Windows has simplified the integration of POS with other office automation tools such as Microsoft Office which you may already be using. The market is full of modern attractive choices. How do you narrow the field?

The first decision most food and beverage operators face is whether or not to go with an open-architecture/(PC) Windows based system. Some of the benefits include ease of training, ease of data transfer to other programs and integration with office automation products (usually Microsoft Office). However, like many powerful tools, the benefits are only fully realized when a commitment is made to learn how to use them.

Windows systems generally require more processing power, memory and support. Though these systems have become well accepted and currently dominate the marketplace in food and beverage POS systems, there are some downsides.

Windows is a less stable platform for food and beverage POS systems and has a higher frequency of failure than proprietary or closed architecture systems such as Unix or DOS. There are several reasons for this. Microsoft Windows was originally designed for office automation, not the harsh restaurant retail environment. If a network fails in an office it is an inconvenience meaning a laser printer or a second terminal is not operating. A failed network in a restaurant can be disastrous. A failed kitchen printer, or a server's terminal, on a Friday evening creates a far greater impact than failed office equipment.

The majority of system failures in restaurants utilizing Windows-based systems are due to electrical power fluctuations, which are unavoidable in a restaurant environment. Therefore, the additional expense for the best possible battery back up and power conditioning equipment is necessary for a Windows-based system and this is a requirement for every single component, including all terminals and each kitchen printer.

The second critical factor that impacts the stability of PC-based systems is the hardware components themselves that make up the computer. Off the shelf PC hardware (open architecture systems) have a higher failure rate than proprietary or custom-configured systems. The failure of a $50 hub or a $100 port card can bring down an entire $30,000 POS system. In addition, the probability of the vendor that sells inexpensive parts having trained professionals available to service failed parts decreases with the price/quality of the part.

> **Like many powerful tools, the benefits are only fully realized when a commitment is made to learn how to use them.**

Therefore, price should not be the major driving force in your purchase decision criteria. System stability and the vendor's ability to implement, maintain and support the system should be high priorities. The issues with power and inexpensive/unreliable components are virtually non-existent in the older proprietary systems. Vendors often built or specified internal parts to withstand the hard restaurant/bar environment.

HOW TO PURCHASE A POINT OF SALE SYSTEM

One of the largest pitfalls in the software selection process is the false belief that all restaurant software is alike and will function well in all types of operations. Fast food, full service, fine dining, clubs, cafeterias, hotels, and catering operations all have different system needs and requirements.

An established restaurant installed a PC-computer-based system including P.O.S., inventory management and recipe costing. It required eight months and additional part-time clerical staff to collect and input all the recipes and other data the system required. Now management is inundated with so much detailed data that they can't separate major food cost problem areas. They inadvertently purchased software designed for a limited menu, fast-food operation. It was not a good fit for a fine dining operation with an extensive menu.

Budget a reasonable amount of time — three to four months—for the selection process.

To avoid selecting unsuitable computer software and/or a P.O.S. system, budget a reasonable amount of time — three to four months — for the selection process. Many first-time computer users emphasize price as the major purchase criterion. This is a mistake because price should not be the first concern. System reliability along with the system's key features and functions should be. The system must meet your specific operational and reporting requirements. This is especially true with back office applications. The vendor's ability to deliver, implement, and provide ongoing system support is of tremendous importance. Adequate planning, knowing what your specific needs are and being able to communicate the information are essential.

REACHING YOUR OBJECTIVES

Plan before you purchase a computer-based P.O.S. system. Define your objectives and system needs. If necessary, hire an expert to assist in determining your hardware and software requirements. To avoid selecting an unsuitable system, focus on software requirements, system stability, and the vendor's ability to deliver, implement and provide system support. The cost-benefit considerations should include the initial purchase price plus the many hidden and recurring costs.

1. **Plan** — Study your operation and determine what style of restaurant you operate. Also who will be using the system and which applications are to be automated. Determine equipment placement location, space requirements, electrical and data cabling requirements. Analyze your past and future growth.

2. **Define Your Requirements** — Considerations include various sizes of computer equipment, single or multiple terminals, number of printers, number of cash drawers, data back-up requirements, power requirements and line conditioning. Concentrate much of your efforts on software requirements. Make note of the various menus, promotions, pricing levels and happy hours. Note how and when you count and cost inventory. Also how you calculate cost of goods. How many bartenders work per shift at peak time? Evaluate your current reporting requirements; gather copies of all the reports and list everyone who uses the reports or the information produced.

3. **Prepare a Request for Proposal (RFP)** — An RFP is a listing of your requirements and specifications written in an organized format. When listing your requirements leave room for written responses. The RFP can be provided to prospective system vendors, who should document their responses. The RFP should become part of the purchase contract. It can be used as a legal document to provide additional protection if a dispute over system capabilities arises at a later date.

4. **Conduct System Demonstrations** — Contact vendors based on your analysis of the RFP responses. Follow-up each RFP response with vendor meetings and system demonstrations. Ask specific

questions and take careful notes. Salespeople are trained to de-emphasize system shortcomings. It is important to identify and decide how to deal with any missing system functions. Address installation, training, and ongoing support requirements.

5 Check References — The point-of-sale system you purchase will impact your operation for many years. When shopping for technology software solutions you are going to be dependent on the salesperson's accurate, detailed and specific answers about the product's capability. The salesperson might be the only vendor contact you meet during the decision making process. There is just enough truth in a stereotype of the fast talking, self-serving salesperson to make any food service technology buyer hesitant. And with your entire operation revolving around getting the right point of sale system, the stakes can be very high in the decision process.

Even with vendor references checked, the credibility of the salesperson should never be taken for granted. Ask for and study the software manuals, seek referrals, and check references. Personally visit a local reference with a similar operation and system configuration that is proposed to you. Talk to the bartenders, servers and lastly, the manager. In addition, using an RFP outline to collect the proper system information should greatly minimize your risks. Going through this process will force the salesperson to deal with issues that his/her prospects rarely ever ask. Stay organized and you'll minimize your risks and protect yourself.

6 Negotiate a Contract — Many contracts are written to protect the vendor from any recourse should the system fail. A professional data processing or management information service consultant can help negotiate on your behalf. Areas to consider include maintenance and support requirements, the implementation schedule, testing, and system acceptance.

7 Implement the System — Identify vendor's areas of responsibility as well as your own. Areas of concern should include pre-installation planning, electrical requirements, cabling, developing new procedures and controls, back-up and recovery, and system testing. Staff and management training is critical. Determine what on-site training services the vendor will provide.

8. Arrange for Support — After the system is installed and operational, ongoing system support will be necessary. Most vendors initially include software support and hardware maintenance, but some do not. Those who do will provide software support for a specified amount of time. Obtain assurances in writing as part of your purchase contract that the vendors will continue to support the software and provide on-site hardware maintenance at reasonable rates.

Implementing an automated point of sale system presents food and beverage operators with benefits that include:

1. Increased Accuracy of Guest Checks and Cash Handling — With a point of sale system, servers are required to place more accurate orders to the bar and kitchen.

2. Security of Guest Checks and Cash Handling — These systems eliminate the possibility of lost guest checks, and each server's cash and credit card sales are tracked.

3. Speed of Service — Remote kitchen and bar printers allow servers to remain longer on the floor serving your guests. This will improve guest satisfaction, productivity, and table turnover.

4. Less Confusion in the Kitchen — P.O.S. reduces the frequency of incorrect items being ordered in the kitchen and at the bar.

5. Improved Price Control — Discounts, happy hour prices, employee meals, and promotions are handled automatically.

6. Theft Reduction — Servers and bartenders must enter sales for all items ordered. Guest check tracking and pricing is automated.

7. Increased Server Friendly Information — These systems present management with critical operational reports in an easy-to-review format.

THE TEN COMMANDMENTS
OF SYSTEM SELECTION

1 Know the vendor and the dealer's reputation — (hardware, software and support). Check for complaints against the service or support department, vendor commitment to products and customers, financial stability, and references.

2 Know the vendor's experience — It is important to verify the experience of the vendor's installers, trainers and salesperson specifically regarding your type of operation.

3 Know the required system's features and needs — What are the owner's and management's objectives? Is there adequate hardware, software, interfacing, training and support requirements?

4 Know the true costs — The hardware and software price, the ongoing costs, such as hardware maintenance, software support, supplies, personnel training,cabling, data communications and electrical requirement costs are all part of the budget.

5 Examine the vendor's proposal — Make sure the proposal addresses your specific system requirements, business needs and goals.

6 Test the system, if possible — Check references, visit another restaurant or bar with the same hardware and software configuration. Preview manuals.

7 Know the system's performance and reliability — Know the speed and response time of the system during peak volume, and the system's track record including upgrades, component reliability and performance.

8 Know the installation and training plan — Purchase agreements should list installation services. Be aware of database design and data entry costs.

9 Negotiate all terms in the contract — Including acceptance and testing criteria. Retain a portion of the final payment until the system is fully functional.

10 Demand ongoing support for hardware and software — Negotiate 7 day, 8am - 2am availability for hardware, on-site maintenance with a 15-minute response time. You should also receive routine software upgrades.

Proposal Cost Summary Schedule

VENDOR: _____

	TOTAL PURCHASE PRICE	ANNUAL MAINTENANCE	ANNUAL SUPPORT	ANNUAL TOTAL
HARDWARE				
SOFTWARE				
TRAINING/INSTALLATION				
SUB-TOTAL				
OTHER CHARGES (SUPPLIES)				
DISCOUNT				
SUB-TOTAL				
TOTAL COSTS				

OTHER ONE-TIME COSTS	COMMENTS:
PRE-INSTALLATION ELECTRICAL/CABLE	
DELIVERY/INSTALLATION	
MISCELLANEOUS	
GRAND TOTAL	

Use a form to keep track of all expense information
from each vendor.

Illustration 19.1

Section Four
Managing
Human Resources

Chapter 20

Hiring Exceptional Employees

A food and beverage operation is an employee-dependent business, entirely dependent on its hourly employees to provide hospitable service to the clientele, market the product, portion the inventory, and handle all of the sales proceeds. Considering the liquid nature of the bar's inventory, it is essential that you make sure your service staff is competent, honest, and have rock-solid attitudes.

There are those who still believe that hiring bartenders is simply a matter of placing a classified ad, opening the front door and making sure you have plenty of sharpened pencils handy. In today's job market that is highly unlikely.

For lack of better terms, the job market in the last five years has gone from a seller's market to a buyer's market. The healthy American economy and a rapidly expanding hospitality industry has created many new bartending jobs. This surplus of opportunities has changed how bartenders view their jobs. Where once there were many applicants for every bar position, now there are numerous openings to choose from. From the operator's perspective, the shoe is now on the other foot.

It is essential that you make sure your service staff is competent and honest.

This reversal of fortune is forcing operators to reevaluate their recruiting, selection and hiring practices. Regardless of the tight employment conditions, it is fundamentally important to consider this a selection rather than a hiring process. The hiring process suggests you're looking for people to fill slots on the staff. The selection process places the emphasis on determining the most qualified and best-suited individuals for the position. The distinction between the two is crucial.

This chapter details how to recruit, interview, and hire employees. It requires intuition, organization, and perseverance to assemble a professional staff. Also, be mindful that there are state and federal regulations governing hiring practices. It is best to have all employee documentation and hiring practices reviewed by your attorney.

RECRUITING QUALIFIED APPLICANTS

There are a number of different methods used to attract qualified job applicants. One frequently relied on method is to place an in the classified section of the local newspaper. Placing a "help wanted" advertisement is legally considered recruitment. There are laws that govern what can and cannot be stated in the copy of the ad. The principle concern when composing an ad is to avoid writing something that could violate federal discrimination laws. It is crucial to only state in the advertisement that you are seeking bona fide occupational qualifications.

The following are points to keep in mind when composing a "help wanted" advertisement.

- Do not state a gender preference. It could be viewed as sexually discriminatory. Do not use language that excludes one of the genders from applying. Use words such as waiter/waitress, server, or host/hostess. The word bartender is applied equally to members of either sex. However, you could use the phrase: male or female bartender.

There are a number of different methods used to attract qualified job applicants.

- Stating an age preference in an ad is discriminatory. You can, however, require applicants for a bartending position to be over the legal drinking age.
- Making the statement in print that an applicant would be required to work Saturdays or Sundays could be grounds for religious discrimination. Likewise, requiring a high school diploma in an ad for a bartender is potential grounds for a charge of discrimination.

There are potential downsides to placing ads in the newspaper, namely that they are often not cost-effective and tend to attract a group of applicants with varying degrees of experience and qualifications. Then you're left with the challenge of screening a large number of people.

One effective method of recruiting is asking for personal references from bartenders on your staff whose opinion you trust. They tend to recommend and personally vouch for people similar to themselves. Ask your bartenders if they know a bartender who is as professional as they are and who would like to work for the company. In most instances their recommendations will yield excellent results. Consider offering a finder's fee to your employees if they recommend an individual and the person is hired and stays on the job past the 90-day probationary period.

There will be about 10% of your staff that won't be contributing their fair share, so always be on the lookout for talented bartenders and servers. Shopping the competition's bartending staffs is another way to recruit bartenders. You have an opportunity to see them in action, serving a comparable clientele in a similar setting. It provides an ideal opportunity to assess their abilities, something akin to an audition.

You never know when the ideal bartending applicant is going to walk through your door. It is therefore important to maintain an active job application file. More often than not, the people who walk into your establishment seeking a bartending job have frequented your club and know the clientele. You know they're motivated to work for you, which makes them people you want to talk to. Interviewing job applicants on a regular basis also helps managers keep their interviewing skills sharp.

EFFECTIVE SCREENING PROCEDURES

Putting together a qualified bartending staff requires time and a good deal of effort. Bartenders are key employees. Selecting the right person for the job on the first pass requires preparation and the ability to learn a lot about a person in a very short period of time.

Putting together a qualified bartending staff requires time and a good deal of effort.

The costs of hiring the wrong bartender can be staggering. It's better to operate short-handed for a period of time and rely on the existing staff to cover the bar than hiring someone unqualified or inappropriate for the establishment. It will be more advantageous in the long run to delay hiring another bartender until the right candidate can be found.

Generic job applications, the type that can be purchased at an office supply store, ask for such general information as to be practically worthless as a screening device. It is better to create your own in-house employment application, one specifically designed for servers of alcohol. Besides asking for basic information, previous work experience and personal references, the application should inquire whether the person has ever been cited for an alcohol-related violation, such as serving a minor or intoxicated person. Applicants should also be asked if they have been certified in an alcohol-awareness program.

Instead of asking applicants what office equipment they can operate or what outside activities they enjoy, the application could ask specific job related questions, such as what are acceptable pieces of identification or the minimum drinking age. Another option is to include short answer questions, for instance what qualities does the applicant possess that qualifies him or her for the position.

It is important to avoid including questions on the job application that could be considered an invasion of an applicant's privacy or discriminatory in some respect. Ask only questions that are directly job-related.

In addition, the job application should contain several key clauses and conditions, one of which is that any misrepresentations made on the application will be considered grounds for immediate dismissal. There should be a provision authorizing the employer to investigate the statements on the application. The application should state that the business is an equal opportunity employer. There should also be the statement that if the individual is hired, the employment would be considered an "at-will" relationship, meaning the employment would be for an indefinite period of time, that either party may terminate the relationship with or without cause, without previous notice and without liability.

Ask only questions that are directly job-related.

It is advisable to have an attorney review the job application prior to use for any liability-incurring statements. All applications submitted should be kept for up to one year. An applicant has 180 days to file a complaint against a prospective employer.

Not everyone who walks through your door looking for employment is suitable to hire. Committing an hour of a manager's time interviewing every job applicant is an unnecessary investment. Thus the need for screening techniques. Screening is intended to save time and effort by eliminating unacceptable and unqualified applicants early in the process.

The appearance of a person's application often reveals as much about his or her level of professionalism and attention to detail as does the written information it contains. It's neatness, completeness, and presentation reflects much about the author. Make note of how the document looks and any impression it might give you about the person.

When you're handed a completed application, ask the individual a few screening questions, such as how many hours a week he or she needs to work, and how much money the person needs to earn a week. Also, find out if the applicant has reliable transportation, and if there are any scheduling conflicts you should be aware of. A few, initial probing questions can often save you from making a poor hiring decision later on.

SUCCESSFUL INTERVIEWING TECHNIQUES

It is important to have a clear vision of the qualities and attributes you're looking for in a bartender, if not, you're likely to end up disappointed. For example, one important aspect is to gauge an applicant's level of stability. While there are exceptions, the more stabilizing factors present in someone's life—things such as being a student, or married with a family—the less likely the person will be to leave or do something to jeopardize his or her job. Likewise, people who tend to stay at their job for more than a year exhibit more stability than those who move from one place to another after only a few months.

Many operators will not interview applicants the same day that they drop off their applications. The intent behind this is to see if the applicants are motivated and organized enough to make an appointed interview. If they're not responsible enough to show up promptly for an interview, why would you presume they'll show up for their scheduled shifts on time?

It is advisable to not conduct interviews at the end of a tough day. Treat the prospective employee with respect and courtesy and make every attempt to put the applicant at ease. One way to accomplish that is to make sure that you conduct the interview in a quiet, undisturbed environment.

Effective interviewing skills are learned. One of the aspects effective interviewers have in common is being a good listener. It's extremely difficult to learn anything about a prospective employee if you're doing most of the talking. Watch the person's facial expressions and body language. Use every valid impression you can to help you make the right choice the first time.

Concentrate closely on the person's behavior and initially focus the conversation on less important fact-finding. Do not appear to be agreeing or disagreeing with what the person is saying. Use pauses to encourage elaboration. Don't cut off the person's answers, but interrupt when necessary.

When conducting an interview, it's important to maintain steady eye contact with the applicant. The eyes often reveal the individual's level of confidence, truthfulness, and character. If the person has difficulty maintaining eye contact, it may provide you some insight into his or her personality.

Undoubtedly the most significant and revealing section of the job application has to do with the individual's previous work

It is important to have a clear vision of the qualities and attributes you're looking for in a bartender.

experience. Look for gaps in work experience, as well as gaps in career and salary. Consider the depth and range of an applicant's stated work experience, and the length of time worked at each establishment. Also, ask the person to explain their reasons for leaving their previous place of employment. These answers are invariably enlightening.

One effective interviewing technique is to require an applicant to role-play several different scenarios. For example, ask the individual to presume that you are showing signs of intoxication and to refuse you further service of alcohol. Management candidates can be asked to fire you for your third policy infraction (the exact cause is unimportant). It is helpful to see how people handle these difficult, stressful situations.

Only ask the application questions that pertain specifically to the job or position being filled. Do not introduce the subject of age, gender, religious preference, race, or physical size or condition into the interview. These are federally protected classes, and can be the basis for discrimination. Avoid questions dealing with the applicant's private life, sexual preferences, and amount or quality of education. Questions about a person's police record, marital status, mode of transportation, living arrangements, health, how long they have lived in the area, or whether they have a "green card" are legally sensitive and should be avoided.

Becoming adept at interviewing requires good organizational skills.

Becoming adept at interviewing also requires good organizational skills. Using a prepared list of questions permits an interviewer to focus and listen to an applicant's responses rather than being distracted about what question to ask next. Probe for the person's limitations. Ask challenging, open-ended questions that require an individual to address his or her professional strengths and weaknesses. Essentially, the more penetrating the question, the tougher it is to answer, the more you'll learn by asking it.

The following are examples of open-ended interviewing questions:

- What is the worst thing your former employer could say about you? What is the best thing?
- What would you do if you caught a fellow employee stealing? As a bartender, what is your definition of stealing?
- What are your major job-related weaknesses? Strengths?
- What do you like most about bartending? What do you like least?
- If you could change one thing about yourself, what would it be?
- How do you feel about female supervisors?

- If you could change one thing about your former manager, what would it be?
- Would you be rehired at your last place of employment?
- Why did you leave your last job?
- Tell me about yourself. Why did you choose this line of work?
- Why do you want to work for our company? Why should we hire you?
- What do you hope to gain from the experience other than employment?
- How long will the job here satisfy you?

During the interview there are a number of key observations to make note of:

- Did the applicant make absurd, unrealistic demands?
- Was the person being overly familiar? Maintaining a conversationally polite manner is appropriate.
- Did the applicant listen well? Did the person show interest in your remarks, acknowledging them with nods and other signals that he or she is alert to what was being said or asked?
- Did the applicant encourage you to do some of the talking? Resist the temptation to take control of the conversation by talking too much.
- Did the applicant demonstrate genuine interest in the job? Did the individual exhibit signs of boredom—impatience, fiddling, doodling, leaning back in the chair, scratching, looking around the room, or looking at his or her watch?
- Did the person overstate his or her qualities? Or is he or she honest enough to say, "I'll need to learn more about that." Did the applicant volunteer any failures or admit ignorance?

To assist the interview process, a standardized interviewing form should be used to record your impressions during an interview. Aside from including the applicant's essential information (name, telephone number, etc.) the form is used to standardize observations regarding the various sought-after qualities and attributes.

Illustration 20.1 is an example of an interview form designed to be used during an applicant's first interview. This form places emphasis on the following: appearance; personality; motivation; energy; pressure handling; honesty; positive attitude; stability; intelligence, and flexibility. The use of a standardized form greatly benefits the two-interview process. Each interviewer will conduct their sessions looking for the same hiring qualities using the same rating system.

First Interview Form

Date: _____ Applicant Name: _____

Position: _____ 1st Interviewer: _____

A. <u>Application — Check for (circle):</u>

1. Presentability	good	fair	poor
2. Completeness	good	fair	poor

B. <u>First Interview Evaluation:</u>

1. Diversity of work history	outstanding	very good	good	fair	poor
2. Scheduling flexibility	outstanding	very good	good	fair	poor
3. Presentability	outstanding	very good	good	fair	poor
4. Personality	outstanding	very good	good	fair	poor
5. Motivation	outstanding	very good	good	fair	poor
6. Energy	outstanding	very good	good	fair	poor
7. Pressure-handlin	outstanding	very good	good	fair	poor
8. Honesty	outstanding	very good	good	fair	poor
9. Positive attitude	outstanding	very good	good	fair	poor
10. Stability	outstanding	very good	good	fair	poor
11. Intelligence	outstanding	very good	good	fair	poor
12. Self-confidence	outstanding	very good	good	fair	poor
13. Friendliness	outstanding	very good	good	fair	poor
14. Enthusiasm	outstanding	very good	good	fair	poor

C. <u>Overall Evaluation:</u>   outstanding   very good   good   fair   poor

D. <u>Recommendation for Second Interview:</u>   definitely   possibly   not desirable

E. <u>First Interview Impressions:</u> _____

_____

_____

_____

_____

F. <u>Reference Check:</u> Rate the overall impression of applicant given by references:

References contacted by: _____ Date: _____

1. Reference #1:	outstanding	very good	good	fair	poor
2. Reference #2:	outstanding	very good	good	fair	poor
3. Reference #3:	outstanding	very good	good	fair	poor
4. Reference #4:	outstanding	very good	good	fair	poor

Illustration 20.1

CHECKING EMPLOYEE REFERENCES

Prospective employees should be asked to supply three or four professional references, people who have first-hand knowledge about the individual's abilities, character, and work ethic. If after the initial interview the applicant seems like a likely candidate, take the time to contact the person's references. Failing to do so may expose you to charges of negligence at a later date. Contact references in the reverse order the prospective employee lists them on the application. People will typically list references in the order they want them contacted.

Ask the reference if he or she would mind verifying some information that the applicant has provided. The comments and observations obtained during a telephone reference check should be listed and kept with the application and interview notes.

The following are questions that are typically asked during a telephone reference check.

    a. Was the applicant employed by you?
    b. How long did he or she work for you?
    c. What did you think of the individual's work?
    d. Is the person trustworthy?
    e. Why did the individual leave your company?
    f. Would you rehire this person?
    g. Do you have any additional comments?

THE TWO-INTERVIEW PROCESS

The selection process is too crucial to rely on only one interview, or one set of impressions to make the hiring decision. It is advisable to interview prospective employees twice and preferably by two different managers. As a result, you'll have someone to compare notes with.

Illustration 20.2 is an example of an interview form designed to be used during an applicant's second interview. This form assesses the same professional qualities that the first interview form focuses on. Each interviewer will conduct their sessions using the same rating system.

Before the second interview, it may be helpful to test an applicant's knowledge of bartending. Include questions about mixology, products, and alcohol-awareness. The results of the test will give you a better idea of the person's level of expertise and, to a degree, his or her stated work experience. If the applicant states that he or she has extensive bartending experience, yet does poorly on a written mixology exam, the person's experience may not be as extensive as claimed.

After a favorable first interview, some operators ask the applicant to go behind the bar and make a few drinks. The intent is not to assess the person's drink-making abilities, rather the idea is to observe how the person moves behind the bar. You can also tell a great deal about a bartender's professionalism by watching him or her open a bottle of wine. It is sort of a practical way to verify experience.

Not everyone has the personality to be a bartender. Likewise, not everyone is compatible with the existing staff. It's important to

It is advisable to interview prospective employees twice and preferably by two different managers.

determine whether the person will fit in with your clientele, fellow-employees, and management team. The ability to remain calm, composed, and emotionally in control is another important bartending attribute to assess.

No matter how experienced a bartender is, there will still be aspects of the employment that require the person to adapt to a new way of doing things. While you're interviewing a prospective bartender, assess how flexible and willing to learn the individual appears to be. Avoid hiring bartenders who think their learning days are behind them.

Even if an applicant provides you with an accurate accounting of his or her work experience, it may portray an incomplete picture

Second Interview Form

Date: _____ Applicant Name: _____

Position: _____ 1st Interviewer: _____

A. Second Interview Evaluation:

1. Diversity of work history	outstanding	very good	good	fair	poor
2. Scheduling flexibility	outstanding	very good	good	fair	poor
3. Presentability	outstanding	very good	good	fair	poor
4. Personality	outstanding	very good	good	fair	poor
5. Motivation	outstanding	very good	good	fair	poor
6. Energy	outstanding	very good	good	fair	poor
7. Pressure-handling	outstanding	very good	good	fair	poor
8. Honesty	outstanding	very good	good	fair	poor
9. Positive attitude	outstanding	very good	good	fair	poor
10. Stability	outstanding	very good	good	fair	poor
11. Intelligence	outstanding	very good	good	fair	poor
12. Self-confidence	outstanding	very good	good	fair	poor
13. Friendliness	outstanding	very good	good	fair	poor
14. Enthusiasm	outstanding	very good	good	fair	poor

B. Professional Impressions:

1. Professional aptitude	outstanding	very good	good	fair	poor
2. Team player	outstanding	very good	good	fair	poor
3. Professional knowledge	outstanding	very good	good	fair	poor
4. Long-term possibilities	outstanding	very good	good	fair	poor

C. Overall Evaluation: outstanding   very good   good   fair   poor

D. Second Interview Impressions: _____

_____

_____

_____

_____

D. Recommendation for Hiring: definitely   possibly   not desirable

Illustration 20.2

of his or her competency. Experience is an intangible commodity. It's important in an interview to determine how the applicant's work experience qualifies the person for the position.

One problem novice interviewers sometimes experience is what's called the "halo effect." They are so impressed with a person's resume that they presume the person is qualified and well suited for the job. You have to look past the individual's work experience and assess their personality and professional attributes.

It's best to give a realistic estimate of how many hours a week a prospective employee might work, and how much the person can expect to earn. Likewise, don't give the applicant an overly optimistic impression of his or her advancement prospects within the company. The person could become disillusioned and resentful as the reality of the situation sets in.

AVOIDING FEDERAL DISCRIMINATION CHARGES

Discrimination is defined as an act, practice or instance of differentiating categorically rather than individually. There are five federally protected classes: race or color; national origin or ancestry; sex/gender; religion and age. Asking questions pertaining to one of these five protected classes on an application or in an interview is legally sensitive and ill advised. Employers also cannot discriminate against the handicapped or American military veterans.

In a federal discrimination case, the burden of proof is on the employer to show "fair use" of the information obtained from an application or in an interview, which is an important reason to only ask questions necessary to make a hiring decision. An applicant cannot bring suit against a business for discrimination unless the person applies for and is denied employment. Selection factors such as height, weight, attractiveness or sexual preference are not federally protected and therefore cannot result in federal discrimination charges.

You are not required by law to provide applicants with the reason(s) why he or she was rejected for a job. The individual should not be told that he or she was qualified, or over-qualified for the position, a statement that would constitute half of a discrimination charge. If the rejected applicant presses for a reason, a prudent response might be, "That position has already been filled," or "We hired the person who best matched the job requirements."

You are not required by law to provide applicants with the reason why he or she was rejected for a job.

DEVELOPING AN EMPLOYEE MANUAL

Employing someone is fraught with legal ramifications. Make a mistake and you could find yourself on the wrong end of a civil lawsuit or in front of the National Labor Relations Board, where nine out of ten employees leave victorious. Suits for wrongful discharge, sexual harassment and racial discrimination are among the most prevalent employment-related litigation with judgments averaging in the six-figure range.

The first line of legal defense is a comprehensive, well-structured employee handbook, one that clearly defines the employees' job descriptions, areas of responsibilities, and all of the operation's policies and procedures. Without it, legally holding employees accountable for their actions is practically impossible.

The employee handbook is similar to an employment contract, **There are** which is how the courts typically view the document. All new **general** employees should receive a copy of the handbook and it is important **operating** to thoroughly review the document with them. Like a contract, **policies that** employees are asked to sign a statement that they have received the **must be** handbook, read it thoroughly, and agree to abide by all of its provi- **included in** sions. **the employee** **handbook.**

The first section of an employee handbook is referred to as the "new hire packet." It should contain material helpful to new employees, including a statement describing the operation's concept, and specific information about the business, such as the names of the owner and managers, operating hours, happy hour information, credit cards accepted, etc.

The new hire packet should also contain a job description for each position, uniform specifications, a current copy of the operation's various menus, price lists and an explanation of the training program. To emphasize their importance, the operation's alcohol service policies and procedures should be covered in the first section for every employee, regardless of position, to become familiar with. These policy statements have to do with the service of alcohol to minors or someone visibly intoxicated.

The second section of the handbook should cover the operation's policies and procedures beginning with the conditions of employment. For example, employment is usually considered an "at-will" relationship, meaning that it is for an indefinite period of time, that either the employee or you may terminate the relationship with or without cause, without previous notice and without liability. The handbook should also state (hopefully the truth) that you are an equal opportunity employer.

There are general operating policies that must be included in the employee handbook. These would include policies such as how soon before a shift can an employee punch-in, how employees are to report their tipped income, what defines full-time employment, policies governing overtime, and how much advance notice is to be given if an employee is sick and cannot cover a shift.

After stating in the handbook how these situations, and numerous others, are to be handled, explain the company's disciplinary policies. List and fully describe what the company considers to be grounds for verbal reprimands or written warnings, and what their cumulative effects will be. Clearly define what actions the business considers to be gross misconduct, and the consequences for abusing alcohol or drugs on-the-job.

Don't make presumptions about what an employee might know about your establishment.

The employee handbook has the potential for becoming more than just a legal document outlining the operation's policies and procedures. It presents a singular opportunity to provide your employees with what is expected of them as professionals and how they can best achieve those expectations.

The handbook should also provide your staff with an understanding of what their responsibilities are as employees of the company. For example, employees are generally expected to respect the confidentiality of company matters. Information they may be privy to regarding the company should be considered confidential and not repeated to others. Employees are expected to help maintain a safe working environment and report any safety-related information to management.

If it is your company policy to regularly evaluate employee performance, then the handbook should describe what factors you use to assess their on-the-job effectiveness. Considerations for promotion and salary increases, such as job performance, work attitude, attendance record, team compatibility and safety record, should also be fully explained.

Nearly everything that you think is important for the staff to know regarding their job should be covered in the handbook. Providing your guests with excellent service is crucial to the operation's success, those service standards and guidelines should be clearly stated in the handbook.

Don't make presumptions about what an employee might know about your establishment. Inevitably the presumption will wind up costing you. If the information is important, discuss it in the handbook. You'll reduce the risk of misunderstanding and ultimately get a more professional staff.

HIRING AND ORIENTATION PROCEDURES

After hiring, but before the employee actually starts working, you must by law have the person's W-4 form, and I-9 (Employee Eligibility Verification) completely filled out. It is highly recommended to start a file on each employee. If an employee is under 18 years of age and has not yet graduated from high school, he or she must have a work permit. This permit should go into the person's work file and must be kept on the premises. He or she may obtain this permit through his or her school. A person who is under 18 and has not graduated from high school should not be permitted to use any power-assisted piece of equipment that could potentially be dangerous to the individual's safety.

All employee time records must be complete. Unless you have time-keeping capability in your point of sale system, time cards and time clocks are recommended. Time clocks are not necessarily required by law, but they do keep accurate time records. Each time card must have the employee's name, hours (regular and overtime), meal breaks and the employee's signature for verification. An audit by the Labor Board could cause a fine if these records are not intact. You must keep all these records for a minimum of three years.

It is your responsibility as the manager to see that an employee's first day at work is a positive experience. Make sure that the individual feels as comfortable as possible. Have the person fill out any necessary forms and give him or her a complete tour of the operation. Spend time with the employee and introduce him or her to the other crew members.

The following is a checklist of the items necessary to include in an employee orientation:

1. **Review the employee's personnel file** — The employee's file should contain a completed job application and completed forms W-4 & I-9.

2. **Scheduling and payroll information** — Thoroughly explain the policies concerning starting time (clocking-in and -out procedures); pay periods; paydays and times; work schedule; over-time; day-off and shift change procedures, and sick time.

3. **Tour of restaurant and bar area** — Orientation to include the main bar(s); dining room(s); kitchen and pantry; restrooms; walk-ins; bulletin boards; first aid kit; prep areas, office and liquor storage room.

4. **Ensure the employee has received materials** — Make sure that the employee leaves the orientation with a menu(s) to study, price lists, employee handbook, training material and schedule, and uniforms and shirts, if applicable.

QUESTIONS LEAD TO ANSWERS WHICH LEAD TO SUCCESS

- Do you place job recruitment ads in the classified section of the newspaper? Are your ads potentially discriminatory?
- How good are you at screening job applicants?
- Does your business maintain an active job application file?
- Do you frequent other beverage operations on the lookout for capable, competent bartenders to recruit?
- Are you and the management staff continually interviewing potential job applicants?
- Do you rely on stock bartending job applications, or have you customized one for your operation?
- Do you keep job applications on file a minimum of 180 days?
- Do you interview job applicants using a standardized interview form?
- Do you interview all potential employees at least twice?
- Do you use a set list of open-ended questions during an interview?
- Do you check all job applicant's references before the second interview?
- Do you test an applicant's knowledge of mixology and products before or during the second interview?
- Do you have a clear understanding of what you're looking for in a bartender?
- Do you know the five federally protected classes with respect to discrimination?
- What do you tell applicants who were rejected for a position when they inquire as to the reasons why?
- Have you developed a comprehensive employee handbook?
- Does your employee handbook clearly outline the operation's alcohol service-related policies and procedures?
- Does your employee handbook clearly outline the operation's general operating procedures?
- Does your employee handbook clearly outline what the grounds are for disciplinary action, including possible termination of employment?

Chapter 21

Maintaining a Positive Work Environment

Human nature dictates that if you show your employees respect and treat them as professionals the staff will respond in kind. Unfortunately the reverse is also true. Mismanaging employees brings out the worst in them. It creates a strained, stressful working environment, one that will affect their attitude, morale and performance.

A food and beverage operation can be an extremely stressful place to earn a living for employees and managers alike. Managers also suffer when working under pressure. There are any number of ways that a manager—for whatever cause or reason— could negatively affect the morale and productivity of his or her employees.

The following are fifteen mismanagement practices. In this context, mismanagement is defined as any managerial action that is unfair, arbitrary, irrational or biased.

1. **Reprimands** — Verbally reprimanding a member of the staff in front of other employees or customers is not only embarrassing for everyone involved, it can drive a wedge between the staff and management. It creates an "us against them" attitude. The right time and place to reprimand or discipline an employee is after the person's shift in the privacy of the office. This will spare the employee humiliation and from having to work the shift with the burden of a reprimand. Naturally, making sure that the basis for the warning is valid is of primary importance.

2. **Misrepresentation** — Initially overselling an employee on the company and the person's role in the future of the business is a form of mismanagement. The employee will inevitably become disillusioned and resentful when reality sets in and the person begins to see the job or company for what it really is. The business is best served by giving a prospective employee an accurate picture of what his or her job will be and what the person can realistically expect to earn. There are serious consequences when employees feel they have been misled regarding financial issues.

3. **Lack of Guidance** — Failing to provide employees with the company's policies and procedures can create an inequitable situation.

> If you show your employees respect and treat them as professionals the staff will respond in kind.

The most effective way to get a group of people to achieve competency is to first inform them exactly what is expected of them. If employees are not given specific guidelines governing their on-the-job performance, management cannot expect them to achieve their full potential as professionals. In addition, it will be more complicated to hold employees accountable for their conduct.

4 • **Inadequate Training** — Failing to furnish the personnel with adequate training and supervision does a disservice to the business and employees alike. The business suffers because the staff will not be as competent and productive as they could. As a result, their ability to earn a decent livelihood is hampered.

5 • **Favoritism** — When a manager demonstrates a preference for certain employees, it inevitably causes feelings of ill will among the other members of the staff. It is unreasonable to expect the other members of the staff to passively tolerate inconsistent treatment, especially if it affects their ability to make a living. Management's objective should be to create a cohesive, tightly knit staff.

6 • **Lack of Maturity** — A manager who exhibits irrational or immature behavior undermines his or her ability to be a strong leader. Examples of inappropriate behavior include being intoxicated at work or making sexual advances toward employees. Respect is an important aspect of authority.

7 • **Lack of Feedback** — Failing to periodically evaluate employee attitudes and performance makes it less likely that the staff will achieve their fullest potential. Periodic evaluations give personnel the opportunity to learn about their on-the-job performance. In addition, any deficiencies can be addressed and a plan can be devised to help the employee overcome the problem.

8 • **Scheduling Inequities** — Few things are more closely associated with an employee's livelihood than the weekly schedule. Unfulfilled scheduling requests, over— or under—scheduling, or preferential treatment towards certain employees can lead to rapid turnover. Fairness, abilities and experience should be the prescribed criteria behind scheduling.

9 • **Lack of Support** — Without positive reinforcement, employee enthusiasm, initiative and motivation are difficult to maintain. Failing to reward or acknowledge an employee's on-the-job performance can be a serious error. Encouragement and positive feedback go a long way in helping employees reach their fullest potential.

> **Failing to furnish the personnel with adequate training does a disservice to the business.**

10 **Admitting Mistakes** — Respect and admiration can be won or lost. Managers who cannot bring themselves to admit that he or she has made a mistake to an employee damage their authority and ability to lead. Perfection is an impossible standard to maintain.

11 **Tolerating Stagnancy** — A food and beverage operation requires a motivated and well-trained staff in order to prosper as a business. One of the most significant reasons for employees to leave a business is lack of advancement and infrequent wage increases. For individuals to remain motivated and enthusiastic they must be challenged and continually prompted to mature professionally. It is a mistake to expect employees to remain inspired and conscientious without management's assistance.

12 **Hinder Earnings** — It is definitely in management's best interest to see that the service employees are adequately compensated for their efforts. The more money they earn, the less likely they'll be to leave the job or do something that puts their employment in jeopardy. The staff may interpret any management decision or policy that hinders the employees' ability to earn a reasonable tipped income as managerial disregard, which will tend to foster discontent.

Encouragement and positive feedback go a long way in helping employees reach their fullest potential.

13 **Lack of Credibility** — Management undermines its credibility when it fails to follow through on stated policy decisions or to rectify problem situations. It sends the negative message to the staff that they cannot necessarily trust what management says it is going to do.

14 **Inconsistent Behavior** — Failing to discipline employees for infractions of policies and procedures, and permitting mediocre on-the-job performance negatively affects staff attitude and morale. Why should employees make an effort to follow the establishment's policies if there are no consequences associated with breaking them? Likewise, if mediocrity is tolerated and some employees' abilities are allowed to remain barely adequate, the entire staff will suffer by association and the operation's professionalism as a whole will be diminished.

15 **Social Involvement** — Becoming socially involved with the staff causes needless entanglements and seriously hampers management's ability to lead effectively. While a warm, congenial relationship between the staff and management should be fostered, outside fraternization or sexual involvement is damaging to the operation.

AVOIDING THE HIGH COST OF BARTENDER TURNOVER

Maintaining a positive work environment is essential to reducing turnover and achieving optimum productivity. It only stands to reason that if you create a healthy working environment your employees will enjoy coming to work and won't want to leave to work elsewhere.

When a bartender leaves your staff, his or her departure will likely weaken the business. It may not be appreciated at the time, but when an experienced employee leaves a service-oriented business the enterprise suffers as a result.

Bartender turnover is a costly occurrence, certainly something to be avoided whenever possible. When a bartender leaves your staff, the beverage operation loses the benefit of the on-the-job training you've invested in the employee, as well as, all of the expertise and experience the individual was able to gain at the position. You must then begin the selection process anew; applications, interviews, paperwork, and training shifts. At the end of the process, the operation must suffer with the new employee's inefficiency.

Maintaining a positive work environment is essential to reducing turnover and achieving optimum productivity.

These costs do not take into consideration the increase in management supervision necessary to see to it that the employee is adequately trained. It is also reasonable to assume that the bartender's departure will negatively impact staff morale, customers' perceptions and gross sales.

One key aspect to reducing turnover behind the bar is to create a positive working environment. Negative pressures and stress can be cumulative in effect and rapidly deteriorate the staff's attitude and professionalism. This can lead to job burnout and turnover. When bartenders and servers stop caring about their on-the-job performance the clientele are the first to suffer, followed closely by the operation as a whole. Without a positive attitude, a bartender's productivity can be expected to drop and liquor cost, spillage and waste to increase.

Creating a positive work environment is essential in reducing turnover and requires managers to use restraint, patience and fairness when dealing with their employees. The following are some suggestions on how to reduce bartender turnover while creating a positive work environment:

Keep Staff Challenged — Professionalism is an ambitious objective, one not easily achieved. Instill within your bartending staff a sense of craftsmanship and a desire to excel at their position.

Continually challenging your bartenders is motivating and will help to stave off on-the-job "burn-out."

2 Solicit Feedback — Bartenders are the resident experts on nearly every subject involving the running of the beverage operation. They are at the point-of-sale of nearly every transaction. They possess firsthand knowledge on how the clientele reacts to your operation's prices, products and promotions, and knows how they compare with your direct competitors'. Getting their feedback will help create a sense of involvement among the staff while tapping into their experience and knowledge.

3 Manage by example — Employees are not managed. Objects are managed, people are led. Managing by example is an essential form of leadership. A manager who voluntarily gets behind the bar during a frantically busy shift is an illustration of an individual managing by example. Leadership is a dynamic and effective means of creating a stable, positive working environment.

4 Help Bartenders Earn More Money — The more money your staff is capable of earning the less reason there will be for any one of them to leave. In addition, the more money your bartenders are earning, the less likely it is that they will risk stealing from the bar.

Managing by example is an essential form of leadership.

Management can play an active role in helping the bartending staff earn more by making sure that servers and cocktail waitresses tip-out to the bar and the bar receives a share of the gratuities earned on transfers to the dining room. A portion of a bartending meeting could be allocated to exchanging ideas on how to increase tips.

5 Work Demands — It is in your best interest to remove any impediments preventing your bartenders from carrying out their job description. For example, bartenders are often required to provide beverage service to patrons seated at the cocktail tables. When business is brisk, it is extremely difficult to wait on the customers at the bar, fill drink orders for servers and still provide good service to patrons seated in the lounge. The more difficult it is for the staff to perform their duties the more hassled they'll be and the more likely they will fall victim to "job burn-out."

6 Provide Benefits — Periodic pay raises are not always feasible, nor the most cost-effective method of providing bartenders with financial incentives. There are other employee benefits that are both affordable and well received, such as day-care or transportation reimbursement, pre- or post-shift meals, dental or health insurance, and profit sharing. You could encourage and financially compensate your employees for continuing their education. It is an excellent means of generating good will, while at the same time creating personal stability within your staff.

7. Provide Support — It is important for the staff to know that you will provide them with immediate support and backing when dealing with the drinking public. In situations where the bartender is forced to refuse further service of alcohol to a patron, it makes it easier to exercise that obligation when your bartenders know they have your full support and assistance. It is crucial that the refusal of service be handled correctly. It is also important that employees maintain their trust in management.

8. Job Descriptions — Do you have employees who are assigned certain tasks or responsibilities that could be better filled by another? For instance, in some establishments bartenders are expected to wait on customers, make drinks for servers, wash glassware, answer the phone and be the cashier for the operation. When it gets busy, they're overwhelmed.

Success is largely dependent on the competence of the service staff.

IMPLEMENTING A BARTENDER TRAINING PROGRAM

Regardless of the concept, the success of a food and beverage operation is largely dependent on the competence of its service staff. Working on the frontlines, they are in every sense of the word your public representatives. What your bartenders don't know can hurt your business. It is imperative to ensure that they are fully trained and held accountable for successfully completing the program.

With turnover and the natural effects of time, you can anticipate that the impact of the training program will lessen. The staff may get careless, take liberties with portioning and stray from the standard recipes. These breeches are costly and exact a toll. The best recourse is a continuous training program.

Training should include all information pertinent to their areas of responsibility. These areas of review and instruction for bartenders include product knowledge, service standards, pricing and recipes, glassware procedures, opening and closing procedures, alcohol-awareness, age identification and safety procedures. A system should be created to track each bartender's progress through the program. Pay raises and advancement within the company can be based on an employee completing the training program.

The following is a synopsis of an effective bartender training program:

1. **Age Identification Training** — Bartenders must be completely familiar with the company's policies surrounding the service of alcohol to minors. In addition, they must be knowledgeable about how to identify minors.

2. **Alcohol Awareness Training** — Bartenders must be completely familiar with the company's policies regarding the service of alcohol. In addition, they must be knowledgeable about how alcohol affects the human physiology and what the visible indicators are of alcohol-induced intoxication.

3. **Bar Food Service** — It is important that bartenders be familiar with the service standards for serving food to guests seated at the bar, and the proper procedures for placing food orders to the kitchen.

4. **Beer Training** — Bartenders must be knowledgeable about the beers featured at the bar. They must know what type of beer each brand is, what it is brewed from, where it is brewed, and what characteristics it possesses.

   Training should include all information pertinent to their areas of responsibility.

5. **Drink Recipes** — It is essential that all bartenders be familiar with the standardized drink recipes. They must have a working knowledge of the ingredients in each recipe, the portions, the bar service glass used, and its price.

6. **Glassware Procedures** — Bartenders must be familiar with the glassware handling and washing procedures.

7. **Opening and Closing Procedures** — Bartenders must be thoroughly familiar with the procedures used to both open and close the bar.

8. **Pouring Procedures** — Bartenders must demonstrate a complete understanding of the bar's policies and procedures regarding portioning and drink making.

9. **Safety Procedures** — Bartenders must be familiar with the company's safety policies and procedures.

10. **Service Standards** — Bartenders must be familiar with the company's service standards and what defines hospitable customer service.

11. **Spirits Training** — Bartenders must be knowledgeable about the premium brands of spirits stocked on the back bar. They must be familiar with what each type of spirit is, what it is distilled from, where it comes from, and what characteristics it possesses. This knowledge is essential if the bartender is to become proficient at marketing premium spirits.

12 **Tableside Service** — It may be necessary for bartenders to occasionally provide guests with tableside service. It is important that each bartender be familiar with serving food to guests seated at a table and the proper procedures for placing food orders to the kitchen. Providing guests with competent service is a learned ability.

13 **Wine Training** — Bartenders must be knowledgeable about the wines featured at the bar. They must be familiar with what type of wine it is, where it is made, whether it is available by-the-glass or only by-the-bottle, and what the wines taste like. Typically servers and bartenders are regularly required to sample all of the operation's wines so that they can offer guests first-hand impressions of each wine offering.

Also consider instituting a cross-training program. There are considerable benefits associated with your food servers being trained how to tend bar, or bar backs knowing how to work the floor and bus tables. Likewise, bartenders should be comfortable with the menu and be capable of serving and properly presenting food menu items. When necessary, bussers should be able to go behind the bar and make espresso or cappuccinos or help wash glassware. Cross-training allows employees to expand their skills to the fullest. Your business benefits by having a more capable, versatile staff, and a smoother running operation.

**How can
you tell if
your new
bartender is
a candidate
for rookie of
the year?**

THE LINE ON TOUTING BARTENDERS

How can you tell if your new bartender is a candidate for rookie of the year or should be sent to the minors? Here are some things to consider:

1 **Pouring Ability** — Can the bartender pour consistently accurate shots? When hurried, does liquor fly every which way or splash off the ice? Does the individual look comfortable behind the bar? Is there grace and fluidity to the person's motions?

2 **Personality** — Does the person have an infectious, likable personality? Does he or she have a ready smile and a good feel for humor? Is the individual receptive to constructive criticism and take direction well? Does the person maintain his or her composure when everyone else seems to be losing theirs?

3 **Knowledge** — Does the person have an aptitude for mixology? Is he or she knowledgeable about the products stocked behind the bar? Is the bartender receptive to learning more about his or her profession?

4 **Service Abilities** — Does the person look to excel at service? Does he or she interact well with the clientele and anticipate their needs? Is the person gracious under fire?

5 **Reliability** — Is the person committed to serving alcohol responsibly? Is he or she conscientious in all aspects of the job? Does the person have what appears to be a stable life outside of work?

EMPLOYEE SCHEDULING CONSIDERATIONS

Scheduling sounds easy. You put the employee names on a piece of paper informing them when you want them to work. You then pay them for the hours they worked. Few things, however, are more closely associated with an employee's livelihood than the weekly schedule. It can cause more headaches than just about any other aspect of running the beverage operation.

There is a natural inclination to want to run a "tight ship" and keep payroll expenses in check. There are, however, serious problems associated with understaffing, not scheduling enough people to handle the anticipated level of business. Aside from subjecting employees to undue stress and burnout, operating with a skeleton crew when it's even moderately busy will cost you sales, the bartender gratuities, and the clientele the level of service they have come to expect. Understaffing is expensive, far exceeding any savings in payroll.

> A schedule should be posted on the same day each week at least seven days before it goes into effect.

Over scheduling a shift is almost as bad. Not only are you wasting payroll dollars, but employees may feel like they are not needed and become careless with their work. Identify areas in which you can reduce labor hours while still maintaining high customer service standards.

To maintain continuity, a schedule should be posted on the same day of every week at least seven days before it goes into effect. There are several reasons to schedule employees two-weeks in advance, rather than the more conventional one-week schedule. A two-week schedule has the stabilizing effect of helping employees to better plan their lives outside of work. The same is true regarding giving employees permanent schedules, meaning they work the same shifts every week. This also allows the bartenders to generate a consistent following. In both cases you can anticipate fewer scheduling conflicts when employees are given more advance notice of their work schedule.

As a matter of policy, all scheduling requests should be made directly to the bar manager. Should a bartender want to change his or her schedule and switch shifts with another bartender, the request must first be approved by management. Unfulfilled scheduling requests, over- or under-scheduling, or preferential treatment towards certain employees can lead to rapid and consistent turnover.

REASONABLE EXPECTATIONS OF YOUR BARTENDING STAFF

One of the basic principles behind being an effective manager is to tell your staff what it is that you expect of them, and then hold them accountable. Your employees can hardly be expected to perform up to a specific level of competency unless they are told exactly what those standards are.

This of course will force you to consider exactly what your expectations of the staff are. Most of us have a vague or general idea of what we want our bartenders to do and how they are to act, but that won't quite cut it. Your employees deserve more than that.

In an effort to jump start the process, the following is a list of what may likely be universally applicable expectations of bartenders. Try it on for size and amend where necessary.

Tell your staff what it is that you expect of them, and then hold them accountable.

1. **Treat Everyone Like a Guest** — Hardware stores have customers. It's an important distinction. When you view our clientele as guests, your attitude will naturally become more gracious and accommodating.

2. **Put the House First** — Don't lose sight of who you're working for. Life gets too complicated when you report for work with a hidden agenda. Keep it simple, look out for the house.

3. **Drink Making is an Art** — Appreciate that not everyone can do what you do. Being a skilled mixologist is something to take pride in. Every drink that you serve should reflect that pride, and be the best drink you can make. Never serve an inferior drink.

4. **Always Give People an Honest Break** — Everyone deserves to be treated fairly. In this context, an honest break means equity in all transactions—no overcharging, underpouring or shortchanging. This means leaving all prejudice and preconceptions at home, and providing genuinely hospitable service without bias or preference. There's no such thing as a second-class guest.

5. **Don't Transfer Stress** — Sure it's busy and you're absolutely swamped, but don't vent that built-up stress at the clientele. It's not

their job to keep track of what you're doing. The crunch will pass.

6. **Ergonomics** — Learn to work smarter, not harder. Do things in the fewest number of steps and in the least amount of motions. It'll save you time and energy, which in turn, will allow you to be more productive and earn more money.

7. **Keep the Bar Clean** — Keeping a commercial bar clean is a challenge, but the alternative is unacceptable. A dirty bar reflects badly on the cleanliness of the rest of the house, and your degree of professionalism.

8. **Economic Power of Fun** — As a bartender you can positively impact how much people enjoy themselves even if they're standing six feet from the bar, so have fun. Be entertaining. Make people smile.

9. **Don't Fret About Tips** — A sure-fire way to step on your tips is to worry about them while you're working. Make good drinks, give the guests great service and your tips will take care of themselves.

10. **When in Doubt, Smile** — Under nearly any circumstance, one of your best courses of action is to keep smiling. Rarely is a smile inappropriate, while a frown or deadpan expression is almost always out of place.

EFFECTIVELY HANDLING CUSTOMER COMPLAINTS

When guests have a complaint they take their complaints with them out the door.

More often than not when guests have a complaint about an operation's product or service they take their complaints with them out the door. In fact people rarely share their criticisms and complaints with the management of nightclubs or restaurants. So when a guest does go out of his or her way to complain, look at it as a rare and valuable opportunity to salvage a relationship and rectify a problem.

Often when guests have a complaint, they express themselves in an abrupt, belligerent manner. It is important that you respond appropriately and not get defensive or take the criticism personally.

The best advise when handling a customer complaint is to allow the principles of common courtesy to be your guide. Show interest and listen carefully to the person's complaint. Refer to the customer by name and always treat the person with respect.

Be genuinely empathetic. Imagine how the customer is feeling. Carefully restate the problem to confirm that you understand the situation. Remain factual to make sure there are no understandings. Apologize for the problem and empathize with the customer: "I understand how you feel, sir, and I am sorry."

Reassure the guest that you will personally take action to remedy the situation. Then see to it that the corrective action is carried out. If a circumstance beyond your control prevents you from solving the customer's problem in a timely manner, inform the guest of the situation and reassure him or her that you will resolve the problem as soon as possible.

If a guest with a complaint approaches someone on your staff, the situation should be promptly brought to your attention. The employee should relay the information about the problem first so that you are fully prepared to assist the customer.

Remember that the majority of dissatisfied customers will not complain, they simply will not come back. On the other hand, when a guest's complaint is handled efficiently and with respect, the situation turns into a positive and the establishment's good will remains intact.

If a guest with a complaint approaches someone on your staff, the situation should be promptly brought to your attention.

HOW TO CRITICIZE EMPLOYEES EFFECTIVELY

Sometimes criticizing an employee's actions or behavior just can't be avoided. For anyone in management, leveling constructive criticism goes with the territory, and unless their empathy meter is pushing empty, it isn't something most look forward to. However, criticism need not leave the recipient permanently scarred and you emotionally disturbed.

To that end, the following are some recommendations on how to criticize effectively, and hopefully, more humanely.

1. **Cool Off** — Let your emotions simmer down before meeting with the person in question. Especially if the criticism needs to be accompanied by a written warning, anger or sarcasm will undermine your objectives.

2. **Lay Down a Cushion** — Start the meeting off by saying something positive about the person's performance or abilities. Aside from cushioning the criticism, it helps set a positive, constructive tone.

3. **Criticize Behavior** — Focus your criticism on the behavior that you want changed, not on the person. The discussion will seem less threatening and you'll likely avoid a defensive reaction.

4. **Make Criticism Work** — Don't use sweeping generalities, such as "you always..." or "you never..." Instead, direct your criticism towards specific behavior, acts or incidents.

5 Be Realistic — Be sure the behavior you're criticizing can be changed. A person's appearance, mannerisms or personality traits often fall outside of what can be modified.

6 Avoid Accusations — Accusations are seldom more than thinly veiled threats. Instead reinforce the message that you want to work with the person to resolve the issue at hand.

7 Be Empathetic — Everyone has felt the sting of criticism before, so show the employee that you do understand his or her feelings.

8 Get to the Point — Don't belabor the issue. State your case as clearly as possible; discuss with the person on how he or she can resolve the problem, and look to conclude the meeting.

9 Seek Understanding — Make sure the person understands the basis for your criticism.

10 Close Strong — At the end, reaffirm your support and confidence in the employee. Help the person leave with his or her self-esteem reasonably intact.

PERIODIC EMPLOYEE EVALUATIONS

The purpose behind periodically evaluating employees is to let them know what you think of their on-the-job performance. The first time to evaluate an employee is after he or she has been working on the job for at least 30 days. You should give the employee an appraisal of the job he or she has been doing, as well as your expectations of the person's future performance. Reviewing an employee's performance each quarter should be sufficient.

An evaluation should start on a positive note, cover any weak or negative points with suggestions for improvement, and end on a positive note to create an air of encouragement. Do not withhold negative comments for fear of hurting an employee's feelings. You are hurting the employee in the long-run by overlooking short-comings or bad habits that could lead to failure or prevent the person from getting a promotion or raise.

It is advisable to use an evaluation form. The use of a standardized form greatly benefits the evaluation process. Every performance evaluation will then focus on the same job factors and use the same rating system. A performance evaluation form is provided in illustration 21.1.

Performance Evaluation Form

Name: _____ Date: _____
Dept: _____ Last Review Date: _____
Position: _____ Time in Position: _____
Period Covered: _____ Report Type: _____ 6 month _____ Probationary
_____ Annual _____ Other _____

Job Factor	Exceeds Requirements	Meets Requirements	Needs Improvement	Comments
Job Knowledge				
Work Quality				
Work Quantity				
Follows Instructions				
Cooperates w/Others				
Dependability				
Safety				
Respect for Property				

Strengths: _____

Areas of Improvement

Plan of Action:
Employee: Supervisor:

Illustration 21.1

WARNINGS, TERMINATIONS AND RESIGNATIONS

If you find it necessary to discipline an employee, always do it in private. Never humiliate someone by criticizing the person in front of his or her fellow employees. Verbal warnings may be sufficient to correct the problem. Be honest, direct and consistent. Make sure that all verbal warnings and written warnings are well documented and filed in the employees' personnel file. If a particular habit or type of behavior is unacceptable in one employee, it should be considered so in all employees.

If an employee's work is substandard, discuss it with the person. Set up a probationary period allowing the employee an opportunity to improve. If the problem persists, a written warning (often called

Employee Separation Report

Employee Name: _____ S.S.#: _____

Address: _____ City: _____ State: _____ Zip: _____

Date Hired: _____ Last Day Worked: _____ Termination Date: _____

Position: _____ Supervisor: _____ Rate of Pay: $ _____

Termination Pay: Vacation: $ _____ Severance: $ _____

Wages in Lieu of Notice: $ _____ Sick Pay: $ _____ Retirement: $ _____

Reason For Separation

Layoff (Lack of Work): Permanent: _____ Temporary: _____ Return Date: _____

Leave of Absence: From: _____ To: _____ Reason: _____

Was separation requested or suggested by management? Yes: _____ No: _____

If "yes," please explain the final incident that led to separation in the space below:

_____

_____

_____

_____

Voluntary Resignation Notice: Yes: _____ No: _____

Reason for Resignation

    Illness/Injury: _____ Other Employment (where: _____)

    Dissatisfaction: _____ Change of Residence: _____ Retired Voluntarily: _____

Marital-Family Obligations: _____ Refused Transfer: _____ Refused Recall: _____

Other (explain): _____

_____

_____

Discharge

Had employee been warned the job was in jeopardy? Yes: _____ No: _____

Reason for Discharge: Unqualified: _____ Violation of Company Rules: _____

    Absenteeism (reported): _____ Absenteeism (unreported): _____ Tardiness: _____

    Insubordination: _____ Negligence, shoddy work: _____ Quarreling, fighting: _____

    Under influence of intoxicant: _____ Incarceration: _____ Failed to report to work: _____

Other (explain): _____

_____

_____

Employee Signature: _____ _____ Date: _____

Manager Signature: _____ Date: _____

Witness Signature: _____ Date: _____

Illustration 21.2

> If you find it necessary to discipline an employee, always do it in private.

job jeopardy) should be issued. Make sure the employee understands the problem and that he or she signs the written notice. If the problem continues, and other means to rectify the situation have been exhausted, there will be little recourse but to terminate the employee.

In the event you find it necessary to terminate an employee, there are some general guidelines to follow in order to protect the company from a potential labor dispute.

Make certain that the reasons for firing the employee are valid. When meeting with an employee who you are about to terminate, it is advisable to hold the meeting with another manager present. The meeting should be well documented and both managers should sign the termination report.

• Once terminated, the person should be paid everything he or she is owed — wages, vacation pay, etc. — immediately upon dismissal, prepared in advance, if possible. If an employee resigns, even without notice, you must pay the person at the next regular payday or before. You may not withhold a person's pay.

An example of an employee separation report can be found in illustration 21.2.

QUESTIONS LEAD TO ANSWERS WHICH LEAD TO SUCCESS

• Do you have a problem with bartender turnover?
• Do you have a mature, emotionally stable and well-intentioned bartending staff?
• Do you have a problem with absenteeism?
• Is there a problem with on-the-job substance abuse in your business?
• Do you have a problem with employees reporting for work impaired or intoxicated?
• Have you created a positive environment in which to work?
• When and where are employees reprimanded and given written warnings?
• Are you forthright with prospective employees regarding their employment prospects?
• Do certain employees on your staff receive preferential treatment?
• Do you periodically evaluate your employees?
• Are your bartenders' schedules fair?
• Do you encourage your employees? Does your staff respect you?
• Are your employees challenged to grow professionally?
• Do you have employees whose abilities and performance can best be described as mediocre?
• Do you solicit your staff's feedback on decisions concerning the operation of the bar?
• Is the amount your bartenders earn a concern of yours?
• Do your employees have a benefit package?

Chapter 22

Preventing Internal Theft

To the uninitiated, the term "shrinkage" may sound harmless, but just the thought of it is enough to make seasoned beverage managers wince and bar owners shudder. Shrinkage refers to the liquor that is lost due to waste, spillage and theft. It is capable of chewing up in excess of 20% to 30% of the bottom line. Bevinco auditors have determined that the average shrinkage is actually 23% on liquor and draft beer, about 10% on wine and 2% on bottled beer. With over 100 franchises throughout North America to draw from, the company has found consistently these figures to be reliable.

For many operators, eliminating shrinkage means the difference between financial success and failure. Theft alone is an insidious source of losses. Opportunities are wide spread for theft behind a bar. Bartenders are often working without direct supervision. They may steal from the bar and its customers because it's easily accomplished, hard to detect, and extremely difficult to prevent on an ongoing basis. The temptations posed by constantly handling large sums of cash and dealing with a liquid inventory can often prove overwhelming. At some point, most bartenders contemplate stealing cash, giving out free drinks, or any one of a multitude of transgressions.

Eliminating shrinkage means the difference between financial success and failure.

Effectively limiting internal theft behind the majority of bars is no easy task, and eliminating it altogether is unrealistic. Regardless of the difficulty factor involved, you must formulate and implement an operational strategy for containing the problem.

This chapter deals with the complex issue of preventing bartender theft. There are several approaches that need to be taken to affect any significant impact on the problem. The first involves tracking pour costs and bartender productivity. These analytical devices are indispensable tools that will provide you with numerous insights.

The strategy also involves implementing an effective inventory control system. The system advanced in this book will let you know exactly what you have in inventory, what you paid for it, where it is, and at what rate it's used. A complete and detailed accounting of the inventory is critical at detecting and deterring internal theft. Consider also the auditing services of Bevinco. It is effectively impossible to rip off the bar without the exact nature of the theft being revealed in the Bevinco reports.

You must also initiate specific measures aimed at alleviating the operation's vulnerability to theft, thereby making it riskier and more difficult for bartenders to steal, while making it easier for you to detect the theft.

The preventative measures mentioned in this chapter are divided into two major sections. The first segment advances numerous employee policies and procedures formulated to help you better control the operation of the bar.

The second section outlines specific preventative measures that you can initiate that address problematic areas of the operation, such as assuring proper portioning, and maintaining effective cash and inventory controls.

Policies and procedures are only effective if they are strictly enforced.

THEFT REDUCTION POLICIES & PROCEDURES

It is important to understand that management policies and procedures by themselves will not stop bartenders from stealing. On the contrary, policies and procedures are only effective if they are strictly enforced. In addition, they must be consistently and uniformly applied to all members of the bartending staff.

Another important consideration regarding policies and procedures is to have employees sign a receipt when hired, that they have thoroughly read and understand the handbook material, and they will perform their duties in strict adherence to the material covered. With this signed receipt, management is in a solid position to hold an employee accountable for any future violation of stated rules governing conduct or financial property.

Not all of the following suggestions regarding policies and procedures will conform to every beverage operation's exact circumstances. An establishment's set directives must be tailored to its own particular needs and requirements.

Bartenders Prohibited From Checking-Out Their Cash at the End of a Shift — In many operations, bartenders are required to reconcile their cash drawers. This entails using the cash in the drawer to compile the bar's opening bank for the following shift, and to itemize the remaining cash proceeds onto a deposit slip. If the bartenders are stealing, the checkout process provides them with an ideal opportunity to safely take out any stolen funds secretly deposited into the register's cash drawer during the course of their shift.

By taking this responsibility away from the employees, management will effectively make it more difficult and riskier for bartenders to withdraw stolen proceeds from the cash register or POS. The bartenders will, as a result, be forced to either pull the money out of the cash drawer during the shift or not use the register as a place for their stolen funds.

2 **Employees Not Allowed To Drink at the Bar When Off-Duty** — While this policy may result in the bar having a few less customers, it will also prevent the bartenders from overpouring, undercharging, or simply giving away free drinks to their co-workers. This is a sound preventative measure, intended to reduce the natural temptation bartenders face when they are put in the position of serving alcoholic beverages to people they work with. In addition, it eliminates the possibility of the establishment's personnel becoming intoxicated at their place of employment.

3 **Bartenders Not Allowed to Participate in the Physical Inventory Process** — The process of taking the bar's physical inventory is solely a management function and should be conducted only by management. Bartenders who are stealing from an operation can use their participation in the physical inventory process to alter the recorded data to offset previous theft. This could be accomplished by overstating the amount of liquor inventory on hand at the end of the month. Overstating the amount of liquor on-hand during the physical inventory process will essentially have the same effect as if the theft never occurred.

4 **Bartenders Not Involved in Ordering, Receiving or Issuing of Liquor** — The ordering, receiving, issuing, and storage of the establishment's liquor inventory should remain the sole responsibility of management. There is no legitimate reason for the bartending staff to be involved in any of these managerial functions. A dishonest bartender could cause immense operational difficulties by altering the establishment's internal inventory systems for illegitimate purposes.

5 **Locked and Secure Inventory** — All of the operation's liquor, beer and wine inventory should be stored in a locked and secure area. It is a sound policy to limit access to the liquor room to management only.

> **If bartenders are stealing, the checkout process provides them with an opportunity to take out any stolen funds secretly deposited into the cash drawer.**

6 **Perpetual Inventory System** — The perpetual inventory system tracks the changes in the liquor room's inventory. You can continually monitor against internal theft by comparing the last entry on a product's perpetual inventory sheet with the actual number of bottles on-hand in the liquor room. The more inventory you store in the liquor room, the more reasons you have to implement a perpetual system.

7 **Banquet Bartenders Not Allowed Behind Main Bar** — The intent behind maintaining two different bartending staffs, one to work catering and banquet functions, the other to work at the main bar, is to prevent banquet liquor inventory from being secretly brought behind the bar's main facility. If that were to occur, a bartender could sell the smuggled liquor, and pocket the entire amount of sales proceeds generated, all done without the operation's cost percentages being negatively affected.

The bar par reading will show if all of the products in the liquor inventory are actually behind the bar in their correct quantities.

8 **Bartenders Required to Take Post-Shift Par Readings** — The operation's bar par sheets will detail precisely how many bottles of each product in the liquor inventory should be behind the bar at any one point in time. The bartending staff should be required to take a bar par reading at the conclusion of the night shift. The closing bar par must take into account the bottles emptied during the course of the shift. The bar par reading will show if all of the products in the liquor inventory are actually behind the bar in their correct quantities. If there is a discrepancy in the bar par reading, it must be investigated immediately, for it may indicate that a full bottle of liquor was stolen from the bar.

9 **"Comp" Sheet Entries Require Managerial Approval** — Bartenders should receive management approval *prior* to preparing a customer's complimentary drink. This policy is intended to stop them from claiming, after the fact, that a drink was given away with management's consent, when in reality the drink was sold and the proceeds of the sale were pocketed.

10 **Absolute Limit of One Transaction Per Drink Ticket** — It should be mandated that bartenders record no more than one transaction per drink ticket. This is considered an essential beverage control. If bartenders are allowed to use one, long running drink ticket to record beverage sales, they will be in an ideal position to steal by not recording all of the drinks actually sold. It is nearly impossible for a casual observer to perceive if the bartender is properly ringing-in each and every sale using a running check.

The best method to alleviate the problem of bartenders stealing unrecorded drinks is to require that they ring in each transaction on a separate drink check.

11 • Enforced "Void Out" Procedures — It should be policy that management approval is first required before a bartender can void-out a drink check. In addition, it is important to stipulate that the bartenders must obtain the approval of the manager on duty before the transaction can be completed.

12 • Established Missing Drink Ticket Penalty — A monetary fine should be imposed in the event a bartender claims to have lost a drink check. The fine should be substantial enough to act as a deterrent against a bartender collecting cash on a hand-written check and destroying it without entering the sale into the register. Destroying the check would eliminate the only evidence that the sale occurred. It is therefore important for management to maintain an accurate ledger of the serial numbers of the drink checks issued to the bar. The ledger will reveal if there are any checks missing.

13 • Tip Jar Procedures — The bartenders' tip jar should be situated well away from the operation's cash register or POS. If the tip jar is located right next to the register, it is far too easy for bartenders to divert stolen funds away from the register and into the tip jar. In addition, bartenders should be prohibited from making change out of their tip jar or taking currency from the tip jar and exchanging it for larger denominations out of the cash drawer. If the bartenders are stealing from the business and using the cash drawer for the stolen funds, they can easily retrieve the money from the register under the pretense of making change. For example, a bartender could take 20 one-dollar bills out of the tip jar, deposit the currency into the register, but instead of taking out a $20 bill in exchange, he or she could remove four $20 bills, withdrawing $60 of stolen funds.

> Bartenders should be prohibited from making change out of their tip jar.

14 • Bartenders Prohibited From Serving Beverages to Service Staff — The intent behind this policy of not permitting bartenders to serve beverages to other personnel is to prevent them from giving employees alcohol. Food servers and cocktail waitresses can easily obtain coffee, iced tea and water to drink from the kitchen or waitress stations. If the bartenders are not allowed to give other employees any beverages over the bar, it will be much more difficult for employees to drink alcohol while on duty.

15 • Manager-on-Duty to Initial All Employee Time Cards — It should be policy that the manager-on-duty must initial all employee time cards when they clock out at the end of their shift. This practice is designed to discourage employee theft through time clock fraud.

16 • **Strictly Enforced "No Sale" Policy** — One of the more uncomplicated methods of theft involves a bartender selling a drink and depositing the proceeds into the register using the "no sale" feature. Unless someone is watching the LCD display, the act usually goes unnoticed. Since the sale wasn't rung into the register, the bartender need only remove the stolen proceeds from the cash drawer when safe to do so. The best preventative measure against this type of theft is to restrict the use of the "no sale" key.

One technique to deterring theft through use of the "no sale" key is to provide the bartenders with an alternative source for making change. A small, inexpensive container, or even a cabinet drawer will suffice. By providing a separate source for making change behind the bar, the bartenders will no longer have a legitimate reason for accessing the cash drawer with the "no sale" key every time someone needs change. This will make it slightly more challenging to steal unrecorded sales and depositing the funds in the cash drawer without entering any sales data.

If bartenders are not allowed to give other employees any beverages, it will be much more difficult for employees to drink alcohol while on duty.

17 • **Ring-in Drink Sale Prior to Service** — One method of reducing the incidence of unrecorded sales is to require bartenders to ring-in a sale of a drink into the cash register prior to service. The transaction is serviced and cleared only when payment has been tendered. This procedure will make it much more difficult for bartenders to give away free drinks or steal unrecorded sales proceeds. To subvert the procedure, a bartender would first have to serve a drink and then go to the register, which would be contrary to standard procedure. It should be noted that this measure is not suited for high volume establishments as it does effectively add another step to the cash register procedures.

18 • **Cash Drawer Count Verification** — Bartenders should be required to verify the amount of money in the bar register's opening bank. This practice will prevent the bartenders from claiming that their opening bank was either over or under the prescribed dollar amount to explain a cash shortage or overage in the register.

On a regular basis, place an extra $5, $10, or $20 bill in the bartender's bank and see if the person informs you of the cash overage. It is a good way to verify if the bartender is counting his bank prior to the shift, as well as providing insight into the person's degree of honesty.

19 •**POS or Cash Register Procedures** — The cash drawer should always remain closed between transactions. Allowing the drawer to remain ajar will completely negate the primary control function of the register. While bartenders should have access to the key that turns the register on, they should not have access to the keys that activate the "x" or "z" reading function. The LCD display should face the public such that anyone seated at the bar can observe what is being entered into the system. The area around the POS or register should remain clear of clutter, such as books, manuals, or stacks of paper. Clutter can be used to hide money, used drink tickets or a ledger system for keeping track of stolen money deposited in the drawer.

20 •**Bartenders Not Allowed to Use "Make-Up" Rings to Correct Errors** — An example of a "make-up ring" is when a bartender incorrectly inputs a $2.50 drink sale as $2.00. To correct the error, another $.50 is rung into the cash register. This technique can be easily manipulated by a bartender for dishonest purposes and should not be allowed.

> **The cash drawer should always remain closed between transactions.**

21 •**Safeguard All POS Passwords** — All management passwords should be kept safe and secure from the bartenders. This will prevent bartenders from being able to open reports and learn what their shift sales are.

22 •**Cash Handling Procedures** — Requiring bartenders to "fan" out a patron's change will make it more difficult for them to short change customers. Bartenders should be required to tell the patron the cost of the order and verbally confirm the amount of money tendered ("That will be $2.50 out of $5.00"). This policy makes it more difficult for the bartenders to defraud the clientele through overcharging or shortchanging. Bartender should also "fan" a customer's change so that the person can at a glance confirm that the correct amount was returned.

23 •**Take an Immediate "Z" Reading After "Last Call"** — At the conclusion of "last call" the manager-on-duty should immediately take the "z" reading of the register or run a sales report of the POS and pull the cash drawer out of the machine. If the bartenders are stealing and using the cash register drawer for stolen funds, this procedure will force them to withdraw the money during the shift while there are still people milling about instead of the relative privacy of closing.

INTERNAL OPERATING PROCEDURES

1 **Bartenders Not Allowed to "Tail" Measurements** — "Tailing" is the practice of letting a bottle continue to pour after the true measure has been reached. Tailing is often used deliberately to overpour the liquor portion used in a drink and should be prohibited.

2 **No Overpouring or Underpouring Liquor Portions Allowed** — Bartenders should be forbidden from overpouring or underpouring the liquor portion in a customer's drink. Likewise, bartenders should be directed not to "top-pour" liquor or "ghost" the alcoholic portion in a blended drink. Both of these techniques are used by bartenders to steal by underpouring the alcohol in a series of drinks.

> **Overpouring or underpouring becomes a non-issue if the Precision Pour control spouts are used.**

Overpouring or underpouring becomes less of an issue when the Precision Pour control spouts are used, and a non-issue with electronic control systems, such as those perfected by the Berg Company.

3 **Standardized Drink Recipes** — Provide the bartending staff with standardized drink recipes. It is absolutely fundamental to the consistency of product and controlling the beverage operation's liquor costs. It should be a matter of policy that bartenders are required to pour only the drink recipes provided by management. This will, for the most part, prevent bartenders from overpouring the alcoholic portion in drinks.

4 **Drink Tabs Secured by Major Credit Card** — If a customer wants to run a drink tab, the bartender should first obtain a major credit card from the customer as a security deposit. This will ensure that the establishment will receive payment in the event the customer walks out without clearing his or her tab.

Another reason to institute this policy is to prevent the bartender and customer from working together to defraud your establishment. This could be accomplished by the bartender claiming that the patron left without clearing his or her tab, when in fact, the person gave the bartender a sizable cash gratuity to let him or her leave without paying the tab amount.

5 **Bartender Required to Record All Transactions on Drink Tab** — Prior to serving a patron another round of drinks, a bartender should be instructed to first record the transaction on the guest's running drink ticket. This policy is intended to make it

more difficult for bartenders to steal by giving away unrecorded drinks. In addition, this policy will make it harder for bartenders to overcharge customers by ringing in a round of drinks onto the running charge that haven't been served.

6 Mandatory Use of a Drop Box — One way to rip-off the house is to present a patron with a previously used check as his or her drink tab. Once the customer pays the total on the check, the bartender pockets the sales proceeds and the sale remains unrecorded. The key for the bartender is to select a previously rung-in check that reflects the right number of drinks and the dollar amount. The most likely scenario is to reuse a ticket reflecting the sale of two rounds of two well drinks, which is statistically a frequent transaction.

A drop box is a lockable box with a slot in the top large enough to slip a drink ticket through. Once a drink ticket has been imprinted it should be deposited into the drop box, thereby preventing it from being fraudulently reused. Any bartender caught in possession of a previously used drink ticket should be suspect.

A drop box is a lockable box with a slot in the top large enough to slip a drink ticket through.

THEFT PREVENTION THROUGH PROACTIVE MANAGEMENT

There are other measures management can use in addition to the previously mentioned policies and procedures to curb employee theft. One strategy is increasing management's presence in the bar. Direct observation is the best method of preventing bartenders from stealing and no one is in a better position to observe that than the manager-on-duty. If an individual is trained to spot specific improprieties and is well versed in the operation's prices, policies and procedures, he or she will be ideally situated to monitor the bartenders' conduct while on-duty.

One costly misconception many managers possess is that the bar is the bartenders' private domain and any manager entering into their inner sanctum is intrusive and operationally disruptive. The fact that the bar facility itself often provides bartenders with the privacy and sanctuary necessary to steal warrants that you need to occasionally intrude into that space. From such a vantage point, it is far easier for a manager-on-duty to detect evidence of internal theft.

When bartenders steal, they need to keep track of exactly how much money they have stashed in the register's drawer. If a bartender makes a mistake, the cash count and the register reading will not balance and it becomes incriminating.

Anything that could be used as a record keeping system should immediately be suspect. Items such as coins, matches, sword picks, or any small object could be used as a token. Tokens are used like poker chips to keep a tally of the amount of money the register's drawer is over. Some bartenders use a written ledger that they keep in their pocket or in a drawer. Anything closely resembling a counting scheme should be immediately investigated.

Other telltale signs of internal theft include an unusual number of "no sale" rings in an evening and the tip jar being inexplicably stuffed to capacity. Another clue would be the cash drawer not being normally maintained. Segregated monies might be hastily deposited proceeds of theft.

More than likely, the manager-on-duty's presence in and around the bar will have an impact on limiting internal theft. The material in this section of the chapter details numerous specific steps which management can use to exert greater control over the actions of the bartending staff and thereby lessen the beverage operation's vulnerability to internal theft.

1 **Mid-Shift "Z" Readings** — The manager should standardly take mid-shift "z" readings. Whether a bartender is suspected of stealing or not, the manager on duty can reduce the opportunity by taking a mid-shift "z" reading. At some point in the shift, the manager should clear the register by taking a "z" reading or run a sales report on the POS and replace the cash drawer with a new bank. If a bartender has deposited unaccounted for funds into the register for safe keeping, the cash drawer count will be "over" when compared to the cash register's sales totals, and the manager has evidence to that effect.

One important element of the strategy is to periodically conduct two mid-shift readings during the course of a night. This will prevent you from being predictable. The bartenders will never be certain which nights you'll take two readings, making it riskier to use the cash drawer for stolen proceeds.

2 **Bottle Tagging** — For establishments with more than one outlet, bottle tagging will make it possible for management to identify each issue bottle of liquor inventory. This is important to prevent employees from smuggling bottles of liquor into the operation and selling the contents to the clientele. Management must routinely check the tags affixed to the liquor bottles to ensure that they are

> The manager-on-duty's presence in and around the bar will have an impact on limiting internal theft.

not being wrongfully removed and reused, or that the inventory issued to one outlet doesn't show up at another of the bars.

Bevinco tags every bottle in the liquor inventory, both as a means of identification, as well as a form of deterrence.

3 Drink Ticket Ledger Maintained — Management should routinely log the serial numbers of the drink checks issued to the bar prior to each shift. When the bartenders turn in their paperwork at the end of the shift, the ledger should be checked to make sure all of the drink tickets issued to the bar are present and accounted for, whether they are used or not. If this ledger is maintained, management will be in a position to determine if any of the bar's drink tickets are missing, and if so, begin the process of investigating its disappearance. A missing drink ticket should be treated as a serious, and potentially costly breach of the operation's stated policies and procedures.

4 Use of Mirrors and Track Lighting — One physical alteration to the facility that will enhance a manager's ability to detect theft is to increase the amount of lighting behind the bar. Track lights are very effective in throwing light on previously dark and secretive area. Mirrors are not only decorative and closely associated with bars, but they also provide managers with a number of angles to view the area.

5 Video Cameras — An effective preventive measure is to install remote video cameras to monitor activity behind the bar. Tremendous technological advancements has made these video surveillance systems both more cost-effective and more effective. There are systems that will show you four different views on the screen simultaneously.

6 Hydrometers — If it is suspected that the bartender might be watering down the liquor inventory, a hydrometer will either confirm or deny those suspicions. It is a device which measures the relative alcoholic content of a liquor, and since the addition of water into the liquor will naturally lower its alcoholic content, a hydrometer will indicate if the particular product in question has been tampered with.

7 Spotting Services — Another option available to management is to enlist the services of a spotting service to scrutinize the operation. Spotters are essentially detectives who, armed with the operation's prices, policies and procedures, will sit at the bar observing the legitimacy of the bartenders' activities.

A missing drink ticket should be treated as a serious breach of the operation's policies and procedures.

Care must be taken when selecting which spotting service to retain as there is a wide disparity in their professional abilities. In addition, bartenders often have a feeling that they are being watched and they will naturally curtail their clandestine activities. In that event, the detectives would submit a clean and misleading report, when in fact, the bartenders might very well be engaged in stealing from the establishment. The opposite is also possible. A spotter could misconstrue what he or she observed and report back to management that the bartenders were engaged in theft, when in reality, they were not.

QUESTIONS LEAD TO ANSWERS WHICH LEAD TO SUCCESS

- Do you employ a spotting service to observe improprieties in the operation?
- Do you prohibit the register's cash drawer from remaining open between transactions?
- Are bartender's allowed to reconcile their cash drawer at the end of the shift?
- Are bartender's allowed to participate in the physical inventory process?
- Can your bartenders open the cash register using the "no sale" key? Under what circumstances are they allowed to use the "no sale?"
- Are your bartenders required to take a daily bar par reading?
- Do you permit bartenders to make change from their tip jars? Are they permitted to exchange coins from their tip jar for currency?
- Are any other hourly employees allowed to go behind the bar other than the bartenders? Do shift managers go behind the bar on a regular basis?
- Is the tip jar located near the cash register?
- Once imprinted, can drink checks be fraudulently reused?
- Do you use a "drop box" as a secure repository for used drink checks behind the bar?
- Does the POS or register L.E.D. display face the public?

- After serving a patron a drink, are bartenders required to state the price of the drink and amount tendered?
- Are bartenders allowed to "tail" or overpour liquor portions?
- Are bartenders allowed to underpour liquor portions? Are they allowed to "top-pour" liquor, the practice of pouring liquor into a glass after the mixer.
- Do you use a two-measure, stainless steel jigger at your bar? Are the jiggers marked in such a way that they cannot be switched surreptitiously?
- Does more than one bartender work out of the same cash drawer?
- Do you permit patrons to open "drink tabs?" Are there measures to ensure that every drink served is recorded onto the tab?
- Is the liquor inventory storeroom locked and secured? Is there limited access to the liquor room?
- Do you regularly conduct a "z" reading and exchange the cash drawer during a bartending shift?
- Do bartenders bring bags, backpacks or purses behind the bar?
- Are there measures in place to prevent employees from falsifying their time cards or inflating their payroll figure by "riding the clock?"

Chapter 23

The Legal Aspects of Serving Alcohol

In every jurisdiction in the United States it is considered a statutory offense for servers of alcohol to cause or contribute to a person's state of intoxication. To remain in compliance with the law, bartenders and servers must refuse further service to any individual exhibiting signs of intoxication. This makes it vitally important that all servers of alcohol understand how alcohol affects the human physiology. They must also be capable of identifying the visible indicators of intoxication and know how to properly deal with a patron who has become intoxicated.

Servers must also be aware that they as well as the business can be held civilly liable for the subsequent actions of an intoxicated patron. This liability is imposed through case law or legislative action, and is generally referred to as the Dram Shop Acts. Loosely defined the Dram Shop Acts are the statutes that establish a civil liability upon servers and licensees when an innocent third party is injured by an intoxicated patron. For a plaintiff to win most Dram Shop suits it must be proven that the server sold alcohol to the patron in question when he or she was already intoxicated, and that the alcohol was the cause of the accident. The intention of the Dram Shop Acts is to place the burden of responsibility onto the server of the alcohol, rather than the consumer or innocent third party.

> **Servers must be aware that they as well as the business can be held civilly liable for the subsequent actions of an intoxicated patron.**

The tactics, strategies and psychology surrounding the service of alcohol are referred to as intervention procedures. Intervention can be defined as a responsible individual placing himself or herself between the consumer and the beverage alcohol. A comprehensive understanding of intervention procedures is the most cost-effective form of insurance protecting the licensee and server alike against the civil litigation or the loss of the operation's liquor license.

THE THEORY OF ALCOHOL EQUIVALENCY

The theory of alcohol equivalency states that there is the same amount of ethyl alcohol in one-ounce of 86.8-proof whiskey, 12-ounces of draft or bottled beer and 5-ounces of table wine. The theory further states that regardless of which product is consumed, alcohol is alcohol, and when ingested, each will produce the same physiological effects and the same relative levels of alcohol-induced impairment.

The controversy over this theory stems from the fact that numerous medical studies reveal that the alcohol in distilled spirits produce significantly faster and higher blood alcohol concentrations than the alcohol present in either beer or wine. Beer and wine contain natural, organic substances not present in distilled spirits that have a buffering effect on the alcohol. This buffering action delays the absorption rate of the alcohol into the bloodstream. The alcohol in beer and wine produces a slower and lower peak in blood alcohol concentration than the alcohol in distilled spirits. Therefore, people are more likely to become impaired or intoxicated faster drinking liquor than beer or wine.

> **The alcohol in beer and wine produces a slower and lower peak in blood alcohol concentration than the alcohol in distilled spirits.**

While it appears that the scientific foundation for the theory of equivalency remains in doubt, it has had a positive effect. It has caused servers of alcohol, as well as the general public, to reevaluate any outdated and potentially dangerous misconceptions about the consumption of beer and wine. People can, and frequently do become intoxicated drinking beer and wine. What is true is that the same amount of discretion must be used when serving beer or wine as it is when serving distilled spirits.

THE ABSORPTION RATE OF ALCOHOL

The amount of alcohol absorbed into a person's bloodstream and the rate at which it enters the system are the two largest factors affecting intoxication. Essentially, the more alcohol absorbed into the bloodstream, the more negatively impaired an individual will become. Likewise, the faster the alcohol is absorbed into the bloodstream, the more rapidly a person will become intoxicated and exhibit signs of impairment. It is important that servers of alcohol understand how alcohol enters the bloodstream and what factors directly affect the rate of absorption.

When a person initially consumes an alcoholic beverage, approximately 2-4% of the alcohol is absorbed directly into the bloodstream while still in the mouth. It then travels to the stomach where another 10-15% is diffused into the bloodstream through the lining of the stomach walls. The remaining alcohol in the stomach, nearly 82-88% passes through the Pyloric junction or valve that is located at the base of the stomach, and enters the small intestine. It is then rapidly absorbed into the bloodstream.

There are five main factors that affect the rate alcohol is absorbed into the bloodstream.

1 **Food** — Food will have a slowing affect on the absorption rate of alcohol. When food and alcohol enter the stomach, the Pyloric valve shuts and will remain closed until the food matter is completely digested. The action of the Pyloric valve keeps the majority of the alcohol away from the small intestine, where the alcohol is most rapidly absorbed into the bloodstream.

After the food is completely digested, the Pyloric valve will open, allowing the food/alcohol mixture to pass into the small intestine. The more food there is in the stomach, the longer this process will take, further delaying the absorption of the alcohol. In addition, some of the alcohol in this mixture passes harmlessly unabsorbed through the small intestine and into the large intestine. Medical studies have shown that when a person drinks with a meal, the rise in blood alcohol concentration is significantly slower and will peak at a lower point.

Food will have a slowing affect on the absorption rate of alcohol.

2 **Type of Food** — The type of food ingested will also play a role in the absorption rate. Fatty foods, such as cheese, nuts, or deep fried items, are difficult for the stomach to digest. These foods remain in the stomach for a longer amount of time. The alcohol will also remain in the stomach, thus further delaying absorption. On the other hand, foods high in carbohydrates, such as pasta, bread, potatoes, rice, and pretzels, are rapidly digested and may actually accelerate the absorption rate of alcohol into the bloodstream.

3 **Use of Drugs or Medicine** — While the simultaneous use of drugs or medicines and alcohol will not actually increase the absorption rate of alcohol into the bloodstream, the combination will significantly alter the individual's reactions to the alcohol. The mental and physiological effects of alcohol are amplified and accelerated when combined with marijuana, amphetamines, barbiturates, cocaine, and cold or allergy medicines. The sale of two or three

drinks to someone under the influence of the aforementioned drugs or medication can rapidly precipitate alcohol-induced intoxication.

4 **Beverage Carbonation** — The presence of carbonation in a drink or beverage will expedite the absorption of alcohol into the bloodstream. Products such as draft or bottled beer, champagne or sparkling wines, and carbonated mixers have a tendency to cause the Pyloric valve to open prematurely, causing the alcohol in the stomach to pass directly into the small intestine where it is rapidly absorbed.

5 **Mood or Disposition** — A person's emotional state can cause the absorption rate to initially decrease. Emotions such as stress, anxiety, worry, or depression will cause the stomach to excrete mucus. This mucus will coat the lining of the stomach walls, preventing any alcohol present from being absorbed either through the stomach lining or in the small intestine.

As an individual begins to relax, the mucus coating will begin to dissipate, and in turn, the Pyloric valve will relax and open, allowing the critical mass of unabsorbed alcohol to virtually "dump" into the small intestine. This rapid influx of alcohol into the small intestine causes a sudden surge of alcohol to be absorbed into the bloodstream, the effect of which is a dramatic acceleration in intoxication.

FACTORS AFFECTING BLOOD ALCOHOL CONCENTRATION

Once alcohol is absorbed into the bloodstream, it is circulated and distributed to all of the organs and tissues in the body. The alcohol is diffused into cells in amounts proportional to their water content. Nerves, muscles, and the brain achieve relatively high concentrations of alcohol, whereas bone and fatty tissue absorb comparatively little.

The higher a person's blood alcohol concentration (BAC), the higher the level of alcohol-induced impairment. It is important that servers of alcohol have a detailed understanding of the factors that will directly affect an individual's BAC. This knowledge will allow them to assess each patron's consumption of alcohol and be in the position to anticipate any potential problems before they arise.

1 **Body Size and Weight** — The absorbed alcohol is greatly diluted by the body's fluids. In a man of average build, the alcohol in an ounce of distilled spirits is diluted to a BAC of approximately 2 parts per 10,000, or 0.02%. In a larger person, this dilution is significantly increased, causing the BAC to be proportionately less. The converse is true about a smaller person.

In addition, the more a person weighs the more body mass available to absorb the alcohol from the bloodstream. Therefore, the higher the body weight, the less a person's BAC will rise per ounce of alcohol consumed.

2 **Body Type** — Due to the fact that fatty tissue will not absorb alcohol, whereas muscle tissue will, a trim and physically fit individual will experience a lower increase in BAC per ounce of alcohol consumed than a person with a higher body fat content.

3 **Gender** — Medical research has found that the stomach lining in women is less effective in neutralizing alcohol than the lining in a man's stomach. Women possess smaller amounts of a dehydrogenase, the enzyme responsible for metabolizing alcohol in the stomach. This enzyme deficiency allows more alcohol to pass through the stomach and eventually into the bloodstream. Consequently, a woman's blood alcohol concentration will rise higher per ounce of alcohol consumed than a man's will.

4 **Rate of Consumption** — The faster a person consumes an alcoholic beverage, the faster his or her BAC will rise and the more rapidly that person will become intoxicated.

5 **Alcohol Content/Potency** — The higher the alcoholic content in a beverage, the faster and higher a person's BAC will increase. A 100-proof liquor will more negatively affect a person than an equivalent amount of 80-proof spirits.

The manner in which the alcohol is prepared will also have an affect on the potency. For example, a martini served straight-up is more potent than a martini served on-the-rocks because the melting ice in the glass will dilute the alcohol. When a drink is blended, all of the ice used in its preparation is blended into the drink, rendering it less potent than a drink served either straight-up or on-the-rocks. The customer will, in actuality, consume more water than alcohol. Finally, because it's prepared using more mixer, a "tall" highball drink is less potent than one prepared in the regular manner.

6 **Type of Beverage** — Medical studies have shown that distilled spirits will cause a person's BAC to increase at a faster rate, and peak at a higher point, than will the alcohol present in either beer or wine.

THE DETOXIFICATION PROCESS

Detoxification is the process by which the body eliminates and disposes of any toxic substance in the bloodstream, such as drugs and alcohol. The body begins to dispose of the alcohol immediately after it is absorbed. Between 2-10% of the alcohol in the blood is detoxified as a result of being exhaled, excreted through sweat, and through accumulation in the kidney and elimination in the urine. Upwards of 90% of the absorbed alcohol in the bloodstream is metabolized and disposed of primarily in the liver.

The body can detoxify alcohol at a rate of approximately one ounce per hour, or one 12-ounce beer, or 4 ounces of white table wine. This roughly translates to a BAC decrease of 0.015% per hour. Coffee, cold showers, or pure oxygen will have no real affect on the rate of detoxification. The only factor that will affect the sobering-up process is time. The one minor exception is strenuous physical exercise and heavy perspiration.

The body can detoxify alcohol at a rate of approximately one ounce per hour.

THE PHYSIOLOGICAL EFFECTS OF ALCOHOL

Alcohol is classified as a depressant, along with tranquilizers, barbiturates, and general anesthetics. Its initial reaction on the physiology at low blood alcohol concentrations is varied. In most individuals, it will produce a prevailing sense of calm, tranquillity, and well-being. In others, alcohol will act as a stimulant, producing feelings of exhilaration, animation, elation, loss of inhibition, unexpected mood swings, talkativeness, and occasional emotional outbursts.

As a person's BAC increases, the alcohol produces a relative state of depression. This depression will deepen with each drink and can contribute to an individual becoming somber, melancholy, arrogant, boisterous, obnoxious, or even suicidal.

Depending on the exact circumstances and the particular individual in question, a person's BAC will rise approximately 0.016-0.04% per ounce of alcohol consumed. An average-sized male will experience a BAC increase of approximately 0.02% per ounce of distilled spirits. An individual's BAC will not peak at its highest level for 15-30 minutes after the individual stops drinking. In addition, the impairing effects of the alcohol will continue to increase approximately 25% for about another hour.

Most people will begin showing signs of intoxication at a BAC of 0.05-0.1%, and it is generally accepted that nearly anyone will demonstrate measurable impairment at 0.2% BAC. At a BAC of 0.4% and above, most will be incapable of voluntary functions and anesthetized into unconsciousness. At higher concentrations an individual is highly susceptible to lapsing into a coma. Between 0.5-1% BAC, the breathing center in the brain and the action of the heart muscle is fatally anesthetized.

THE VISIBLE INDICATORS OF INTOXICATION

The practical reality surrounding the service of alcohol is that the only means a server or bartender can use to determine the level of a patron's alcohol-induced impairment is through direct observation, making note of the recognizable signs of intoxication. The effects of drinking alcohol impairs a person's judgment, ability to concentrate, coordination, neuromuscular functions, sensory perceptions, and reflexes. As a person continues to drink, the gradual effects of the alcohol become increasingly more apparent. These alcohol-induced affectations are easily identified, and in many cases, glaringly obvious.

The only means a server or bartender can use to determine the level of a patron's alcohol-induced impairment is through direct observation.

While alcohol will affect people differently, there are four identifiable stages someone passes through when becoming intoxicated. It is imperative that servers and bartenders recognize these observable indications associated with each stage of alcohol-induced impairment. It may be the only viable means of gauging a patron's level of intoxication.

• **1st Stage of Impairment** — Noticeable Alteration of Behavior
    As alcohol gradually begins to affect the physiology, a person may begin to lose his or her inhibitions. A person may become noticeably emotional and demonstrate sudden and unexpected mood swings. Essentially, in this initial stage there is a general relaxation of behavior patterns.
    Visible indicators of this first stage may include:
• Reversed personality behavior; uncontrolled emotional displays or outbursts; sudden, unexpected mood swings; displays of immaturity; excessive profanity; acting in an annoying and irritating manner; crude or rude behavior.

- Becoming increasingly louder, boisterous, animated, agitated or entertaining; overtly friendly with other customers or employees; excessive touching.
- Brooding, detached, solitary or anti-social behavior; leaving a group to drink alone; somber or melancholy appearance.

• 2nd Stage of Impairment — Temporary Dissociation

Alcohol will almost immediately begin affecting the higher brain functions, such as clear thinking, logic, learning, remembering and judgment. As an individual's blood alcohol concentration steadily increases, sensible action and rational thinking will steadily diminish.

Visible indicators of this second stage may include:
- Increased rate of consumption; ordering more-potent drinks; careless with money, leaving money unattended for long periods; offering to buy drinks for total strangers.
- Diminished alertness; inability to make fine discriminations; making irrational, unsubstantiated statements.
- Complaining about drink strength, preparation or price; displays of bravado, confrontational, argumentative, aggressive or belligerent behavior.

• 3rd Stage of Impairment — Impairment to Normal
Brain Function

Alcohol has an adverse effect on brain activity and will diminish reactions and impair normal brain function. As BAC increases, activities which normally require no conscious thought, such as lighting a cigarette or speaking clearly, gradually become more difficult.

Visible indicators of this stage may include:
- Loss of concentration and sequence of thought; digressing or trailing off and not finishing sentences,
- Lessened eye contact; eyes glassy and unfocused; pupils dilated,
- Slurred speech; exaggerated or deliberate speech,
- Difficulty handling cigarettes; lighting the wrong end of a cigarette,
- Drowsiness; drooping eyelids; excessive yawning.

• 4th Stage of Impairment — Loss of Dexterity and
Muscle Control

As the alcohol in the bloodstream gradually affects the central nervous system, a person's coordination will steadily deteriorate and diminish to the point where simple tasks become challenging.

Hand/eye coordination, dexterity, and motor functions are severely impaired.

Visible indicators of this fourth stage may include:
- Increased clumsiness in handling small objects like coins, lighters and cigarettes,
- Spilling drinks; inability to find mouth with the glass,
- Difficulty maneuvering around furniture; loss of balance; lessening ability to stand or sit upright,
- Unsteady gait; weaving, swaying, stumbling, staggering.

GUIDELINES FOR SERVING ALCOHOL

Without question, bartenders and servers are in the best position to make the decision whether or not to serve a patron another drink. Considering the legal ramifications it is imperative that they consistently make the right decisions. Failure on their part to exercise sound judgment can have severe consequences for all concerned. Everyone involved in the operation must have an unwavering commitment to serving alcohol responsibly and protecting the safety of the clientele, as well as the public-at-large.

The intent of alcohol-awareness training is to provide servers with a sound, factual basis to make informed service-related decisions. It is critical they become comfortable exercising their right and obligation to refuse further service to anyone visibly intoxicated and to have the skills to confidently handle this type of situation when it occurs.

The primary service rule regarding the sale of alcohol should always be, "When In Doubt, Don't Serve." While this may seem oversimplified, it is the best guideline available. It is important to forego the sale if there is any doubt as to the sobriety of the patron. You can ask no more from your staff than to exercise their best judgment in these situations. There is too much at stake to base the decision whether or not to serve alcohol on anything less.

It is advisable for servers to keep a mental count of how many drinks a patron has consumed. The number of drinks consumed will provide an approximation of how much alcohol a patron has ingested. This information will prove beneficial when supporting the decision to refuse further service.

Bartenders and servers should also be instructed to never serve alcohol to someone not yet present. Frequently, two customers will sit down at the bar and order three drinks, one of which is for a third person out parking the car or perhaps in the restroom. In this situation, the bartender should only serve the two patrons present, and wait to prepare the third cocktail until the other person arrives. This third individual could very well be a minor, or someone already intoxicated. Unfortunately, this is an all too common ploy to illegally obtain alcohol.

It is essential that the staff understand that management will support their decision to refuse further service of alcohol to any customer. This support will make it considerably easier for them to exercise their judgment and cut off a patron when necessary. In nearly every instance, the server is in a better position than the manager-on-duty to assess a customer's sobriety. Therefore, management should always be willing to support a server in his or her effort to refuse further service.

It is essential that the staff understand that management will support their decision to refuse further service of alcohol to any customer.

Bartenders and servers should be informed that while you will not overrule their decision to refuse further service to a customer, you do reserve the right to overrule their decision to serve alcohol. Considering the magnitude of what is involved, the safest and most conservative position should always prevail.

What makes refusing further service complicated and often intimidating is that alcohol has a destabilizing effect on a drinker's emotional state. It is difficult to anticipate whether a customer will acknowledge the refusal calmly or react in an agitated or belligerent manner.

Tact and diplomacy are the two strongest attributes a server can possess. When refusing further service, it is important to avoid using inflammatory language or assuming a judgmental, disapproving attitude. Telling someone under the influence that he or she is drunk or intoxicated will likely provoke an incident.

Bartenders and servers should make a concerted effort to avoid embarrassing the patron by keeping their voice quiet and remaining sensitive to the customer's feelings and predicament. However, they are to remain firm about refusing the individual further service of alcohol. Their tone should be authoritative without being overbearing or condescending.

Regardless of what is said when "cutting off" a customer, the simpler the approach the easier it will be to intervene in the future. An important part of intervention training is for bartenders and servers to be familiar with how to best accomplish the task in the fewest words. The more automatic it becomes to deliver the lines, the more comfortable they will be when obliged to refuse a patron further service.

Essentially, a patron can be refused further service of alcohol either before or after he or she has become intoxicated. The approach the bartender or server takes will depend on the customer's level of impairment.

Informing a guest that he or she is being refused another drink is better received and less involved when done before the person reaches the point of intoxication. The best tactic to adopt in this situation is to serve the guest his or her drink and then inform the patron that it will be his or her last drink of the evening. For instance, a person orders a drink and the bartender knows that it will be the last one that can be safely served to the person that night. When the bartender serves the customer the cocktail, he or she should lean forward and quietly say, "Here you are . . . drink this one slowly because it's the last one I can serve you tonight."

In essence, the person is only being denied further service of alcohol, and is not being deprived the opportunity to "nurse" what will be his or her last drink of the evening. This approach will cause little embarrassment for a patron, and will usually not cause a negative response.

The approach the bartender or server takes will depend on the customer's level of impairment.

Telling someone who is already intoxicated that he or she will not be served any more alcohol is a straightforward proposition. In the fewest words possible the bartender or server should inform the patron that in his or her best judgment the person has already had enough to drink and will therefore not be served any more alcohol. There is no need to add any thing else to the statement. It is direct and to the point.

The message says that it was the bartender's or server's decision based on his or her best judgment. It does not accuse the patron of being drunk. If the statement is delivered properly, it will probably not foster a negative reaction. If the refusal is met with a negative reaction, the manager should be notified immediately. It is management's responsibility to handle these kinds of customer situations.

After a customer has been "cut off," the other bartender(s) on duty should be notified of the refusal of service so they do not mistakenly serve the individual another drink. In this case, miscommunication can be as damaging as inaction.

The bartender's or server's role in the procedure ends when the owner or manager is informed of the situation. It is then up to management to see that the situation is handled correctly, allowing the bartender or server to resume his or her duties.

At this time management should arrange alternate means of transportation for the guest to get home. The options available are to either call a taxi cab to drive the customer home, or assist the patron in calling a friend or relative to take protective custody, so to speak. It is important that the intoxicated person not get behind the wheel of his or her car.

AGE IDENTIFICATION AND REQUESTING PROPER ID

One of the most serious problems facing eating and drinking establishments is the service of alcohol to minors. There are severe legal ramifications for serving alcohol to a minor. If nothing else, self-preservation dictates that the business must institute strict policies and procedures prohibiting underage patrons from purchasing and consuming alcohol on the premises.

Compounding the situation is that typically bartenders, cocktail waitresses, and food servers have an aversion carding guests prior to serving alcohol. It's an understandable reluctance. Checking identification is a clumsy, unpleasant, and time-consuming procedure. In addition, there is always the possibility that a person will become defensive and confrontational.

The vast majority of operators enforce a policy that servers must card any guest ordering alcohol who appears younger than 30 years old. The staff absolutely must be trained how to quickly spot a minor. While looks can be deceiving, and many people appear younger or older than their years, there are several guidelines to consider when estimating a person's age.

1. **Type of Apparel** — Younger people often wear clothes imprinted with the name of a college or University, musical group, or sports team. Minors frequently wear high school rings, ID bracelets, trendy watches and "pop" jewelry.

2. **Physical Appearance** — A generally youthful appearance, bad complexion, and trendy hair styles might suggest someone in his or her late teens or early twenties. Exhibitions of immature behavior could also indicate that a person is under the legal drinking age.

3. **Drinking Habits** — Individuals under the legal drinking age are likely to sit in corner booths or in dark areas near the back of the house so as to avoid being conspicuous. They are more likely to attempt to purchase alcohol early in the evening or late at night and

to pay with cash. Because they have limited drinking experience, minors often order draft or bottled beer, or basic drinks such as Rum and Coke, Tequila Sunrise, Seven & Seven, etc.

4. **Presenting Identification** — Usually minors won't bring along a purse or wallet and will only have one piece of ID, this to avoid being placed in the position of having to produce a second piece of identification.

5. **Costumes and Make-Up** — Halloween and costume parties pose singular problems with respect to age identification. Masks and heavy use of theatrical make-up can make people look older than their years. Formal attire, make-up, and jewelry can also make a person appear older, making New Year's celebrations and wedding receptions particularly challenging.

HOW TO REQUEST PROPER IDENTIFICATION

The first line of defense is to card everyone who looks under 30 years as they enter the door. This is typically the responsibility of a doorman or security guard. Bartenders and servers must be made to understand that even checking identification at the door doesn't relieve them of the responsibility to card young looking guests at the bar. Servers of alcohol are always responsible for establishing that a guest is of legal drinking age. If in doubt, a bartender or server should always ask for ID.

When carding someone, the simplest approach is the best. The approach should be something along the lines of, "I need to see ID before I can serve you alcohol." If the person balks, a good response would be, "Sir, it's the law", or "It's management policy." The delivery of these lines should be fluent and automatic. There is no need for extra dialogue or apologies, both of which only tend to complicate matters.

The employee should request that the guest remove the identification ID from the wallet or other similar enclosure. After the patron has offered identification, the bartender or server should check the date of birth and verify the individual is of legal drinking age. They should also compare the photo on the piece of identification with the presenter's actual appearance.

If there is any doubt as to the authenticity of the identification, the employee should ask the person questions pertaining to the information on the ID. If the server is unconvinced, he or she should request a second piece of identification.

SPOTTING FAKE IDs

A piece of identification must contain a picture of the bearer to be considered legally acceptable for the service of alcohol. There are primarily four acceptable forms of identification: a valid state-issued driver's license; a state-issued Identification Card; a United States Military Identification Card; and a valid United States passport. University/college picture identification, bank cards, and credit cards are not acceptable forms of ID for establishing legal drinking age.

Legally acceptable pieces of identification are usually laminated, tamper-proof and issued by a bona fide government agency. They provide a complete physical description of the bearer. A piece of identification needs to be signed to be considered legally acceptable.

Most fake or altered identification is doctored such that it will pass visual inspection under normal lighting conditions. Backlighting will often reveal alterations to a piece of identification. Shining a flashlight through the item from the underside will quickly reveal erasures and deletions.

Drivers' licenses are the most frequently altered or fraudulent form of identification. The following points are important to check when inspecting a driver's license:

1. **Picture** — Look for proper quality of lighting (balanced lighting/few shadows); clarity of focus (image not blurry); proper subject centering (person in middle of the frame/upper torso on up); background in photo inconsistent with normal government issue (not solid color or photographic screen); non-standard posing (head should be erect and eyes looking forward); picture should be flush with license (feel for raised edge around photograph).

2. **Laminate** — Look for cracks, splits, cuts, or open edges; over-sized laminate (standard laminate no more than 1/4 inch past edge of document); laminate trimmed unevenly/crooked.

3. **Printing** — Look for printing not straight; type appears photocopied versus printed (look for obvious photocopying on back of license); blurry edges on type face; multiple type sizes or faces.

4. **Miscellaneous** — Look for newness of the identification (fake identification is more likely to appear new); if the identification is not laminated it will feel like photo film paper (look on back for manufacturer's name—Eastman Kodak, Fugi, etc.); surname used on the bogus identification is usually easily pronounced (common names are easier to remember).

QUESTIONS LEAD TO ANSWERS
WHICH LEAD TO SUCCESS

- Is there Dram Shop legislation in force in your state?
- Has your staff been briefed on the civil liability surrounding the service of alcohol?
- Does the operation conduct on-going alcohol-awareness and intervention training?
- Have all of the servers been instructed on how alcohol affects the physiology?
- Have all of the servers been trained on the various factors that affect absorption rate?
- Have all of the servers been trained on the various factors that affect blood alcohol concentration?
- Have all of the servers been trained how to identify the indicators of intoxication?
- Are all of the servers familiar with the operation's guidelines on serving alcohol?
- Have all of the servers been trained how to request identification and how to spot minors?
- Have all of the servers received training on how to spot fake identification?

Chapter 24

Protecting Customer and Employee Safety

Like cooking with grease, the potential for a major flare-up between people drinking alcohol seemingly goes with the territory. Acts of violence on your licensed premises pose a significant problem. You are legally obligated to protect the physical safety and welfare of your guests and employees. Whether a person was the aggressor or victim, each must be protected from harm and injury. The days of telling combatants to "take it outside" are long gone.

You will need to instruct your staff on how you want them to respond to fights on-premise. Are they to physically intervene or back off and call the police? What are they to do if weapons are involved?

It is critically important to stop fights before they start.

ON-PREMISE SECURITY

Unfortunately in this business, there will be times when a patron has had too much to drink and then becomes loud, disruptive or starts trouble of some sort. It is critically important to stop fights before they start. One of the things to remember is that most people provoked to the point of contemplating violence are intoxicated. Ensuring the safety of your guests as well as the public-at-large is one of the primary reasons for insisting that your bartending staff strive to prevent guests from becoming intoxicated.

One of the best ways to avoid a fight from breaking out is to be aware of what is going on in the bar. Keep an eye out for trouble. Arguments typically precede an outbreak of violence. When a verbal altercation erupts, intervene in a friendly, yet firm way to defuse the situation. The individuals involved must be told that this sort of behavior will not be tolerated and they will have to immediately disengage and "cool off," or leave the premise. Never imply that they should take their "argument outside," your "licensed premises" includes the parking lot.

See if you can get one of the patrons involved to leave the premises. If they both refuse, threaten to call the police. Often just the threat works well enough. If you do call the police, inform them that there is not an emergency but that you have asked a customer to leave and they have not done so.

Once the police arrive, the patron(s) should again be asked to leave. If they refuse to leave in the presence of a police officer, then the person will be charged with trespassing and can be charged with a misdemeanor.

In the event that a fight breaks out, call the police immediately. Make sure customers are ushered to a safe area so that they do not risk getting injured. Never allow a customer to break up a fight. Should the person become injured as a result, the business may potentially be held liable. Do not become physically involved, or allow employees to get involved in the altercation. You may defend yourself or an employee only, and absolutely only, if you are physically attacked.

In the event that a fight breaks out, call the police immediately.

Under no circumstances are you to provide aid in a fight, provide weapons, or use excessive force. Excessive force means physically throwing someone out of the bar, slamming someone against a wall, striking someone, or physically restraining someone. Such acts may result in physical injury and expose the company and personnel involved to civil liability or criminal prosecution.

Should a weapon be brandished, the police should be immediately called. Try to keep the situation from getting more out of control. Your immediate concern should be for your personal safety, and the safety of your employees and clientele. Do not allow an employee or guest to become involved. Urge your employees and guests to get down and lie on the floor. Everyone under your influence should be made to understand that there is to be absolutely no attempts at heroics.

Once the police have arrived, it is important to give them as much detail about the circumstances surrounding the incident as possible. Make sure to document all details of the fight. Provide a full description of the patrons involved. Record all of the events leading up to the fight. Make sure to document the level of intoxication of the patrons involved.

ESTABLISHING ARMED ROBBERY PROCEDURES

Armed robberies present the most dangerous and hazardous of situations. The brazen nature of the crime immediately suggests the perpetrator(s) are desperate and inured to the risks involved. At a staff meeting, instruct employees how to respond during this type of crisis situation, in effect, instituting "robbery procedures."

Until you've had a gun pulled on you, it's difficult to imagine how terrifying an armed robbery actually is. The unfortunate reality is that a bar, nightclub or restaurant are prime targets for armed robbery-high profile, high visibility, cash businesses.

Employees should greet customers with good eye contact. According to the police, robbers are overtly concerned about being identified after the fact. They should make note of anything suspicious, a bulge under a jacket or someone unusually nervous or agitated. It is illegal in this country to allow a weapon onto a licensed premise.

Armed robberies present the most dangerous and hazardous of situations.

The operation is most vulnerable at closing, a time when there is the most cash on-hand and the fewest employees on-premise. As a precaution, it is advisable that the manager on-duty leave the establishment with the other closing employees. There is safety in numbers.

In the event of an armed robbery, urge that your staff remain calm, alert and observant. Panic will only heighten the danger. Emphasize that their safety and welfare is your primary concern. Money can be replaced, human life cannot. The perpetrator's instructions and commands are to be followed completely and without hesitation. The robber should be told about other employees or customers on the premises. Someone unexpectedly interrupting the robbery-in-progress presents a real danger.

The employees should make slow, deliberate movements; they are not to do anything sudden. Instruct them to tell the perpetrator in advance everything they are about to do and to keep their hands within sight. If they need to place their hands where the robber can't see them, they should tell the perpetrator what they're doing. In addition, they shouldn't stare directly into the robber's eyes. It will heighten his anxieties and general state of paranoia. During a robbery, employees should open the cash register and back away, allowing unobstructed access to the money.

Avoid confrontation and do not openly resist. Employees should cooperate fully with the robber. They are to give him any cash or supplies on demand. There should be no resistance or attempt to deceive him concerning the amount or location of what he asks for. However, they should not volunteer any information. The employees should always comply with the robber's wishes and never do anything to increase the tension of the situation. Armed robbers are typically extremely nervous, jittery and feel the surging effects of adrenaline. There is also the possibility that the person is under the influence of drugs or alcohol, or both. Any act of defiance will likely escalate into violence.

While the robbery is in progress, employees should make note of the perpetrator's physical characteristics, such as height, weight, the color of his eyes, skin, etc. Recognition of small, unchangeable details is extremely helpful to the police. They are to look for any distinguishing features, such as a scar, mark or tattoo. Did the perpetrator speak with a lisp or have an accent? Did he walk with a limp? Was he is right or left-handed? Even knowing what kind of jewelry the person was wearing can be of assistance.

> **While the robbery is in progress, employees should make note of the perpetrator's physical characteristics.**

Information regarding the weapon used is also beneficial. If it was a handgun, was it a revolver or automatic? Did it have a long or short barrel? What color was it?

Finally, do not follow the perpetrator. When he leaves, the employees should only attempt to see which direction he left in. If possible, they are to observe the make, model and color of his car and the license number.

DEVELOPING AFTER-THE-EVENT PROCEDURES

Contact the police as soon as it's safe to do so. It's extremely important to leave the crime scene undisturbed. Avoid handling anything that the perpetrator may have touched, preserving any fingerprints left behind.

Before the police arrive, get the names and addresses of any witnesses to the crime. Request that they remain until the authorities arrive. Also, it is important that employees be debriefed that same evening if at all possible. Sometimes employees have second thoughts about becoming involved and cooperating with the police. Without the employees' formal statement, prosecution is next to impossible.

Write down pertinent facts immediately. Each person should write down all the information he or she remembers without discussing it with anyone else. Give the police your complete cooperation when they arrive.

Do not discuss details of the incident until all questioning has been completed. Secure the names and addresses of all persons present at the time of the robbery. Assist the police or investigators as needed.

SECURITY PRECAUTIONS

The back of the facility is where your operation and employees are most vulnerable. Halogen security lights that illuminate the rear of the building and parking lot are an excellent deterrent. The area around the rear door should be free of anything behind which someone could hide.

Hold-up alarms, security video cameras and other security-related systems are effective and provide a measure of reassurance. These systems should be tested regularly to ensure that they are operational. Any equipment not in working order should be repaired immediately; its breakdown could be the result of criminal machination. Conspicuous notices should be posted that the premise is wired with an alarm system. This alone may prove to be a sufficient deterrent.

The back of the facility is where your operation and employees are most vulnerable.

Bank deposits should be made daily, at different times of the day, and if possible, at different bank branches. Avoiding a predictable routine is paramount. An alternative to you making bank deposits is to retain a bonded courier or armored car service. Never allow employees to make your business deposits.

Keep the amount of currency in the register to a minimum. Make numerous cash drops during the course of operations, pulling excess currency, usually large denominations, out of the register. Not only will this lessen any potential loss, but also a drawer stuffed with cash attracts undue attention.

Front and rear doors should be locked at the earliest opportunity. Exterior signs should be turned off upon locking the front door, and not just prior to departing from the operation for the night. Before closing, check all entry points and anywhere someone could hide in your business, including the stalls in the rest rooms.

Be suspicious of any unsolicited phone calls from a security company canvassing for sales prospects. Bona fide security companies don't operate in this manner. The caller is more likely "casing" your operation, probing for weaknesses and hoping you'll divulge security-related information.

The following are security precautions to consider implementing:

- Always be alert during opening and closing times and exercise sound judgement. Call the police immediately if when opening the establishment you find the doors unlocked. Do not enter the store alone prior to arrival of the police. Allow the police to completely check out the establishment.
- Do not unlock doors except during posted hours. Allow only known people inside before opening.
- When counting money the office door should remained closed and locked, and keep interruptions to a minimum. Never count money in public view.
- At no time during business hours should any employee leave the register or point of sale system unattended. Allow only "on-duty" employees in work areas. Keep the delivery, storeroom, liquor room, and office doors closed and locked at all times.

- Be aware of any suspicious people loitering in or around your place of business. Be wary of people breaking large bills. If the bartender has no problem cashing a $100 bill he must have an extreme amount of available cash on hand, enough to risk a hold-up. Withdraw as much cash as possible before 11:00 PM, leaving the rest for one trip after closing.
- Immediately after closing, lock up the money. Allow no one in the licensed premises after closing. Leave the register empty, open and visible at night. Make sure all exterior lights are on and working properly.
- If you terminate an employee who has keys and alarm codes, or should the employee resign voluntarily, get the locks and codes changed immediately. Do not leave keys to the business where anyone unauthorized will have access to them.
- Do not keep more than one day's deposits on hand. Do not leave the deposit "laying around." Get it to the bank, or leave it locked up. Do not leave the deposit in your car.
- Never schedule people to work alone in the store. This is a bad security risk. People observed to be working alone are prime targets for robbery.
- When closing for the night, make sure all doors and exits are locked. Check restrooms and storage rooms, etc., where a potential robber could hide or wait for you to close the store. Split employees into two groups when leaving the bar after closing.

SAFETY PROCEDURES

Ensuring the safety of your employees and guests is fundamentally important. Aside from the obligation you have as an employer to safeguard their welfare and safety, a safe work place results in fewer mishaps and injuries, which is essential to creating a positive work environment.

Therefore, for the safety of your guests and employees, the following safety procedures should be adhered to without exception.

Clothing Requirements

- All employees should wear clothes that fit properly and that allow them to move easily and comfortably.
- All employees should avoid wearing jewelry that might catch on something and cause employees injury.
- All employees should wear shoes that have closed heels and toes. They should have an appropriate heel height for balance and comfort. Shoes should also provide good ankle support and have good traction.

Lifting Heavy Objects

- The proper procedure for lifting heavy objects, such as kegs of beer or cases of beer, begins with spreading the feet apart, one foot in front of the other, squatting down as close to the object as possible.
- The object should be grasped with the palms of the hands, keeping the arms close to the body. This will allow the individual to use the strength in his or her legs and will prevent the person from straining their back.
- The chin should remain tucked.
- Finally, in some instances, it will be safer for two people to lift some objects rather than one.

Equipment Safety

- All machinery should be used in the manner in which it was originally designed.
- The manufacturer's operating instructions should be strictly followed at all times.
- It is imperative that all machinery be checked to ensure that it is in proper working order prior to use.
- Equipment should always be turned off and unplugged after it is used and before it is cleaned.
- Hands should be kept clear while operating all equipment.

Ensuring the safety of your employees and guests is fundamentally important.

- Employees should be familiar with and well trained regarding all attachments for the machinery prior to use. The employee should ensure that the right attachment is being used and that it is in good working order. If repairs are needed or attachment(s) require routine service, employees should notify you or a manager of the situation immediately.
- All equipment should be properly cleaned after each use.

Cutting and Knives

- Knives should be used with care and extreme caution.
- Knives should be held firmly. Cutting should be done with a balanced, rocking motion.
- Knives should always be carried with the blade pointed down and the blade flat against the body.
- If a knife is dropped, it should be allowed to fall as opposed to trying to catch it.
- Knives should be handed to another person handle-end first.
- Do not submerge knives in water when washing such that they are hidden in the sink. Do not leave knives unattended in a sink full of water where someone unsuspecting may reach into the water and be injured.

Employees should be familiar with and well trained for the machinery prior to use.

Ladder Use

- Ladders should be set-up well out of the way of foot traffic.
- Be sure that ladders are secure and properly positioned prior to use.
- Never let anyone stand on the top step of a ladder as it is extremely unstable and dangerous.
- When climbing, the hands should be used for balance. Ladders should never be climbed with hands full. Supplies should be passed to or from someone standing below.

Customer Safety

- All spills, broken glass or broken dinnerware should be cleaned up immediately.
- Floors should be routinely mopped after business hours. In the event of a spill when the business is open, using a dry mop won't leave the floor slippery afterwards.
- In the event a glass breaks in the vicinity of your station's ice bin, completely empty the ice and thoroughly clean the stainless steel bin. Your customers' safety should never be placed in jeopardy by presuming that no broken glass flew into the ice bin.
- Periodically examine furniture and floor coverings to insure they are in good condition.

- Exterior walkways must always be clear of debris and in good repair.
- Security lights in the parking lot should be properly maintained and in good working order.

⊙ •Restaurant Safety

- The operation's first aid kit should always be fully stocked and maintained in good order.
- Employees should know the location and condition of all fire extinguishers in the restaurant.
- Employees should know how to operate the fire extinguishers quickly and safely.
- Fire exits must be well marked and remain clear and free of obstruction.

QUESTIONS LEAD TO ANSWERS WHICH LEAD TO SUCCESS

- Have the employees been instructed how to properly respond to an act of violence or fight on-premises?
- Have the employees been instructed that the parking lot is considered a part of your licensed premises?
- Have you established procedures for employees to follow in the event of an armed robbery?
- Have the employees been briefed on after-the-event procedures?
- Have you reviewed your company's security precautions?
- Have the employees been instructed on the company's safety procedures?

RESOURCES

Following is a list of the companies, products and people that made *Successful Beverage Management* a success. We recommend that you contact these companies concerning their products and services.

If there is a product in the book that you have trouble finding which is not listed, contact the publisher for further information.

Berg Company
2001 S. Stoughton Road
Madison, WI 53716
phone: 608.221.4281
fax: 608.221.1416
email: sales@berg-controls.com
website: www.berg-controls.com
Products: Berg All-Bottle Liquor
Control System, Berg Tap 1 System

Bevinco
250 Consumers Road, Suite 1103
Toronto, Ontario
Canada M2J 4V6
phone: 416.490.6266
fax: 416.490.6899
email: info@bevinco.com
website: www.bevinco.com
Product: Bevinco Auditing Services

Libbey, Inc.
300 Madison Ave.
Toledo, OH 43604
phone: 419.325.2100
fax: 419.325.2367
web site: www.libbey.com
Products: Libbey Glassware

Precision Pours, Inc.
3650 Annapolis Lane North, Suite 140
Plymouth, MN 55447
phone: 800.549.4491
phone: 763.694.9291
fax: 763.694.9343
email: 3ball@precisionpours.com
web site: www.precisionpours.com
Product: Precision 3 Ball Pours

Steve Goumas, consultant
Madison Group
5821 East Larkspur Drive
Scottsdale, AZ 85254
phone: 480.443.0555
fax: 480.483.6306
email: MadisonGrp@aol.com

CastleBay
Design ~ Miguel Castillo
Tucson, AZ
phone: 520.954.0594
email: cbsgd@aol.com

INDEX

Need more tools?

If your bar sales are $500,000 and you reduce your costs by just 2%, that's $10,000 added to your bottom line. Now that doesn't even take into consideration all the ways you can increase your sales.

This package has been carefully chosen with reducing and controlling costs, and increasing sales in mind. We are so confident that it will work for you that we offer an unconditional money back guarantee.

THE ULTIMATE BAR MANAGEMENT LIBRARY III

is a must have for the profit minded manager and operator. Includes the all new *Successful Beverage Management* book and *Successful Beverage Management Forms Booklet*. It provides you with all of the pieces you need to operate your bar profitably. And now we've added the wine training no establishment should be without. *Plus* we've stream-lined the bartending training in our limited edition of *The Commercial Bartender's Training Manual*. Incorporating all of these products results in a profitable bottom line. The benefits of consistency will be found in training, service, product and cost controls. You will increase your profits, guaranteed. You'll also improve hiring procedures, reduce theft, increase creativity and have everything running more smoothly.

Includes: The Bartender's Companion Drink Recipe Guide, Increasing Bar Sales: Creative Twists to Bigger Profits book, the 2nd edition of Preventing Internal Theft book, The Commercial Bartender's Training Manual, Successful Beverage Management: Proven Strategies for the On-Premise Operator, the Successful Beverage Management Forms booklet, The Wine Expert Video Package & a one year subscription to the American Mixologist online ezine (weekly online newsletter).

For more information on these products visit www.BarMedia.com.

A $205 value Just $173.95*
Save 15%!
PLUS get *The Original Guide to Margaritas and Tequila* with every Ultimate. **FREE!**
THIS ALL NEW PACKAGE WILL MAKE YOUR OPERATION CLICK!

*Plus $15 shipping & handling. Prices are good thru 06/15/01.